FIVE

Compiled and Edited by
The Auxiliary of University Hospitals
of Cleveland

STAR

To benefit the
University Ireland Cancer Center
at University Hospitals of Cleveland

SENSATIONS

Designed by Ade Skunta and Company
Photography by Beth Segal Photography

ACKNOWLEDGEMENTS

Grateful acknowledgement is made to the following for permission to reprint previously published material:

From *Cooking For All Seasons*, copyright © 1991 by Jimmy Schmidt. Reprinted by permission of Macmillan Publishing Company.

From *The Wolfgang Puck Cookbook*, copyright © 1991 by Wolfgang Puck. Reprinted by permission of Random House, Inc.

From *Cooking for a Crowd*, copyright © 1988 by Susan Wyler. Reprinted by permission of Harmony Books, a division of Crown Publishers, Inc.

From *CITY Cuisine*, copyright © 1989 by Susan Feniger and Mary Sue Milliken. Reprinted with permission of William Morrow & Co., Inc.

From *Tailgate Parties*, copyright © 1984 by Susan Wyler. Reprinted by permission of Harmony Books, a division of Crown Publishers, Inc.

From *The Mansion on Turtle Creek Cookbook*, copyright © 1987 by Dean Fearing. Reprinted with permission of Grove/Weidenfeld.

From *A La Carte*, copyright © 1991 by Wolfgang Puck. Reprinted with permission of Random House, Inc.

From *Authentic Mexican*, copyright © 1987 by Rick Bayless and Deann Groen Bayless. Reprinted with permission of William Morrow & Co., Inc.

From *Baking with Jim Dodge*, copyright © 1991 by Jim Dodge. Reprinted by permission of Simon and Schuster.

From *Art Culinaire*, copyright © 1991 by Franz Mitterer. Reprinted by permission of Culinaire, Inc.

Text copyright © 1991 The Auxiliary of University Hospitals of Cleveland

Design copyright © 1991 Ade Skunta and Company

Photography copyright © 1991 Beth Segal Photography

Published by The Auxiliary of University Hospitals of Cleveland, a volunteer organization to render service to the hospital and its patients, and to assist the hospital in promoting the health and welfare of the community in accordance with objectives established by University Hospitals of Cleveland, 2074 Abington Road, Cleveland, OH 44106

Printed in U.S.A. by Great Lakes Lithograph Company, Cleveland, Ohio

ISBN 0-9630749-0-3

10   9   8   7   6   5   4   3   2   1

*The Auxiliary of University Hospitals
of Cleveland gratefully acknowledges
the generous support of*

SOCIETY NATIONAL BANK

*which provided the funding
for this first printing*

and to

THE PLAIN DEALER
WHITE CONSOLIDATED INDUSTRIES, INC.
ORLANDO BAKING COMPANY

*whose underwriting helped defray
the additional costs of
this project.*

*Because of this corporate support,
all proceeds from the sale of this book directly benefit*

THE UNIVERSITY IRELAND CANCER CENTER
AT UNIVERSITY HOSPITALS OF CLEVELAND.

Our symbol, which previewed at the first Five Star Sensation benefit in 1987, is used throughout the cookbook to highlight those chefs who came to Cleveland and generously donated their time and talents to benefit University Hospitals of Cleveland.

MY FRIENDSHIP WITH CLEVELAND BEGAN IN 1987 WHEN I WAS ASKED TO HELP PLAN A FOOD AND WINE BENEFIT FOR THE UNIVERSITY HOSPITALS OF CLEVELAND.

That year, many of America's best chefs came to Cleveland to prepare their restaurants' most wonderful dishes. To complement our delicious meals, vintners from around the country provided the finest wines from California to the Midwest and Atlantic. But what made our appetizing event a *true* Five Star Sensation were the people of Cleveland, who added their overwhelming enthusiasm for food and wine to the recipes and made the evening a celebration. It was a resounding success and each chef and winemaker looks forward to their annual trip to Cleveland.

Over the years, we collected so many savory recipes from each of the chefs, it seemed only natural that they should end up in a cookbook called *Five Star Sensations*. From "down-home" midwestern cooking to some of the most sophisticated and elegant, yet easy to prepare dishes, this collection has something for every cook. With such a broad range of recipes, I am sure you will discover your own "five star sensations."

Bon Appetit!

WOLFGANG PUCK

To heal.

To teach.

To discover.

SINCE OUR FOUNDING IN 1866,
University Hospitals of Cleveland has pursued a mission of healing,
teaching, and discovering, thus making us one of the country's
premier academic medical centers.

In our 125th year, under the auspices of the Auxiliary of University
Hospitals of Cleveland, we are proud to sponsor yet another successful
project: the publication of *Five Star Sensations,* a new community
cookbook.

This book is more than a collection of great recipes. It represents
the spirit of committed volunteers who worked for more than a year
to create a sensational product. The Auxiliary of University Hospitals
continues to provide an invaluable contribution of time and talent
for the hospitals' benefit.

Proceeds from the sale of *Five Star Sensations* directly benefit the
University Ireland Cancer Center. Well known for sensitive, supportive
patient care as well as cutting-edge research, the Ireland Cancer
Center is one of only 12 National Cancer Institute Clinical Cancer
Centers in the United States.

Thank you on behalf of the University Ireland Cancer Center and
University Hospitals of Cleveland.

Sincerely,

James A Block MD.

JAMES A. BLOCK, M.D.
PRESIDENT AND CHIEF EXECUTIVE OFFICER

THE AUXILIARY OF UNIVERSITY HOSPITALS IS PLEASED TO PRESENT . . .

Cleveland's newest community cookbook. *Five Star Sensations* is an outgrowth of University Hospitals' successful food and wine benefit. What began as a festive evening of dining has culminated in a book to be enjoyed—long after the party's over.

Our cookbook, *Five Star Sensations*, evolved from a desire to raise funds for the University Ireland Cancer Center at University Hospitals, and like charity, it began at home—ours. We collected recipes from many of America's most renowned chefs and combined them with recipes from some of Cleveland's finest cooks. We spent over eighteen months requesting recipes, testing them and re-testing them. We devised standards based on preparation by qualified cooks and a systemized rating for presentation and palate. We are confident that you will find a variety of new and interesting recipes.

We would like to express our appreciation to the Cleveland community for its generous support in this endeavor, and we take great pleasure in knowing that you will find this a *five star* cookbook filled with *sensational* recipes.

LEE EDWARDS
Cookbook Committee Chairman

LAURA THOMSON *Testing Chairman*	PEGGY RATCHESON *Assistant Testing Chairman*
LLOYD TAPLIN *Design Chairman*	MARCIA FLOYD *Assistant Design Chairman*

MARGARET SIMON   CHARLOTTE RILEY   MARY WARD
Editor   *Assistant Editor*   *Index Author*

MARY RYDZEL   MARY BETH SCHNEIDER
Marketing Chairman   *Assistant Marketing Chairman*

Cookbook Committee

Diana Armstrong
Sosamma Berger
Melinda Bickers
Margie Biggar
Barbara Bohlman
Barbara Bratel Collier
Debbie Daberko
Sarah DeFino
Becky Dunn
Lee Edwards
Marcia Floyd
Ann Gelehrter
Ann Gillespie
Colleen Gotherman
Claudia Gruen
Colleen Hanna
Ann Holtzman
Sheila Jacobs
Muffy Kain
Nancy Keithley

Jane Kern
Bambi Kramer
Pamela LaMantia
Rosemary Macedonio
Vickie Majoras
Lois McCartan
Claire Morgan
Candy Murdock
Shirley Nook
Sue Omori
Robin Oppmann
Madeleine Parker
Jane Pinkas
Pat Pogue
Anah Pytte
Peggy Ratcheson
Gail Resch
Charlotte Riley
Mary Rydzel
Sue Sackman
Mary Beth Schneider

Carol Sherwin
Sue Sherwin
Laura Shields
Linda Shuck
Margaret Simon
Gretchen Smith
Joyce Neiditz-Snow
Janet Sterrett
Lloyd Taplin
Laura Thomson
Linda Turner
Dianne Vogt
Mary Ward
Candy Weil
Sherry Whiting
Trudy Wiesenberger
Jane Wood
Kathie Young
Rebecca Reynolds-Young
Barb Zola

Advisory Committee

Denise Fugo   Wolfgang Puck   Zona Spray   Susan Wyler

9

Recipe Modifications
for Healthier Eating

꿯 Healthy eating has become the hallmark of contemporary American cuisine. Light, natural, nutritious foods and the lifestyles that go with them are becoming increasingly a part of the American way of life. Yet even the most vigilant cook strives to present elegant, flavorful dishes, occasionally even succumbing to a sinfully rich dessert or two.

The *Five Star Sensations* cookbook is a collection of recipes from the community's finest cooks and America's most renowned chefs. Many of the recipes are inherently light and nutritious; other recipes that reflect our community's rich cultural heritage and family traditions have been presented in their original form. The recipes use almost exclusively fresh, natural ingredients, and with a little thought, can be modified to "lighten" their fat, salt and sugar contents without sacrificing flavor.

Listed on these two pages are our suggestions for modifying recipes to achieve healthful and delicious results.

Increasing Fiber Content

Substitute cut-up vegetables for bread when stuffing chicken, fish or turkey.

Substitute brown rice for white rice, being sure to increase cooking time accordingly.

Decreasing Salt Content

Use reduced sodium soy sauce.

Use salt-free beef and chicken broth.

Use garlic and onion powders instead of salts.

Reducing Cholesterol and Fat

Trim meats of all visible fat. Remove skin from poultry before cooking and reduce cooking time by 1/3 to 1/2 to avoid overcooking.

Broil, bake, roast, stir-fry or poach meats, poultry and fish rather than pan-fry or deep-fry.

Sauté with broth, wine or water whenever possible. Sauté vegetables in a small amount of bouillon instead of fat.

Marinate in wine, tomato juice, beer, broth or bouillon instead of fat.

When making stocks, soups or stews, cook in advance, chill and remove all hardened fat.

To thicken cream soups, purée some of the vegetables in broth and combine with skim milk instead of cream.

In recipes calling for mayonnaise, use 1/2 light mayonnaise and 1/2 low-fat yogurt, or substitute nonfat products.

Substitute low-fat plain yogurt for sour cream (in equal proportions).

Reduce the amount of fat in baked goods by 1/3 to 1/2. Whenever possible, use vegetable oil or soft margarine instead of butter.

Substitute 2 large egg whites for 1 whole egg or 3 large egg whites for 2 whole eggs.

Decreasing Sugar Content

Use other spices and extracts to add flavor when reducing the amount of sugar.

To reduce sugar in sweet breads, cakes and cookies, use naturally sweetened fruits such as raisins, dates or bananas for flavor.

Replace 1/3 of sugar in baked goods with nonfat dry milk.

Wild Mushroom Strudel

For that special occasion.

Yield: 8-10 appetizer servings

1/2 pound fresh shiitake or
    oyster mushrooms
1/2 pound fresh button mushrooms
6 scallions, sliced
3 tablespoons butter
3 tablespoons dry white wine
2 tablespoons diced pimiento
2 tablespoons chopped
    fresh parsley
1/4 teaspoon sage
1/4 teaspoon pepper
1/8 teaspoon thyme
1 egg yolk
6 sheets phyllo dough, thawed
1/3 cup melted butter
2 tablespoons bread crumbs

⇝ Preheat oven to 400°F. Finely chop all mushrooms. Cook mushrooms and scallions in butter for 5 minutes over medium-high heat. Add wine and continue cooking until liquid has evaporated.

Remove from heat and add pimiento, parsley, sage, pepper and thyme; cool 10 minutes.

Mix the mushroom mixture and the egg yolk in a food processor or blender. Set aside.

Place a layer of phyllo dough on a baking pan and brush with melted butter. Top with second sheet of phyllo and brush with melted butter. Repeat this process, using all 6 layers of dough. Sprinkle the bread crumbs over the layered phyllo. Spread the mushroom mixture over the bread crumbs.

Cut the stack in half lengthwise. Working quickly, roll each stack, jelly-roll style, beginning with the long side. Brush each roll with melted butter and cut diagonal slits 1-inch apart, almost through the pastry.

Bake for approximately 15 minutes. Serve directly from the oven or at room temperature.

— Denise Grcevich

Shiitake Mushrooms
stuffed with spinach

Yield: 12 servings

1/2 pound fresh shiitake
    mushrooms
1 package (10 ounces) frozen
    chopped spinach, thawed
    and drained
2 ounces bleu cheese, crumbled
2 ounces feta cheese, crumbled
1 tablespoon butter, melted
Parmesan cheese
Lemon slices for garnish

⇝ Rinse mushrooms and pat dry. Remove stems and chop.

Mix stems with spinach and cheeses and fill mushroom caps.

Melt butter and drizzle over stuffed mushrooms.

Sprinkle with Parmesan cheese and broil for 3 to 5 minutes, until cheese is lightly browned.

Serve on small plates and garnish with sliced lemon.

— Molly Bartlett
silver creek farm

Mushroom Palmiers

A feast for the eyes.

Yield: 5 dozen

5 tablespoons butter
18 ounces mushrooms,
    finely chopped
1-1/2 medium onions,
    finely chopped
1 teaspoon fresh lemon juice
2 tablespoons all-purpose flour
1-1/2 teaspoons crumbled,
    dried thyme
Salt and pepper to taste
3 frozen puff pastry sheets,
    thawed
2 eggs, beaten with 4 teaspoons
    water (glaze)

૎ Melt butter in a heavy skillet over medium-high heat. Add mushrooms and onions and cook until juices evaporate, about 8 minutes. Mix in lemon juice, flour and thyme and continue cooking 2 to 3 minutes. Season with salt and pepper. Remove from heat and cool.

Spread one-third of mushroom mixture evenly over one pastry sheet. Beginning at the short side, roll up, jelly-roll style, to center. Roll the other side in the same fashion to the center. Press the two sides together and transfer to baking sheet. Repeat the process for the remaining 2 pastry sheets. Cover and chill until firm, at least 1 hour or overnight.

Preheat oven to 400°F. Slice pastry in 1/4-inch thick slices using a sharp, serrated knife. Arrange slices, cut-side down, on ungreased baking sheet, spacing one inch apart. Brush with glaze. Bake about 20 minutes or until golden brown.

This recipe can be prepared a week ahead of time and frozen. Thaw before slicing and baking.

—Debra Arthur

SAUTÉ OF SHIITAKE MUSHROOMS
WITH HERBS

*Great first course with phyllo shells or as
a sauce for salmon steaks.*

YIELD: 12 SERVINGS

FILLING
1 pound shiitake mushrooms,
    stems removed
1/2 cup (1 stick) unsalted butter
6 shallots, peeled and finely
    chopped
1/2 cup Madeira
2 to 3 tablespoons finely chopped
    fresh tarragon
1 cup crème fraîche*
Salt and pepper to taste

PHYLLO SHELLS
5 sheets phyllo dough, thawed
1/3 cup butter, melted

** Crème fraîche may be purchased
ready-made at specialty stores.*

≥ To make filling, slice mushrooms. Melt butter in pan, add shallots and sauté over medium-high heat until translucent. Add mushrooms and cook over medium heat until they begin to soften. Add Madeira and cook until sauce is reduced. Add tarragon, crème fraîche, salt and pepper. Keep warm for serving.

To make phyllo shells, preheat oven to 350°F and lightly grease a standard (12) muffin tin. Take phyllo dough and cut it in rounds to fit the muffin cups. Fill each tin with 5 layers of dough, brushing each layer with melted butter. Bake until golden brown, approximately 15 minutes. Fill with mushroom mixture.

— PAMELA GROSSCUP

GRAVLAX
WITH MUSTARD DILL SAUCE
Classic Scandinavian starter.
YIELD: 12 SERVINGS

1 small (3-1/2 pound) salmon, cut in half lengthwise, with head and bones removed, skin and tail intact
1/4 cup coarse salt
1/4 cup brown sugar
2 tablespoons crushed peppercorns
1 tablespoon crushed juniper berries (optional)
1 large bunch fresh dill, coarsely chopped
1 lemon, sliced

MUSTARD DILL SAUCE
5 tablespoons Dijon-style mustard
1-1/4 teaspoons dry mustard
3-1/2 tablespoons sugar
2-1/2 tablespoons distilled white vinegar
1/3 cup plus 1 tablespoon vegetable oil
3-1/2 tablespoons finely chopped fresh dill

֍ Rinse and dry salmon, being sure all bones have been removed.

Mix salt, sugar, peppercorns and juniper berries and rub this mixture into the flesh of the salmon. Place one half of the fish, skin-side down, in a glass dish. Cover with chopped dill. Place the other salmon half, skin-side up, on top of the first and cover with waxed paper or foil.

Weight the fish with a plate and a heavy object, pressing the halves together to make sure the weight is evenly distributed. (Soup cans work well as weights.)

Refrigerate for a total of 48 hours, turning every 12 hours.

To serve, drain juice from salmon and pat dry. Slice paper-thin on the diagonal and garnish with lemon slices.

To make Mustard Dill Sauce, mix mustards, sugar and vinegar in a small bowl. Add oil slowly while beating with a wire whisk. Stir in chopped dill, cover and refrigerate.

Serve with buttered whole-wheat bread or pumpernickel slices.

— MAYNARD THOMSON

HOT CRABMEAT PUFFS

*All-time favorite of the
Mayfield Women's Club.*

YIELD: 36 APPETIZERS

MINIATURE CREAM PUFFS
1 cup water
1/2 cup margarine or butter
1 cup all-purpose flour
Salt to taste
4 eggs

CRABMEAT FILLING
1 package (8 ounces) cream
    cheese
1 tablespoon milk
1/2 teaspoon horseradish sauce
Pepper to taste
1 can (6-1/2 ounces) crabmeat,
    drained
1/2 cup slivered almonds, toasted
2 tablespoons finely chopped
    onion

❧ Preheat oven to 400°F. Bring water and margarine to a boil. Add flour and salt. Stir vigorously over low heat until mixture forms a ball. Add eggs, one at a time, beating until smooth. Drop teaspoonfuls of batter onto ungreased baking sheet. Bake for 30 to 35 minutes and remove from baking sheet.

Lower the oven temperature to 375°F. Combine softened cream cheese, milk, horseradish sauce and pepper. Mix until well blended. Stir in crabmeat, almonds and onion.

To assemble cream puffs, cut tops from cream puffs and fill with crab mixture. Replace tops. Bake for 10 minutes and serve.

Easier than it looks. Be sure to make cream puffs small.

—SUE BUMGARDNER

CRAB LOUIS

An old standard.

YIELD: 6 SERVINGS

SAUCE LOUIS
1 cup mayonnaise
2 tablespoons grated onion
Cayenne pepper to taste
1/3 cup heavy cream, whipped
2 tablespoons chopped parsley
1/2 cup chili sauce
1 tablespoon lemon juice

1 to 1-1/2 pounds crab meat,
    fresh or frozen
1 head iceberg lettuce, shredded
2 to 3 tomatoes, thinly sliced
Artichoke hearts, canned
    or frozen
1 hard-cooked egg,
    finely chopped

❧ Whisk all ingredients for Sauce Louis in a medium-size bowl. Refrigerate until ready to use.

Pick over crab meat, leaving the meat pieces as large as possible. Arrange a bed of shredded lettuce on 6 individual salad plates and place a mound of crab meat on each.

Encircle the crab meat with halved tomato slices and wedges of artichoke hearts. Sprinkle generously with egg. Chill thoroughly and serve with Sauce Louis.

Sauce would make excellent dip for grilled fish or a delicious Thousand Island dressing.

—CHEF RENATO BERTOLO
MAYFIELD COUNTRY CLUB

CRAB CAKES
WITH CRACKED MUSTARD SAUCE
YIELD: 8 SERVINGS
OR 4 ENTRÉE SERVINGS

CRAB CAKES
1/2 pound scallops
1 egg white
4 tablespoons unsalted butter
1/2 teaspoon salt
1/4 teaspoon pepper
1/3 cup whipping cream
1/2 cup peeled, seeded and diced
    yellow peppers
1/2 cup peeled, seeded and diced
    red peppers
2 tablespoons chopped parsley
2 tablespoons chopped chives
1 pound crab meat, free of shells
All-purpose flour
Butter for frying

SAUCE
1/2 cup white wine
1/2 cup fish fumet (may
    substitute clam juice)
1 cup whipping cream
1/4 cup coarse grained mustard
2 tablespoons chopped chives

🐚 Place scallops and egg white in container of food processor. Purée until smooth. Whip butter, salt and pepper in a mixing bowl until smooth. Add scallop purée, tablespoon by tablespoon, until well combined. Mix in cream, beating at slow speed. Transfer to large bowl. Add peppers, parsley, chives and crab. Fold to combine. Form into 8 cakes, place on parchment or waxed paper and refrigerate for 2 hours.

Combine white wine and fumet and simmer over medium-high heat, cooking until reduced by half. Add cream and simmer until thickened to coat back of spoon, about 10 minutes. Strain into another saucepan.

Lightly dust crab cakes with flour. Melt butter in heavy skillet over medium-high heat. Add crab cakes, cooking until golden and hot. Drain on paper towels.

Return sauce to simmer over high heat. Add mustard. Spoon sauce on plate and sprinkle with chives. Position crab cakes in center. Serve.

Previously published in *Cooking For All Seasons,* Macmillan copyright ©1991, by Jimmy Schmidt, reprinted with permission.

— CHEF JIMMY SCHMIDT

Five Star
APPETIZERS

CRAB

Cocina Del Sol
28565 Northwestern Highway
Southfield, MI 48075

The Rattlesnake Club
300 River Place
Detroit, MI 48207
313-567-4400

Tres Vite
2203 Woodward Avenue
Detroit, MI 48201
313-964-4144

MOULES MARINIÈRE

A traditional Belgian treat.

YIELD: 4 SERVINGS
OR 2 ENTRÉE SERVINGS

2 pounds mussels
4 tablespoons butter
1 cup chopped onion
1 cup chopped celery
4 tablespoons chopped parsley
1 cup white wine

❧ Scrub mussels and set aside. Melt butter in pot large enough for all ingredients. Add onion, celery and parsley and simmer 10 minutes. Add wine and simmer 5 minutes. Add mussels and cover. Steam until all mussels open, approximately 15 minutes. Do not eat mussels that remain closed after steaming.

Remove from heat and serve with sauce.

Be sure to serve with crusty bread to soak up the sauce.

—CYNTHIA BAILEY

SCALLOPS WITH MUSHROOMS

YIELD: 6 SERVINGS

1/2 cup (1 stick) butter or
   margarine, divided
1 cup sliced mushrooms
3 tablespoons chopped shallots
1 tablespoon chopped garlic
1 pound fresh bay scallops
1/2 cup bread crumbs
1/2 cup chopped parsley
Salt and pepper to taste

❧ Preheat oven to 450°F. Melt 1/4 cup of butter or margarine in small skillet and add mushrooms, cooking until they wilt.

Add shallots and garlic and continue cooking another 2 to 3 minutes. Place this mixture in a mixing bowl and cool.

Add 2 tablespoons of the remaining butter, scallops, bread crumbs, parsley and salt and pepper. Blend well.

Fill 6 seafood shells or ramekins with the seafood mixture and place them on a cookie sheet.

Melt remaining butter and drizzle over scallops. Bake in preheated oven for 10 minutes and brown under the broiler for 1 minute.

—RETT LEWANDOWSKI

PICKLED SHRIMP

*A very easy, elegant way
to serve cold shrimp.*

YIELD: 10 SERVINGS

3 pounds shrimp, cooked,
    shelled and deveined
2 bunches scallions, chopped
    (tops included)
7 bay leaves
2 heads red-tipped leaf lettuce
    for garnish

MARINADE
1-1/4 cups vegetable oil
3/4 cup white vinegar
4 tablespoons capers and
    some juice
1 large clove garlic, minced
1/8 teaspoon salt
Dash of hot pepper sauce

  Alternate shrimp, scallions
and bay leaves in a non-metal
dish or pan. Mix marinade and
pour over shrimp. Cover and
refrigerate for 24 hours.
    Drain marinade before
serving. Toss shrimp, scallions
and bay leaves. Serve as a first
course on plates lined with
red-tipped leaf lettuce.

— SHIRLEY SHAPERO

This recipe is featured on the color
cover of the Appetizers section tab.

PANCHO SAUCE

*A tangy sauce that
goes well with ground sirloin,
cold shrimp or crab.
The original recipe was developed
by Chef "Pancho" at the
London Chop House in Detroit.*

YIELD: 1-1/2 QUARTS

3 cups ketchup
1-3/4 cups chili sauce
1/4 cup dry mustard
1/4 cup horseradish
1/4 cup lemon juice
3 tablespoons wine vinegar
2 tablespoons Worcestershire
    sauce
10 drops hot pepper sauce
6 pepperoncini*
1-1/2 teaspoons ginger
1/2 cup mayonnaise
Salt and pepper to taste

*Pickled pepper found with relishes
in the supermarket.*

  Combine ketchup and
chili sauce in saucepan and
simmer over medium heat for
about 45 minutes, until reduced
in volume, stirring occasionally.
    Add remaining ingredients,
except mayonnaise, and stir well.
Cook for 2 minutes.
    Add mayonnaise and stir
well. Remove mixture from heat
and pour into jars; salt and pepper
to taste. Refrigerate until ready
to use.

*This sauce may be stored for several
months in the refrigerator.*

— GEORGE J. DUNN

Five Star
APPETIZERS
SEAFOOD

GRILLED SHRIMP

With spicy options.

YIELD: 4-6 SERVINGS

1 pound green shrimp
Juice of 1 lemon
1/4 cup olive oil
5 cloves garlic, crushed
10 drops hot sauce (optional)
2-3 tablespoons chili powder
     (optional)

&❧ Peel, devein and butterfly shrimp, leaving on tail shell if desired. Mix lemon, oil and garlic in a glass dish. For a spicy version, add either one of the optional ingredients to the marinade. Add shrimp and stir gently. Marinate shrimp for at least 1 hour. Skewer, if desired. Grill over hot coals 2 to 3 minutes per side. Do not overcook!

Serve with Pancho Sauce; see page 21.

— LAURA THOMSON
— REBECCA REYNOLDS-YOUNG

BAHAMIAN SHRIMP

Coconut lends flavor and texture.

YIELD: 15-20 SERVINGS

1 pound (about 25) medium
     shrimp
1/2 cup all-purpose flour
1/2 teaspoon salt
Pepper to taste
3/4 cup beer
Oil for frying
1 cup shredded unsweetened
     coconut

ORANGE SAUCE FOR DIPPING
1/4 cup orange marmalade
4 teaspoons Dijon-style mustard
2 tablespoons orange juice

&❧ Clean shrimp, leaving on tail shells; drain on paper towels.

Combine flour, salt and pepper. Stir in beer, adding more if mixture looks too thick.

Heat 1-1/2 inches of oil in saucepan. Dip shrimp, one at a time, in beer batter, allowing excess to drip off. Dredge in coconut and fry until brown. Drain on paper towels.

Combine orange marmalade, mustard and orange juice and serve as a dipping sauce.

— ROBIN OPPMANN

BLACKENED SHRIMP
WITH HONEYED DIJON MUSTARD

YIELD: 2 SERVINGS

8 to 10 large shrimp
Blackening spices (1/4 teaspoon
     each: paprika, salt, onion
     powder, garlic powder,
     ground red pepper,
     white pepper, black
     pepper, thyme, oregano)
Oil for sautéing
1 small clove garlic, minced
2 teaspoons honey
2 teaspoons Dijon-style mustard
1 tablespoon butter
Chopped parsley for garnish

&❧ Heat cast-iron skillet until smoking.

Season shrimp with blackening spices (for a spicier dish, use more). Sauté in a small amount of oil over medium-high heat until shrimp turn pink. Add garlic, honey and mustard; mix well, then add butter. Swirl pan until butter is mixed through. To serve, arrange in a spiral on a plate and garnish with chopped parsley.

— VINCE HULSMAN

When similar recipes were submitted, acknowledgement was given to each contributor.

22

LOBSTER WITH SWEET GINGER

YIELD: 2 SERVINGS

1 piece fresh ginger,
   approximately 1 inch
2 cloves garlic, minced
3/4 cup plum wine or port
2 tablespoons rice wine
   vinegar
2 tablespoons peanut oil
1 lobster (2 pounds), split
   lengthwise
2 tablespoons unsalted butter
4 scallions, cut into 3/8-inch slices
1 to 2 teaspoons curry powder
1/4 cup dry white wine
1/2 cup fish stock
1/2 teaspoon dried hot chili flakes
1 tablespoon Chinese black
   vinegar or balsamic vinegar
1/2 cup heavy cream
Salt and freshly ground black
   pepper to taste

❧ Preheat the oven to 500°F. Peel the ginger, reserving the peels, and cut the ginger into fine julienne strips. Cut the peels into coarse julienne strips and set aside. In a small saucepan, cook the ginger (not peels) and garlic with 1/2 cup of the plum wine and the rice wine vinegar, until 1 tablespoon of liquid remains. Remove the saucepan from the heat and reserve.

Place a heavy oven-proof 12-inch skillet over high heat until it is very hot. Add oil and heat it almost to the smoking point. Carefully add lobster halves, meat side down. Cook 3 minutes. Turn over and add 1 tablespoon of the butter. Continue to sauté until lobster shells get red and butter is nutty red.

Transfer lobster to the oven for about 10 minutes, or until just cooked. Remove from oven, remove the lobster from skillet and keep warm. Add scallions, ginger peels and curry powder to the skillet. Sauté mixture lightly for 10 to 15 seconds, then whisk in the remaining plum wine and the white wine, stock, chili flakes and vinegar. Reduce the liquid to 1/2 cup. Add cream and reduce it by half. Add any liquid from the julienne of ginger, then whisk in remaining tablespoon butter. Salt and pepper to taste.

Crack lobster claws, then drain any liquid from claws and body. Arrange the lobster halves on a warm platter, meat side up. Strain the sauce over each lobster; sprinkle the reserved sweet ginger on top.

Previously published in *The Wolfgang Puck Cookbook*, Random House, copyright ©1986, by Wolfgang Puck, reprinted with permission.

—CHEF KAZUTO MATSUSAKA

Chinois on Main
2709 Main Street
Santa Monica, CA 90405
213-392-9025

Deep Fried Shrimp with Toast

YIELD: 8-10 SERVINGS

6 slices bread, toasted
1 pound shrimp
1 ounce pork fat
1 egg white
1 teaspoon salt
1 teaspoon sugar
1 tablespoon cornstarch
1/2 teaspoon sesame oil
1/8 teaspoon black pepper
Vegetable oil for frying
Tomatoes, scallions and
    coriander for garnish

PEPPER SALT
1/2 teaspoon five-spice powder*
1/2 teaspoon Szechuan pepper
    powder* or black pepper
1 tablespoon salt

*Available in Asian and
Oriental markets.*

❧ Remove crusts from bread. Crush bread to make fine crumbs.

Shell and devein shrimp. Clean in cold, salted water and drain.

Place shrimp, pork fat, egg white, salt, sugar, cornstarch, sesame oil and black pepper in container of food processor and process until mixture is minced.

Form the mixture into approximately 24 balls and roll each in bread crumbs.

Deep fry shrimp balls in hot oil for approximately 5 minutes or until golden brown. Drain on paper towels.

Place shrimp balls on serving platter and garnish with tomatoes, shredded scallions and coriander.

To prepare Pepper Salt, mix five-spice powder, Szechuan pepper powder and salt in a small skillet. Stir-fry over high heat for approximately 1 minute. Remove to a small saucer and pass with shrimp.

—ROBERT LIN
HUNAN GOURMET

Sweet and Sour Chicken Wings

*A milder, sweeter
Cleveland alternative
to Buffalo hot wings!*

YIELD: 6-8 SERVINGS

2-1/2 pounds chicken wings
1/3 cup vegetable oil
1/3 cup cider vinegar
1/2 cup brown sugar
1 can (12 ounces) unsweetened
    pineapple juice
3/4 cup ketchup
1 tablespoon soy sauce
1 teaspoon mustard
1/8 teaspoon salt

❧ Brown one-third of the wings at a time in oil in skillet over medium-high heat. Remove as they brown.

Drain fat from skillet and add vinegar, sugar, juice, ketchup, soy sauce, mustard and salt. Boil gently for approximately 5 minutes.

Add wings and simmer, covered, for approximately 15 minutes. Turn wings, uncover and cook for another 15 minutes. Skim fat if necessary.

—MARILYN ALTHANS

EGG ROLLS
YIELD: 8 SERVINGS

SAUCE
1 teaspoon salt
2 teaspoons sugar
2 tablespoons oyster sauce
2 teaspoons cornstarch
1/4 cup chicken broth

FILLING
2 cups cooked ham or
    barbecued pork, thinly sliced
5 medium dried mushrooms
1 cup bamboo shoots
2 scallions
3 stalks celery
1 cup shredded cabbage
1/2 pound bean sprouts
Peanut oil
1 package egg roll wrappers
1 egg

∾ Combine sauce ingredients and pour over meat. Set aside.

Soak mushrooms in hot water for 10-15 minutes to soften. Remove stems.

Slice bamboo shoots, mushrooms and scallions into matchsticks. Slice celery on the diagonal. Rinse and drain bean sprouts.

Heat wok over medium-high heat and add 1 tablespoon of oil. Stir-fry the following ingredients separately, adding more oil as needed:

Bean sprouts . . . 1 minute
Celery and
   Mushrooms . . 2 minutes
Bamboo shoots . . 2 minutes
Cabbage . . . . . . 2 minutes

Lastly, stir-fry meat and sauce mixture until sauce thickens, approximately 2 minutes. Return all cooked vegetables and uncooked scallions to the wok. Mix well and cool.

Place 1-1/2 tablespoons of the filling near one corner of egg roll wrapper. Fold once or twice on the diagonal, then fold over ends to enclose filling. Finish rolling and seal egg rolls by brushing with egg.

Deep fry in peanut oil until golden brown. Drain on paper towels and serve warm.

— STEPHEN KLEIN

Five Star
APPETIZERS

Mexican Chili Cheese Logs

Spicy crowd pleaser.

YIELD: 9 DOZEN SERVINGS

2 eggs
4 slices thinly sliced white bread,
    torn into pieces
1 beef bouillon cube dissolved
    in 1 tablespoon hot water
1/2 cup salsa
2 tablespoons instant
    minced onion
1 teaspoon salt
1-1/2 teaspoons oregano leaves
1-1/2 teaspoons chili powder
1/2 teaspoon ground cumin
2-1/2 cups (10 ounces) shredded
    sharp Cheddar cheese
2 cloves garlic, pressed
1-1/4 pounds hot pork sausage
1 pound ground turkey
2 cans (4 ounces each) whole
    green chilies
1 can (4 ounces) sliced black
    olives, drained
3/4 teaspoon cumin seeds

☙ Beat eggs in large bowl. Add bread, bouillon mixture, 1/4 cup of salsa and onion. Let stand for 5 minutes.

Mix salt, oregano, chili powder, ground cumin, 1 cup of cheese, garlic, sausage and turkey with hands until blended.

Turn mixture out onto a 20 × 12-inch piece of foil. Pat meat into an 18 × 10-inch rectangle and divide into thirds, 10 × 6-inches each.

Split chilies, discard seeds and drain on paper towels. Flatten 2 chilies and arrange down center of each rectangle. Sprinkle with olives, cumin seeds and remaining cheese.

Starting from long side, lift meat off foil and tightly roll rectangle into a cylinder; firmly pinch meat together at seams and ends to seal in cheese. Repeat process for other two logs.

Place logs in greased 15 × 10-inch rimmed baking pan; brush tops with remaining 1/4 cup salsa. Bake, uncovered, in a 350°F oven for 45 minutes or until meat feels firm.

Cool, wrap in foil and refrigerate at least 8 hours or up to 3 days. Cut chilled logs into thin slices. Serve with tortilla chips and additional salsa.

This can be frozen for 2 months.

— RYN CLARKE

Mexican Caviar

*Olé! Sensational
south-of-the-border starter.*

YIELD: 8-12 SERVINGS

2 cans (4 ounces each) chopped
    ripe olives, drained
2 cans (4 ounces each) chopped
    green chilies, drained
2 tomatoes, peeled, seeded,
    chopped and drained
8 scallions, minced
2 cloves garlic, minced
2 teaspoons olive oil
2 teaspoons red wine vinegar
1 teaspoon pepper
Salt to taste

☙ Combine ingredients, making sure olives and tomatoes are well drained. Do **not** use a food processor. Chill overnight.

Drain through a slotted spoon if necessary and serve with tortilla chips.

— ROBIN OPPMANN

SPICY AVOCADO DIP

Tasty and not too spicy.
Can be made "hotter"
by using hot green chilies.

YIELD: 2-1/2 CUPS

3 ripe tomatoes, peeled, seeded
   and chopped
1 can (4 ounces) diced green
   chilies
2 cloves garlic, minced
1 bunch scallions, finely chopped
1/2 cup cider vinegar
1/3 cup vegetable oil
1/2 cup chopped fresh cilantro
1/2 teaspoon salt
2 ripe avocados, peeled, seeded
   and diced

∓ Mix all ingredients except
avocado in tightly covered container. Store in refrigerator at
least 4 hours and add avocado
just before serving.

Serve as a dip with tortilla chips
or as a salsa for grilled meats and
fajitas.

—MARY SUSAN LYON

BLACK-EYED PEA AND PEPPER SALSA

Easy, zesty appetizer
with a Southwestern flavor.

YIELD: 5 CUPS

2 cans (15 ounces each)
   black-eyed peas, rinsed
   and drained
2 sweet red peppers, diced
1 jar (11-1/2 ounces) hot salsa
4 tablespoons olive oil or
   vegetable oil
4 tablespoons red wine vinegar
3 tablespoons minced onion
2 tablespoons snipped fresh
   parsley
1 tablespoon minced jalapeño
   chilies

∓ Combine all ingredients
and refrigerate. Allow flavors to
blend in refrigerator for 2 hours
or overnight.

Serve with corn chips or tortillas.

—ELIZABETH MARTIN

Five Star
APPETIZERS

Brie and Herb Cheeses in Pastry

YIELD: 12-20 SERVINGS

1 sheet frozen puff pastry
    (10 × 9-inches), thawed
1 wheel (14 ounces) Brie
1 package (4 ounces) garlic and
    herb semi-soft cheese
1 egg, beaten
1 tablespoon water

“ Lightly flour a board and roll out puff pastry. Place Brie in center of pastry and spread the semi-soft cheese on top of the Brie. Bring the pastry up around the sides and over the cheese, wrapping completely and trimming excess pastry. (Make sure the pastry is sealed tightly or the cheese will seep out in baking.) Turn over and place the cheese pastry seam-side down on a shallow baking dish.

Combine egg and water and brush over top of pastry. The cheese pastry may be prepared a day ahead and refrigerated. Bring it to room temperature before baking.

Bake in 375°F oven for approximately 30 to 35 minutes or until golden brown. Let stand 10 minutes before serving.

—CYDNEY WEINGART BADDELEY

Swiss Cheese Fondue

An old favorite.
Great with apple slices.

YIELD: 6-8 SERVINGS

1 clove garlic, whole
1-1/2 cups Chablis
1 tablespoon lemon juice
1/2 pound Emmentaler cheese,
    grated
1/2 pound Gruyère cheese, grated
2 tablespoons cornstarch
3 tablespoons kirsch
1/8 teaspoon cayenne pepper
1/8 teaspoon nutmeg

“ Rub the inside of a 1-quart fondue pot with cut surface of garlic. Pour Chablis and lemon juice into fondue pot and heat until it begins to steam, but do not boil.

Combine Emmentaler and Gruyère cheeses and cornstarch. Add to wine mixture in small amounts, stirring constantly with a wooden spoon, until cheese is melted.

Add kirsch, cayenne and nutmeg, stirring to mix well. Bring to a boil.

Serve with French bread cubes, apple slices or fresh vegetables.

—ANDREW MIKUSZEWSKI

MASCARPONE WITH PESTO
Rich, tasty and colorful.
YIELD: 18 SERVINGS

TORTA
3 pounds mascarpone, at room
    temperature
1 pound butter
2 cups minced sun-dried
    tomatoes packed in oil
    and well drained

PESTO
2 cups loosely packed fresh
    basil leaves
4 cloves garlic
Salt to taste
1/2 cup Parmesan cheese
1/2 cup olive oil
3 tablespoons pecorino cheese
    or Parmesan cheese
3 tablespoons butter
1/4 cup pine nuts

ᴥ Line bottom of 9-inch springform pan with parchment paper.

Cream mascarpone with electric mixer, add butter and continue to mix until smooth. Set aside.

Place all Pesto ingredients into container of food processor and blend until smooth.

Pour one-third of mascarpone mixture into bottom of prepared pan. Cover with one-third of sun-dried tomatoes and then spread with one-third of Pesto. Repeat layers, ending with Pesto.

Cover and refrigerate overnight. Unmold and serve with crackers.

—BONNIE DAVIS CATERING
BEACHWOOD, OHIO

Five Star
APPETIZERS
CHEESE

Scottish Sausage Rolls

Popular for Scottish
New Year celebrations.

YIELD: 28 ROLLS

PASTRY
2 cups all-purpose flour
1/2 pound (2 sticks) frozen
    margarine
1/2 cup ice water

SAUSAGE FILLING
2 pounds lean bulk sausage
    meat (whole hog preferred)
1 cup finely chopped onion
1 cup crushed saltine crackers
2 eggs, beaten

To make pastry, grate frozen margarine into flour. Add ice water to make dough. Roll out on floured board and divide dough into four equal portions.

To make filling, mix all ingredients and divide into four equal portions.

To assemble sausage rolls, roll out one portion of pastry to a 21 × 5-inch rectangle. Take one portion of sausage filling and lay it evenly across the width of the pastry. Brush edges of pastry with water. Roll pastry around sausage filling and seal well. Cut the long strip into seven 3-inch sections. Repeat this process for remaining three portions.

Place rolls on cookie sheets. Brush with beaten egg and prick top with a fork. Bake on middle rack in 350°F oven for 1 hour. Check at 30 minutes and drain grease.

— MAY GILCHRIST

Lahmajune
(LA-MA-JOON)

Middle Eastern pizza.

YIELD: 24 SERVINGS

12 medium-size rounds of pita
    bread
1 pound lamb, ground from
    shank or shoulder with fat
    removed
1 large can (28 ounces) crushed
    tomatoes (or equivalent fresh)
2 medium onions, finely chopped
1/2 cup minced parsley
1 red pepper, finely chopped
1 green pepper, finely chopped
2 tablespoons tomato paste
2 tablespoons all-purpose flour
1 tablespoon fresh or 1 teaspoon
    dried mint
1 tablespoon fresh or 1 teaspoon
    dried sweet basil
2 teaspoons salt
2 teaspoons paprika
1/2 teaspoon garlic powder
    (optional)
1/4 teaspoon cayenne pepper
    (optional)
Lemons

Split pita bread around edges to produce 24 shells. Combine all other ingredients, blending with meat. Spread mixture on pita bread, covering entire shell. Bake at 400°F for approximately 18 minutes.

Sprinkle with a few drops of fresh lemon juice. Cut each pita round into quarters. Serve with a lemon wedge.

— BERGE TOOKMAN

FRITTATA OMELET

Italian-style omelet.
Quicker than it looks!

YIELD: 15-30 SERVINGS

1 cup chopped scallions
2 tablespoons olive oil
1 tablespoon butter or margarine
8 ounces prosciutto or
    smoked ham, finely chopped
8 ounces cappicola, finely
    chopped
8 ounces Genoa salami,
    finely chopped
10 eggs, lightly beaten
1 cup chopped red and green
    peppers
1 cup shredded Swiss cheese
1/2 cup grated Parmesan cheese
8 to 10 cherry tomatoes, finely
    chopped and drained
2 tablespoons chopped fresh basil
2 tablespoons chopped fresh
    parsley
2 tablespoons minced dried
    tomatoes
1/8 teaspoon ground black pepper
3 tablespoons butter or margarine

❧ Sauté scallions in olive oil and 1 tablespoon butter or margarine over medium-high heat until tender, about 5 minutes. Add prosciutto, cappicola and salami; simmer 5 minutes, stirring frequently. Drain on paper towel.

Place scallion-meat mixture in a large mixing bowl. Add beaten eggs and stir to combine. Add remaining ingredients and mix well.

Melt 3 tablespoons butter over medium-high heat in a 12-inch skillet (or two 6-inch skillets). When butter begins to foam, add egg mixture. Reduce heat to low and cook slowly for 15 minutes or until outer edges are firm. (To test firmness, run rubber spatula around outer edge of pan.) Top of frittata will be slightly runny. Remove skillet from heat; place under the broiler unit and broil 3 to 4 inches from heat source until top of frittata is firm and golden brown, about 3 minutes. Slide frittata onto large round platter and let stand for 15 minutes.

Serve hot, at room temperature or refrigerate overnight and serve cold. Slice into 15 appetizer portions or 30 hors d'oeuvre-size portions.

Garnish with parsley and a tomato rose, if desired.

Recipe adapted from Zona Spray Cooking School.

—JAN CHAPMAN

Five Star
APPETIZERS

CLEVELAND WHITE BREAD
Old-fashioned favorite.
YIELD: 1 LOAF

1/2 ounce cake of yeast or
    1 package active dry yeast
2 tablespoons warm water
1/8 teaspoon sugar
3 cups bread flour
1 cup skim milk or water
1-1/2 teaspoons salt
1 tablespoon sugar
1 tablespoon vegetable oil

꙳ Grease a 9 × 5 × 3-inch loaf pan; set aside.

Dissolve yeast and 1/8 teaspoon sugar in warm water until bubbly.

Combine flour, milk, salt, 1 tablespoon of sugar and oil in a large bowl. Stir in yeast mixture and mix well. (If dough is sticky, gradually add more flour, 2 tablespoons at a time.)

Place dough in greased bowl; turn dough to coat all sides. Cover with a moist towel or cloth and let rise in a warm place until double in size, approximately 1-1/2 to 2 hours.

Turn dough out on a lightly floured board and knead until dough is smooth and elastic.

Allow dough to rest, covered with a moist cloth in a warm place, approximately 45 minutes. Form dough into a round shape and let rest covered in a warm place for an additional 20 minutes.

Place dough into prepared loaf pan and let rise in warm place until nearly doubled in size, approximately 1-1/2 hours.

Bake in preheated 400°F oven for approximately 35 to 40 minutes or until nicely browned. Cool on wire rack.

— JOSEPH E. MARTANOVIC

BEER BREAD
Quick and easy.
YIELD: 1 LOAF

1/4 cup sugar
1 can (12 ounces) beer, at room
    temperature
1 egg
3-1/2 cups self-rising flour

꙳ Preheat oven to 375°F. Grease and lightly flour a 9 × 5 × 3-inch loaf pan.

Mix sugar, beer and egg in large mixing bowl. Gradually add flour and stir just long enough to blend. Pour into prepared loaf pan and bake for approximately 45 minutes or until nicely browned. Cool on wire rack before slicing.

— ALEX GYEKENYESI
GATTO'S SHAKER MARKET

WHOLE-WHEAT BREAD

A grainy delight.

YIELD: 2 LOAVES

1 package active dry yeast
1/2 cup warm water
3 cups whole-wheat flour
1/4 cup wheat germ
1 teaspoon salt
1/2 cup honey
1/4 cup dark molasses
1 egg
1/3 cup butter, melted
1 cup boiling water
1 cup buttermilk or sour milk
1/3 cup chopped dried fruit
    (optional)
1 cup oats
4 to 6 cups all-purpose flour

Add yeast to warm water. Set aside. Mix wheat flour, wheat germ and salt. Add honey, molasses, egg and melted butter. Stir in boiling water and buttermilk; mix well. Add yeast mixture and stir. Add dried fruit, if desired. Stir in oats and flour, a little at a time. Knead for 10 minutes.

Place in greased bowl, turning dough to coat; cover with a damp towel. Put in a warm place and let rise 2 hours.

Punch down dough, divide in half and place in two greased 8-1/2 × 4-1/2 × 2-1/2-inch loaf pans, or it can be formed into 2 round loaves on a greased baking sheet. Cover with damp towel, put in a warm place and let rise 1 hour more.

Bake in 375°F oven for 45 minutes.

—ANDY KROTINGER

Five Star
BREADS

MULTI-GRAIN BREAD

Hearty and satisfying.

YIELD: 4 LOAVES

1 cup cornmeal
1-1/2 tablespoons salt
2/3 cup dark molasses or dark
    brown sugar
1/2 cup vegetable oil
3 cups water
4 packages active dry yeast
2 cups whole-wheat flour
1-1/2 cups rye flour or whole-
    wheat flour
1/4 cup sesame seed (optional)
5 to 6 cups unbleached flour

➤ Combine cornmeal, salt, molasses, vegetable oil and 2 cups boiling water in a large bowl. Let stand until lukewarm, approximately 30 minutes.

Dissolve yeast in 1 cup warm water and let stand for 10 minutes. Stir into cornmeal mixture.

Add whole-wheat flour, rye flour and sesame seed. Mix at low speed with electric mixer until blended, then at high speed for 3 minutes. Add enough unbleached flour to make a soft dough. (Dough will be sticky.)

Turn out on a lightly floured surface and knead for 10 minutes, adding unbleached flour as needed.

Place dough in a large, greased bowl, turning once to coat. Cover and let rise until double in size, approximately 1 to 1-1/2 hours.

Punch down dough. Divide into 4 parts and shape into loaves. Place each loaf into a greased 9 × 5 × 3-inch loaf pan. Cover and let rise until double in size, approximately 45 to 60 minutes.

Preheat oven to 375°F and bake for 35 to 45 minutes.

—JANET STERRETT

POORI

Indian fried bread.
Great with curry.

YIELD: 10 SERVINGS

3 cups all-purpose flour
1 cup whole-wheat flour
1/4 teaspoon salt
3 to 4 tablespoons margarine
    or butter, melted
Water
Vegetable oil for frying

➤ Combine flours. Add salt and melted margarine or butter.

Gradually add enough water to make a stiff dough. Refrigerate for 30 minutes.

Remove from refrigerator and form into small balls. Flatten the balls into small, thin discs. Deep-fry in vegetable oil until brown and crispy. Drain on paper towels and serve hot.

—DR. SOSAMMA BERGER

IRISH SODA BREAD

*Raisins and caraway
make this special.*

YIELD: 1 LOAF

4 cups all-purpose flour
1/4 cup sugar
1 teaspoon salt
1 teaspoon baking powder
1 teaspoon baking soda
1/4 cup (1/2 stick) butter
    or margarine
1/2 cup raisins, plumped
3 tablespoons caraway seed
1-1/2 cups buttermilk
1 egg yolk (optional)

இ Preheat oven to 325°F. Grease and flour a 2-quart oven-proof dish or a 9-inch black, cast-iron skillet.

Stir flour, sugar, salt, baking powder and baking soda into a large bowl. Cut in butter until mixture is crumbly and resembles coarse meal.

"Plump" raisins by simmering them in water to cover for 1 to 2 minutes, then drain. Add raisins and caraway seeds to flour mixture.

Add buttermilk, stirring until dry ingredients are moistened. Turn onto lightly floured surface and knead gently until dough is smooth (10 to 12 strokes). Shape dough into a ball; place in prepared 2-quart dish. Cut a 4-inch slit, about 1/2-inch deep, in center of loaf. If desired, brush surface with beaten egg yolk.

Bake for 1 hour and 15 minutes or until a toothpick inserted in the center comes out clean. Remove from oven. Cool thoroughly on a wire rack. Slice very thin to serve.

— SISTER ROSARIE

Five Star
BREADS

CARROT BREAD

YIELD: 1 LOAF

2 cups all-purpose flour
2 teaspoons baking soda
2 teaspoons cinnamon
1/2 teaspoon salt
3 eggs
3/4 cup vegetable oil
1-1/2 cups sugar
2 cups grated carrots
1 teaspoon vanilla
1/2 cup chopped nuts (optional)
1 cup raisins or 1/2 cup each,
    raisins and shredded
    coconut (optional)

&. Lightly grease and flour a
9 × 5 × 3-inch loaf pan.
    Sift flour, baking soda,
cinnamon and salt in a large bowl.
    Beat eggs, gradually adding
oil and sugar.
    Combine all ingredients
and pour into prepared loaf
pan. Allow the mixture to sit
for 20 minutes before baking to
prevent cracking.
    Bake in 350°F oven for
1 hour. Cool in pan for 15 minutes
before turning out on rack.

— PAMELA LaMANTIA
— DR. AGNES LINA
— MICHELLE MORSE

ZUCCHINI BREAD

*A sweet solution
for summer bounty.*

YIELD: 2 LOAVES

3 eggs, beaten
3 cups all-purpose flour
2 cups sugar
1 cup vegetable oil
2 cups grated zucchini
1 cup chopped nuts and/or raisins
1 cup crushed pineapple,
    drained (optional)
1/2 cup sour cream
1 teaspoon vanilla
1 teaspoon cinnamon
1 teaspoon baking soda
1/4 teaspoon baking powder
1 teaspoon salt
Confectioners sugar (optional)

&. Preheat oven to 350°F.
Lightly grease and flour two
9 × 5 × 3-inch loaf pans or one
large bundt pan.
    Sift flour and combine all
ingredients, except confectioners
sugar, and mix well by hand.
Pour batter into prepared pans
and bake for 1 hour or until a
toothpick inserted in the center
comes out clean. Remove from
pans and sprinkle with confectioners sugar.

— KATHY BAKER
— LAUREL SHIE BOWLES
— FLORA TUISKU

COCONUT BREAD

YIELD: 1 LOAF

1 cup shredded unsweetened
    coconut
3 cups all-purpose flour
1 tablespoon baking powder
3/4 cup sugar
1/2 teaspoon salt
1 egg
1-1/2 cups milk
1 teaspoon vanilla

&. Preheat oven to 350°F.
Lightly grease a 9 × 5 × 3-inch
loaf pan.
    Place shredded coconut
on an ungreased cookie sheet
and toast until golden, about
5 minutes. Be careful it does
not burn.
    Sift flour, baking powder,
sugar and salt into a large bowl.
Stir in coconut.
    Beat egg in small mixing
bowl; add milk and vanilla. Stir
egg mixture into dry ingredients.
Mix thoroughly, but do not
beat. Pour batter into prepared
pan and bake for 1 hour and
10 minutes or until a toothpick
inserted in the center comes
out clean.
    Cool on wire rack and
serve warm or toasted.

— MELANIA ADAMCIO

*When similar recipes were submitted,
acknowledgement was given to each contributor.*

CRANBERRY NUT BREAD

A holiday treat.

YIELD: 1 LOAF

2 cups all-purpose flour
1/2 teaspoon salt
1-1/2 teaspoons baking powder
1/2 teaspoon baking soda
1 cup sugar
1 egg
2 tablespoons butter, melted
1/2 cup orange juice
2 tablespoons lemon juice
1/2 cup chopped walnuts
1-1/2 cups whole raw cranberries
3 tablespoons grated orange rind

☙ Preheat oven to 350°F. Grease and lightly flour a 9 × 5 × 3-inch loaf pan.

Sift flour, salt, baking powder, baking soda and sugar in a large bowl; set aside.

Beat egg in small bowl and stir in the remaining ingredients. Mix well.

Fold egg mixture into flour mixture and spoon into prepared loaf pan. Bake for approximately 1 hour or until a toothpick inserted in the center comes out clean.

Cool in pan for 15 minutes; turn out on wire rack to cool completely.

— LYDIA B. OPPMANN

STRAWBERRY BREAD

Great with cream cheese.

YIELD: 2 LOAVES

4 eggs
1 cup vegetable oil
2-1/2 cups sliced fresh strawberries or 2 boxes (10 ounces each) unsweetened frozen strawberries, thawed and drained
3 cups all-purpose flour
2 cups sugar
1 tablespoon cinnamon
1 teaspoon salt
1 teaspoon baking soda
1-1/4 cups chopped pecans or other nuts

☙ Preheat oven to 350°F. Grease and lightly flour two 9 × 5 × 3-inch loaf pans.

Beat eggs lightly. Add oil and strawberries and mix well.

Sift flour, sugar, cinnamon, salt and baking soda into a large bowl. Add egg and strawberry mixture, blending until dry ingredients are just moistened. Stir in nuts.

Pour batter into prepared loaf pans. Bake for 50 to 60 minutes or until a toothpick inserted in the center comes out clean.

Cool in pans for 10 minutes before removing, then turn out on wire rack and cool completely.

— EDNA BURKLE
— HAZEL JENNINGS
— NANCY SHENKER

Five Star
BREADS

CHUNKY APPLE MUFFINS

Moist and dense.

YIELD: 24 MUFFINS

1 cup raisins
1 tablespoon brandy (optional)
4 cups peeled and coarsely
    chopped apples
1 cup sugar
2 large eggs, lightly beaten
1/2 cup vegetable oil
1-1/2 teaspoons vanilla
2 cups all-purpose flour
3 teaspoons cinnamon
2 teaspoons baking soda
1 teaspoon salt (optional)
1-1/4 cups coarsely chopped
    walnuts

෯ Preheat oven to 325°F.
Lightly grease two standard
(12) muffin tins. Soak raisins in
brandy and set aside.

Combine apples and sugar.
Add eggs, oil and vanilla and
stir well.

Mix dry ingredients in a
separate bowl. Add apple mixture,
raisins and walnuts, and mix
lightly.

Divide into prepared muffin
cups and bake for 20 to 30
minutes or until a toothpick
inserted in the center comes
out clean.

—NANCY HALPIN

PUMPKIN GINGERBREAD MUFFINS

A fall favorite.

YIELD: 12 MUFFINS

6 tablespoons butter, softened
1/3 cup dark brown sugar
1/3 cup sugar
1 egg
1/2 cup mashed pumpkin
1 tablespoon molasses
1-1/2 cups all-purpose flour
1/2 teaspoon salt
1/2 teaspoon baking soda
2 teaspoons baking powder
1 teaspoon ground ginger
1 teaspoon cinnamon
1/4 teaspoon ground cloves
1/8 teaspoon ground cardamom
1/2 cup milk or buttermilk
1 tablespoon corn oil
1/2 cup currants
1/2 cup chopped walnuts

෯ Preheat oven to 350°F.
Lightly oil muffin tin.

Cream butter and sugars.
Add egg, pumpkin and molasses;
set aside.

Sift flour, salt, baking soda,
baking powder and spices in a
large bowl. Add pumpkin mixture
to dry ingredients. Pour in
buttermilk and mix well. Stir in
oil, currants and nuts.

Fill muffin cups two-thirds
full and bake for 25 to 30 minutes
or until a toothpick inserted in
the center comes out clean.
Remove from pan after 2 to
3 minutes and serve immediately.

—LAURA STERKEL GRANT

BLUEBERRY MUFFINS

These don't last!

YIELD: 12 MUFFINS

1/2 cup butter, softened
1-1/4 cups sugar
2 eggs
2 cups all-purpose flour
2 teaspoons baking powder
1/2 teaspoon salt
1/2 cup milk
2 cups fresh blueberries, picked
    over and washed
3 teaspoons sugar for topping

෯ Preheat oven to 375°F.
Lightly grease muffin tin or
line with paper baking cups.

Cream butter and sugar in
a large bowl. Add eggs, one at a
time, beating well. Stir in flour,
baking powder, salt and milk.
Crush 1 cup of the blueberries
and add them to the batter.
Gently fold in the remaining
1 cup of blueberries.

Pour batter into muffin tin
and sprinkle with sugar. Bake
for approximately 30 minutes
or until a toothpick inserted in
the center comes out clean.
Serve warm.

—MRS. ROLAND D. CARLSON
—PAMELA LAPISH
—GAIL RESCH

*When similar recipes were submitted,
acknowledgement was given to each contributor.*

BANANA SWEET ROLLS

*A little work, but well
worth the effort!*

YIELD: 30-36 ROLLS

DOUGH
2 packages active dry yeast
1/2 cup warm water
1 cup milk
1/4 cup margarine
1/4 cup sugar
1/2 cup sour cream
1 teaspoon salt
1 cup oat bran
1 egg
1 banana, mashed
4-1/2 to 5 cups flour

FILLING
1/2 cup brown sugar
1 teaspoon cinnamon
1/2 cup sliced almonds
1 tablespoon margarine,
    melted

GLAZE
1 cup confectioners sugar
7 teaspoons milk
1/4 teaspoon almond extract

&❧ Add yeast to warm water and allow to stand 10 minutes.

Combine milk and margarine in saucepan over low heat. Pour mixture into a large mixing bowl; add sugar, sour cream, salt and oat bran. Allow to stand for 5 minutes to soften the oat bran. Add egg, banana and yeast mixture. Mix well.

Blend in flour to form a soft dough. Turn onto a lightly floured surface and knead until smooth (about 10 minutes). Place dough in an oiled bowl, cover with a damp cloth and allow to rise in a warm place for 1 hour.

Combine brown sugar, cinnamon and sliced almonds in a small bowl; set aside.

Knead dough and turn it onto a lightly floured surface. Divide in half and allow to rest for 10 minutes. Roll out half of the dough into a 15 × 10-inch rectangle. Brush with half the margarine and sprinkle with half the sugar mixture. Roll up, jelly roll-style, beginning with the long side. Seal edges. Cut into 1-inch slices and place, cut-side down, onto greased baking pans approximately 1 inch apart. Repeat with remaining dough. Cover and allow to rise for 45 minutes.

Preheat oven to 375°F. Bake for 16 minutes or until rolls are golden. Mix glaze ingredients and spread over cooled rolls, if desired.

— MARY WARD
COOKBOOK AUTHOR

Five Star
BREADS

41

BAKED FRENCH TOAST

Elegant brunch idea.

YIELD: 6-8 SERVINGS

4 cups graham cracker crumbs
    or corn flake crumbs
1-1/2 teaspoons cinnamon
3 teaspoons brown sugar
4 to 5 eggs (or egg substitute)
2-1/2 cups milk
1 teaspoon vanilla
12 slices day-old bread
    (white, French, raisin), sliced
    into halves
1/2 cup (1 stick) butter or
    margarine, melted

℞ Preheat oven to 450°F.
Lightly grease a cookie sheet
and set aside.

Place cracker crumbs in a
shallow pan and mix in cinnamon
and sugar. Set aside.

Beat eggs until foamy. Stir
in milk and vanilla. Dip bread
in egg mixture, turning once to
allow bread to soak up liquid,
then dip in crumb mixture and
coat thoroughly.

Place bread in a single
layer on prepared cookie sheet
and drizzle with melted butter
or margarine. Bake for 10 to 12
minutes or until lightly browned.

—MICHELLE L. SANSON

SWEDISH PANCAKES

A delicate crêpe.

YIELD: 4 SERVINGS

4 eggs
3/4 cup milk
3/4 cup all-purpose flour
1 teaspoon salt
1 tablespoon sugar
Butter

℞ Put all ingredients, except
butter, in container of blender
or food processor and process
on low until smooth, about 20
seconds.

Heat 1 tablespoon of butter
in a 10-inch omelet or crêpe
pan. When butter is brown and
scant, add 1/4 cup of batter and
swirl to coat bottom of pan. Cook
over medium-high heat until
shiny, about 30 to 45 seconds,
and flip. Repeat this process for
each pancake.

Roll up and serve with
butter, syrup or confectioners
sugar. For an extra special
Swedish treat, serve with
lingonberries or preserves, or
serve as a dessert with ice cream.

—CAROLYN CAPLAN

ZELLA'S CRESCENT ROLLS

Rich whole-wheat rolls.

YIELD: 32 ROLLS

2 packages active dry yeast
2 cups water
1 cup shortening
1/2 cup sugar
1 cup All-Bran cereal
2 teaspoons salt
2 eggs
6-1/2 cups sifted all-purpose flour

❧ Mix yeast with 1 cup warm water until dissolved. Set aside.

Combine shortening, sugar, All-Bran cereal and salt in a large bowl. Add 1 cup boiling water and stir until shortening is melted. Cool until lukewarm. Add eggs and yeast mixture. Stir in flour and mix until smooth. Cover and refrigerate overnight.

Divide dough into four equal parts and roll each into a 9-inch circle. Cut each circle into eight pie-shaped wedges and roll each wedge into a crescent shape. Place on a lightly greased cookie sheet, curving slightly, and allow the rolls to rise for 2 hours.

Bake in 450°F oven for 15 minutes or until lightly browned. Serve warm.

These freeze well.
— AILEEN FORD

NO-CHOLESTEROL POPOVERS

YIELD: 12 POPOVERS

6 egg whites
1 cup skim milk
2 tablespoons margarine, melted
1 cup all-purpose flour
1/4 teaspoon salt (optional)

❧ Preheat oven to 375°F. Spray or grease a standard size (12) muffin tin.

Beat egg whites in a large bowl at medium speed until frothy. Beat in milk and margarine until blended. Add flour and salt; beat until batter is smooth.

Fill each muffin cup about three-quarters full. Bake 50 minutes, then quickly make a small slit in the top of each popover to let out steam. Bake 5 minutes longer. Remove from muffin tin and serve piping hot.

This recipe can be easily cut in half for six servings. Best prepared an hour before serving, but can be made in the morning and reheated.

— MRS. MARC E. GRAVES

Five Star
BREADS

Zitny Rohlicky Rye Rolls

Vary the shapes for fun!

Yield: 24-36 rolls

2 cups lukewarm milk
1/4 cup brown sugar
1/2 teaspoon baking soda
2 tablespoons molasses
2 teaspoons salt
2 egg yolks, beaten
1 cake (0.6 ounces) fresh yeast
2 cups blended rye flour
1/4 cup vegetable oil
3-1/2 cups all-purpose flour
1 egg, beaten
Caraway seeds
2 tablespoons butter, melted

❧ Mix all ingredients, except butter, in the order given.

Lightly grease a large bowl. Place dough in bowl and turn to coat. Cover with a towel and let rise until double in bulk, **two times,** approximately 1-1/2 to 2 hours for each rising.

Make into rolls (see suggestions below) and let rise again, approximately one hour.

Brush with beaten egg and sprinkle with caraway seeds. Place on a lightly greased cookie sheet and bake in a 425°F oven for 12 to 15 minutes or until brown. Remove from oven and immediately brush with melted butter.

For knots, break off a small portion of dough and roll by hand into an 8-inch strip. Tie in a loose knot.

For braids, break off three pieces of dough and roll by hand into three 12-inch strips. Braid, securing well at both ends.

For figure eights, break off a piece of dough and roll by hand into a 12-inch strip. Form into a circle and twist once into a figure 8.

— Mary Rydzel

Old-Fashioned Chewy Pretzels

Fun to make with the whole family.

Yield: 16 pretzels

1 envelope active dry yeast
1-1/2 cups lukewarm water
2 teaspoons sugar
3/4 teaspoon salt
4 cups all-purpose flour
1 egg, beaten
Coarse salt

❧ Preheat oven to 400° F. Lightly grease a cookie sheet.

Soften yeast in 1/2 cup lukewarm water and 1 teaspoon sugar.

Combine remaining sugar, salt and flour in a large bowl. When the yeast mixture begins to bubble, add it to the dry ingredients, along with the remaining cup of water. Turn dough out on a lightly floured surface and knead until it is soft and smooth.

Do **not** let dough rise. Immediately divide dough into 16 pieces. Roll each piece into a 1/4-inch thick rope. Shape like a pretzel and pinch ends together. Place seam-side down on prepared cookie sheet, brush with egg and sprinkle with coarse salt. Bake for approximately 15 minutes or until golden brown. Serve with melted cheese or mustard for dipping.

Try these optional ingredients to make your own traditional family pretzel: corn flakes, sesame seeds, poppy seeds, Parmesan cheese or garlic powder.

— Claudia Gregorek

FRENCH ONION TART

*An appealing blend
of colors.*

YIELD: 8 SERVINGS

CRUST
1/2 teaspoon active dry yeast
1/2 cup lukewarm water
1 teaspoon salt
1-1/2 cups all-purpose flour
1 teaspoon olive oil

FILLING
1 pound Spanish onions, chopped
1/2 cup olive oil, divided
2 teaspoons Dijon-style mustard
1/4 pound Gruyère cheese, grated
3 to 4 ripe tomatoes
4 ounces black olives, pitted
    and sliced
1 teaspoon basil

৯ Dissolve yeast in lukewarm water in a large bowl. Set aside 2 to 3 minutes.

Mix salt with flour and add to yeast mixture. Add 1 teaspoon olive oil. Mix thoroughly and turn out on floured surface. Knead for 10 minutes. Place dough in a large, oiled bowl, turning once to coat. Cover with towel and let rise in a warm place until double in bulk.

Sauté onions in 1/3 cup olive oil until browned. Cool.

Punch down dough and roll into a circle to fit a 9-inch tart pan. Place in pan and spread mustard on dough. Top with onions and grated cheese.

Core and halve tomatoes. Cut each half into six wedges and arrange on tart, filling spaces between tomatoes with sliced olives. Sprinkle tart with basil. Drizzle with the remaining olive oil and set tart in warm place until dough rises slightly above pan.

Bake in 375°F oven for 30 to 35 minutes. Serve warm or at room temperature.

—CLARENCE GALLMANN

Five Star
BREADS

STUFFED ITALIAN-STYLE BREAD

A colorful treat.

YIELD: 8-12 SERVINGS

1 large round loaf of bread
1/3 cup olive oil
1 tablespoon unsalted butter
3 large eggs, lightly beaten
    with salt and pepper to taste
1/4 pound Italian salami, sliced
1/2 pound provolone cheese,
    sliced
1 jar (14 ounces) roasted red
    peppers, drained and dried
    on paper towels
1/3 pound mozzarella cheese,
    sliced
1/4 pound mortadella, sliced
1 package (10 ounces) frozen
    spinach, thawed and
    squeezed dry
1/4 pound prosciutto, sliced
1 teaspoon dried herbs (Herbes
    de Provence, oregano, etc.)

∾ Preheat oven to 350°F. Cut off the top of the bread and set aside. Cut around the inside of the bread, leaving about a 1-inch shell, and carefully remove the inside of the bread. (Save for another use.) Brush the inside of bread with about 3 tablespoons olive oil.

Melt butter over medium-high heat in a skillet the approximate size of the bread and add eggs to make an omelet. Allow the eggs to set on the underside. Flip and continue to cook until done. Remove from heat and set aside.

Line the hollow bread with all of the salami, half of the provolone, half of the roasted peppers and all of the mortadella.

Spread the spinach in an even layer and top with all of the mozzarella. Add the second half of the roasted peppers and top with the omelet, trimmed to fit. Add the prosciutto and the other half of the provolone cheese.

Sprinkle with herbs and drizzle with the remaining olive oil. Replace the top of the bread and wrap it in foil. Place on a cookie sheet and bake in foil for approximately 1 hour.

Unwrap bread and continue to bake an additional 15 minutes or until bread is crisp. Cut in wedges.

Serve warm or at room temperature.

—SUSIE HELLER

PM Magazine's Pizza on the Grill

A light, crisp crust with a rich, woodsy flavor.

YIELD: 2 LARGE, THIN-CRUSTED PIZZAS

1 package dry yeast
3/4 cup very warm water
2 cups flour (a combination of
    white and wheat, if possible)
1/2 teaspoon salt
2 medium yellow peppers
    (mild or hot)
2 medium sweet green peppers
12-ounce piece hot Italian
    sausage in casing
4 large ripe tomatoes, sliced
1 medium onion, sliced
2 cups sliced mushrooms
2 cups shredded cheese
    (mozzarella, Romano,
    Parmesan)

❖ Dissolve yeast in water for 5 minutes. Add flour and salt and mix. Knead for 2 or 3 minutes until flour is well blended. Allow to rest in a warm place.

Meanwhile, preheat charcoal grill to very hot (450°-475°F). Adjust grill grid to 8 inches above source of heat.

Place peppers and sausage on grill. Cover grill; roast peppers and sausage for 15 minutes, turning 3 or 4 times.

While peppers and sausage cook, roll pizza dough to fit two 12-inch, well-greased pizza pans. Top pizzas with tomatoes, onion and mushrooms.

Remove peppers from grill and place into a paper bag (to facilitate removal of skin). Remove sausage to a cutting board. Place 1 pizza pan on grill. Cover and allow to cook for 5 minutes. Slice sausage thinly. Remove skin from peppers and cut into strips.

Gently slide pizza from pan directly onto the grill surface. Top pizza with half the sausage, peppers and cheese. Cover and continue to cook for 15 to 20 minutes until cheese melts. Remove to a cutting board and divide into 6 slices.

Repeat with other pizza.

— MARY WARD
COOKBOOK AUTHOR

Five Star
BREADS

47

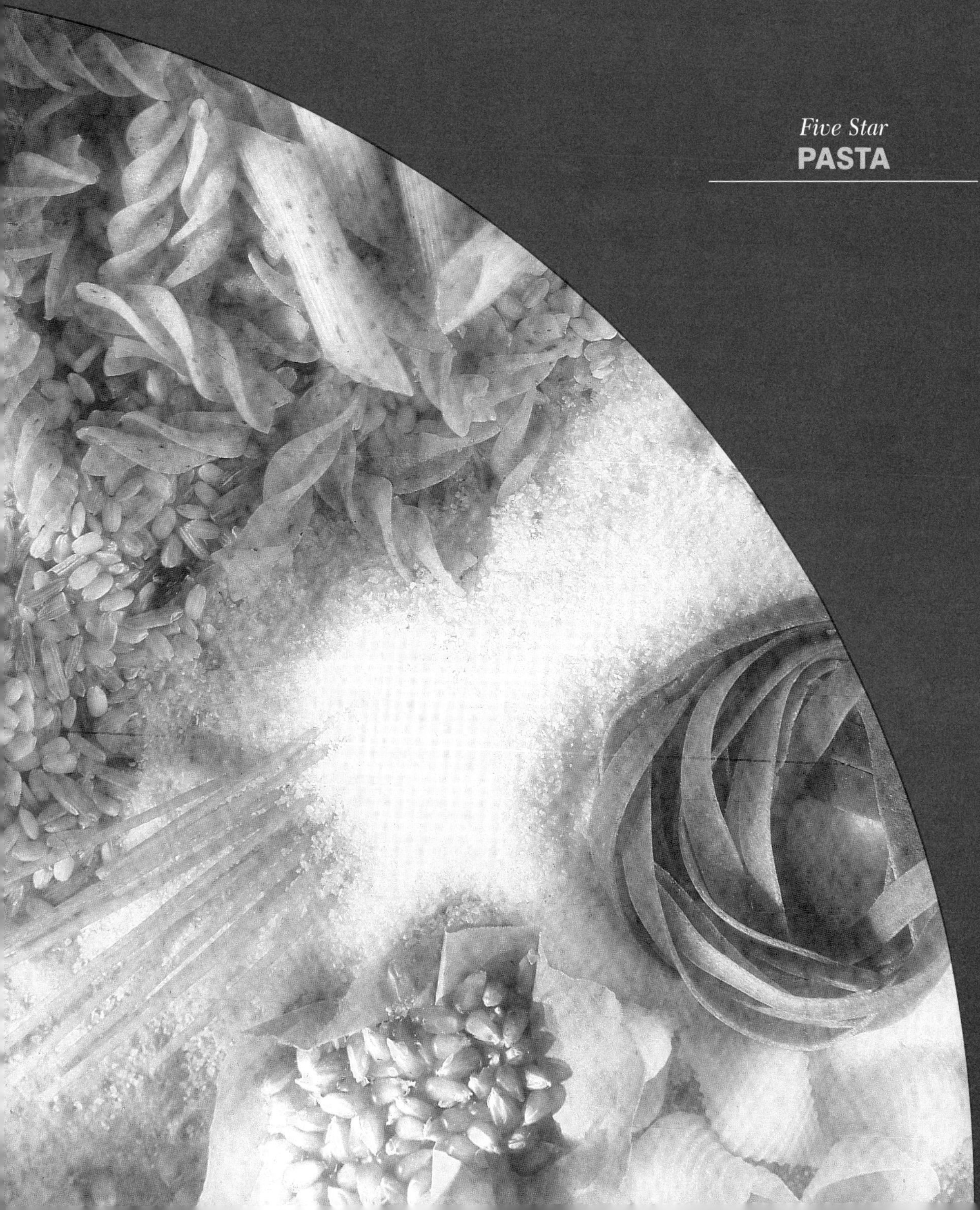

Five Star
PASTA

Pasta with Stuffed Tomatoes and Goat Cheese

Excellent first course.

YIELD: 8 SERVINGS

8 small tomatoes
Salt to taste
12 ounces goat cheese
1/4 cup olive oil
2 cloves garlic, minced
1 cup chopped basil leaves
1 pound angel hair pasta
2 tablespoons butter
1 tablespoon lemon juice
Whole basil leaves

∾ Preheat oven to 400°F and lightly grease a 3-quart oven-proof dish.

Slice the tops off the tomatoes; set aside. Scoop out the tomato seeds, sprinkle with salt and turn upside down on paper towels for 1/2 hour to drain.

Cream goat cheese and oil in a mixing bowl. Add garlic and chopped basil leaves, mixing well. Fill tomato shells with cheese mixture and replace tops of tomatoes. Place in prepared dish and bake for 15 minutes. **Do not overcook as tomatoes will collapse.**

Bring a large pot of salted water to a boil and add angel hair pasta. Cook until tender but not limp, about 5 minutes. Drain pasta and toss with butter and lemon.

To serve, place tomatoes on a large platter and surround them with the pasta. Garnish with fresh basil leaves.

—CLAIRE MORGAN

Fettucine with Tomatoes, Basil, Capers and Goat Cheese

Also delicious as an appetizer for eight.

YIELD: 4 SERVINGS

2 tablespoons olive oil
1 tablespoon butter
3 large vine-ripe tomatoes, peeled and coarsely chopped
4 fresh basil leaves or 2 teaspoons dried basil, chopped
2 tablespoons capers
1 pound fresh fettucine
1/4 pound goat cheese, sliced into rounds
Pepper to taste

∾ Heat oil and butter in a large skillet. Add tomatoes, basil and capers. Cook until tomatoes are just soft.

Cook fettucine in boiling salted water until al dente. Drain and remove to serving platter.

Pour sauce over fettucine and top with thin slices of goat cheese. Mill fresh pepper on top and serve immediately.

—JAMES T. BARTLETT

PASTA WITH TOMATOES, CHEESE AND SOUR CREAM

A dish the children will love.

YIELD: 4-5 SERVINGS

2 cups macaroni bows, shells
   or twists
3 tablespoons olive oil
1 cup minced onion
1 can (14-1/2 ounces) tomatoes
   with liquid
1-1/2 teaspoons dried oregano
1-1/2 teaspoons dried basil
Salt and pepper to taste
1 cup sour cream, at room
   temperature
1 cup shredded American cheese
Butter

❧ Preheat oven to 350°F. Lightly grease a 9-inch square baking dish.

Cook pasta in boiling water until just tender and drain.

Sauté onion in olive oil over medium-high heat until limp. Add canned tomatoes with liquid, oregano, basil, salt and pepper, and cook slowly, approximately 10 minutes.

Combine cooked pasta, tomato mixture, sour cream and cheese in a large bowl. Spoon into prepared baking dish. Dot with butter. Bake until mixture is bubbly and top is golden, approximately 20 minutes.

— CAROL SPARK FULOP

ASPARAGUS AND FARFALLE PASTA

YIELD: 4 SERVINGS

6 ounces bow-tie (Farfalle)
   pasta, blanched
5 tablespoons butter, divided
Salt and pepper to taste
3/4 cup heavy cream
1/2 cup grated Parmesan cheese
1 tablespoon chopped fresh
   basil, divided
12 asparagus spears, blanched
2 tomatoes, diced
Chopped fresh parsley
Shaved Parmesan cheese

❧ Toss pasta with 2 tablespoons butter and season with salt and pepper. Add cream and bring to a boil over medium-high heat. Add grated Parmesan cheese and 1-1/2 teaspoons basil.

Sauté asparagus with remaining butter, season with salt and pepper. Set aside. Arrange pasta on serving plates, top with tomatoes, parsley and shaved Parmesan cheese. Surround with asparagus spears, sprinkle with remaining basil and serve.

— CHEF LUCIEN VENDÔME

Five Star
PASTA

Stouffer Hotels and Resorts
Corporate Office
29800 Bainbridge Road
Solon, OH 44139
216-248-3600

PASTA WITH PESTO AND SEAFOOD

YIELD: 4 SERVINGS
OR 6-8 APPETIZER SERVINGS

3 cloves garlic or more to taste
3/4 teaspoon salt
1-1/2 tablespoons pine nuts
1-1/2 cups fresh basil leaves
1/3 cup plus 1 tablespoon olive oil
1/3 cup grated Parmesan cheese
1/2 cup dry white wine
Juice of 1/2 lemon
Salt and pepper to taste
1 pound bay scallops or peeled
    raw shrimp, cut in half, or
    a combination
1 pound capellini or vermicelli

❧ Place garlic, salt, pine nuts and basil in food processor fitted with a steel blade. Begin processing and gradually add 1/3 cup oil until ingredients have been reduced to a paste. Add cheese and process until blended; set aside in a large mixing bowl.

Place wine, lemon, salt and pepper in a saucepan and bring to a boil. Add the shellfish and simmer until barely cooked, 3 to 5 minutes. Drain, reserving the cooking liquid.

Bring a large pot of water to a rolling boil. Add one tablespoon of olive oil. Add the pasta and cook, stirring with a fork to separate the strands, for 5 to 7 minutes or until al dente.

Drain the pasta and immediately add it to the pesto, tossing thoroughly. Add the reserved cooking liquid, gradually, and toss. Finally, add the shellfish and toss gently.

Serve immediately or refrigerate and serve cold.

—PEGGY CALDWELL
AND DAN ELLIOTT

Toasted Vermicelli with Onions and Mushrooms

Yield: 6 servings

8 ounces fideo or vermicelli coils
1/2 onion, finely minced
4 tablespoons butter
1/4 pound mushrooms, finely chopped
2-1/2 cups rich chicken broth
Salt and pepper to taste

ঌ Toast fideos in a 350°F oven approximately 8 minutes or until golden brown. Set aside.

Sauté onion in 2 tablespoons butter until onion is soft. Add mushrooms and continue sautéing until mushrooms are tender. Set aside.

Melt remaining 2 tablespoons butter in a saucepan and add chicken broth, salt and pepper. Bring mixture to a boil and add toasted fideos. Reduce heat and simmer until fideos are tender and liquid is absorbed, about 10 minutes. Add onion and mushroom mixture and toss to combine.

—Claudia Gregorek

Spinach Sauce
for pasta
A close relative to pesto.
Yield: 6-8 servings

1 pound pasta

SPINACH SAUCE
1 pound fresh spinach
8 sprigs fresh flatleaf parsley
2 cloves garlic
2 tablespoons pine nuts
4 tablespoons extra virgin olive oil
1 teaspoon salt
1/2 teaspoon pepper
Freshly grated Parmesan cheese for garnish

ঌ Cook pasta in boiling salted water until al dente. Drain and pour into serving bowl.

Wash spinach and place in container of food processor. Add parsley, garlic, pine nuts, oil, salt and pepper and purée for 2 minutes.

To serve, toss pasta with sauce and pass Parmesan cheese for garnish.

—Zona Spray
THE ZONA SPRAY COOKING SCHOOL

Five Star
PASTA

PENNE ALL' ARRABBIATA
MACARONI PENS WITH ANGRY SAUCE
Robust, "hot" taste from Tuscany.
YIELD: 4 SERVINGS

1 pound penne

ANGRY SAUCE
Extra virgin olive oil
2 cans (14-1/2 ounces each)
    Italian-style stewed tomatoes
1 large clove garlic, scored
    top and bottom
1 teaspoon crushed hot red
    pepper*
1/8 teaspoon salt
1 teaspoon oregano
1/2 large, sweet red pepper,
    chopped
1 small onion, chopped

Warning: This is what makes the sauce "angry." Use less if you are not used to hot foods.

⇢ Heat just enough oil to cover the bottom of a large frying pan. Add all ingredients for Angry Sauce and bring to a simmer over low heat. Simmer for 1 hour, stirring occasionally, until ingredients lose their identities and sauce is smooth.

Cook penne in boiling salted water. Boil until pasta softens but retains some resilience. Drain pasta, transfer to serving platter and cover with sauce.

Angry Sauce can be prepared ahead of time and refrigerated or frozen and reheated for later use.

— PAUL J. VINCENT

PENNE COLORATE
A colorful pasta.
YIELD: 4 SERVINGS

4 cups frozen artichoke hearts
2 teaspoons lemon juice
1 pound penne
1 large onion, chopped
1 green pepper, chopped
1 yellow pepper, chopped
2 cloves garlic, minced
4 tablespoons olive oil
2 red ripe tomatoes, chopped
1 teaspoon salt
1/8 teaspoon pepper
1 teaspoon chopped fresh parsley
1/2 cup grated Parmesan cheese

⇢ Thaw, drain and slice artichoke hearts and place in a bowl with lemon juice.

Cook the pasta in a large pot of boiling salted water until al dente and drain.

Sauté the onion, peppers and garlic in olive oil in a large skillet over medium-high heat until onion is translucent. Add drained artichoke hearts and chopped tomatoes and cook for 20 minutes or until reduced. Season with salt and pepper. Add parsley and stir through.

Toss the pasta with the sauce and sprinkle with cheese.

— LORETTA PAGANINI
LORETTA PAGANINI
SCHOOL OF COOKING

PASTA PRIMAVERA

Springtime treat.

YIELD: 6 SERVINGS

1/2 cup (1 stick) margarine
1 medium onion, finely chopped
2 large cloves garlic, pressed
1 pound fresh asparagus spears,
    diagonally cut in
    1/4-inch pieces
6 ounces cauliflower, cut in
    1/4-inch pieces
1 medium zucchini, cut in
    1/4-inch pieces
1 carrot, halved and cut in
    1/8-inch pieces
1/2 pound fresh button
    mushrooms, thinly sliced
1 cup half and half
1/2 cup chicken stock
2 tablespoons chopped fresh basil
1 cup tiny frozen peas, thawed
5 ounces baked ham, chopped
5 scallions, finely chopped
Salt and pepper to taste
1 pound linguine
1 cup grated Romano cheese
2 to 3 plum tomatoes, cut in
    wedges for garnish

ﳢ Heat a large skillet. Add margarine and onion and sauté for approximately 2 minutes.

Add garlic, asparagus, cauliflower, zucchini and carrot and stir-fry over medium-high heat another 2 minutes. Add mushrooms and continue to sauté another 2 minutes.

Increase heat and add half and half, chicken stock and basil. Bring to a boil and cook until liquid is slightly reduced, about 3 minutes.

Stir in peas, ham and scallions and cook to heat through, about 3 minutes. Season with salt and pepper.

Cook pasta in a large pot of boiling salted water until al dente. Drain.

Combine all ingredients and toss. Turn out onto large serving platter and garnish with wedges of fresh plum tomatoes.

—HELEN L. JUDGE

Five Star
PASTA

GIOVANNI'S
PANSOTTI DI MARE CON SALSA DI NOCE
Delicious pasta with seafood. Not for the novice cook.
YIELD: 4 MAIN SERVINGS OR 8 APPETIZER SERVINGS

PANSOTTI
1-1/2 to 2 cups all-purpose flour
1 egg
1 teaspoon salt
1/2 to 3/4 cup water

FILLING
2 shallots, minced
1 cup sliced shiitake (or button)
    mushrooms
2 tablespoons butter
2 tablespoons white wine
5 ounces sea scallops
3 ounces halibut
1/8 teaspoon cayenne pepper
Salt to taste
Freshly ground pepper
1/3 cup heavy whipping cream
4 ounces uncooked shrimp,
    peeled, deveined and
    chopped
1 egg for sealing pasta squares

SAUCE
2 ounces unsalted butter
1 cup heavy whipping cream
2-1/2 ounces chopped walnuts
1-1/2 ounces Parmesan cheese,
    grated
1/8 teaspoon nutmeg
Salt to taste
Freshly ground pepper
3 egg yolks

CABBAGE MIXTURE
1/2 pound bacon, minced
1/2 head savoy cabbage, julienned
Salt to taste
Freshly ground pepper
Basil leaves for garnish
Walnuts for garnish

☙ Pour the flour onto a board; make a well and break the egg into it. Add salt and blend with fork; add water and mix until the dough is smooth and soft. Form the dough into a ball and wrap it in a sheet of plastic wrap. Refrigerate for 30 minutes.

Sauté the shallots and mushrooms in butter in a heavy skillet over medium-high heat until limp, about 3 minutes. Add wine and cook another 3 minutes. Cool slightly and put into container of a blender or food processor. Add scallops, halibut, cayenne, salt and pepper. Process until blended but not puréed. Add the heavy cream in a steady stream while the processor is running until the consistency of heavy pudding is achieved. Pour into a mixing bowl. Fold in the chopped shrimp.

Roll pasta into thin sheets or use a pasta machine on a setting of "5."

To fill the pasta, cut pasta into 3-1/2-inch squares and place a dollop of the seafood filling atop the pasta. Moisten the perimeter of the pasta square with egg wash and lift the corners toward the center to form a point. Seal the edges together by pinching them lightly. Cook the pansotti squares in boiling salted water for 4 to 5 minutes. Drain.

To make sauce, heat butter and cream in a saucepan over medium heat until bubbling. Add walnuts, cheese, nutmeg, salt and pepper; then whisk in egg yolks immediately to avoid curdling. Keep warm.

To serve, sauté bacon until crisp; add cabbage and sauté until limp; add salt and pepper to taste. Divide cabbage onto four plates as a bed for the pasta squares. Place 8 to 9 pansotti atop the cabbage and sprinkle with a portion of the sauce. Garnish with basil leaves and additional walnuts.

—CARL QUAGLIATA
GIOVANNI'S
CLEVELAND, OHIO

Stuffed Pasta with Walnut Basil Sauce

Unusual nutty flavor.

Yield: 8-10 servings

40 large pasta shells for
   stuffing (1-1/2 pounds)

FILLING
1 pound Swiss chard or escarole,
   boiled until tender and well
   drained
2 plum tomatoes, peeled
1/2 pound ricotta cheese
1/4 pound Gorgonzola or bleu
   cheese
Extra virgin olive oil

WALNUT BASIL SAUCE
2-1/2 cups fresh basil leaves
3 cloves garlic
4 large plum tomatoes, diced
1/3 cup Parmesan cheese
3/4 cup fresh walnuts
10 tablespoons extra virgin
   olive oil
Salt and freshly ground pepper
   to taste

Cook shells according to package directions. Drain and cool.

To make filling, hand chop the Swiss chard and tomatoes until fine. Combine with ricotta and Gorgonzola cheeses until ingredients form a stiff paste.

Lightly stuff shells with filling. Place into a large, well greased baking dish(es). Drizzle with olive oil.

To make sauce, combine basil, garlic, tomatoes, Parmesan cheese and walnuts in container of food processor or blender and slowly add olive oil. Do not let the mixture turn to a paste; try to keep the texture fairly coarse. Add salt and pepper. Heat in the top of a double boiler, making sure not to overcook.

To serve, preheat oven to 400°F. Cover shells with foil and heat for 15 minutes. Serve with hot sauce.

—Jerome F. Weiss

Five Star
PASTA

ANGEL OF HEARTS

A heavenly pasta.

YIELD: 4 SERVINGS

1/4 cup extra virgin olive oil
4 cloves garlic, minced
1 cup julienned shiitake
    mushrooms
4 chicken breast halves (6 ounces
    each), boned, skinned and
    cut into 1-inch strips
1 cup all-purpose flour
1 cup quartered artichoke hearts
1/2 cup sweet vermouth
1 cup chicken stock
1/4 cup lemon juice
1 cup heavy cream
1 cup grated Parmesan cheese
1 pound angel hair pasta
1 teaspoon tarragon leaves
    for garnish

ও Sauté garlic and mushrooms in olive oil in a 10 to 12-inch skillet. Remove from skillet and set aside.

Dredge chicken strips in flour and sauté in same skillet until golden brown. Remove and set aside with mushroom mixture.

Add quartered artichoke hearts to skillet and sauté until golden brown. Add to chicken mixture.

Deglaze the skillet with sweet vermouth, stirring to mix juices and sediment. Add chicken stock and lemon juice and continue cooking for 1 minute. Return chicken, mushrooms and artichoke hearts to skillet and continue cooking. Add heavy cream and Parmesan cheese. Stir and simmer for approximately 5 minutes.

Cook angel hair pasta in pot of boiling salted water for 6 to 8 minutes. Drain.

Place pasta on a large serving platter and top with chicken and sauce. Garnish with tarragon leaves and serve warm.

To add color to this recipe, try a spinach or tomato pasta. Pimiento and paprika can also add a devilish look to this heavenly recipe.

—JONATHAN S. JUHASZ
KIRTLAND COUNTRY CLUB

Alfred Portale's Goat Cheese Ravioli with Tomatoes, Thyme and Garlic

Yield: 4-6 servings

DOUGH
5-1/4 cups all-purpose flour
Salt as needed
4 egg yolks
4 whole eggs

FILLING
1 pound fresh goat cheese
2 whole eggs
Salt and freshly ground pepper

GARNISH
3 ounces rich chicken stock
1 recipe garlic butter
1/2 cup peeled, seeded tomatoes,
    cut into 1/4-inch dice
1 tablespoon chopped parsley
1 tablespoon chopped chives

GARLIC BUTTER
8 ounces butter
1 or 2 cloves minced garlic
1/2 teaspoon fresh savory
1/2 teaspoon fresh thyme
Salt and freshly ground
    black pepper

To make the dough, place flour, salt, egg yolks and eggs into container of food processor. Mix lightly. Add few drops water and pulse machine to bring together as a mass. Turn out onto a floured board and begin to knead approximately 10 to 15 minutes. Cover dough with plastic and allow to rest in refrigerator 1 hour before rolling and cutting.

To make the filling, cream the cheese and eggs. Season mixture with salt and freshly ground pepper. Roll out pasta on machine's lowest setting and make ravioli in the usual way.

To prepare garlic butter, cream all ingredients and adjust seasonings.

To serve, cook ravioli in boiling salted water until tender. Place chicken stock in small saucepan, bring to a rapid boil and whisk in herb butter. Add tomato dice and taste for seasonings. Arrange ravioli on warm soup plates, spoon a little sauce around and sprinkle with fresh parsley and chives.

— CHEF ALFRED PORTALE

Five Star
PASTA

The Gotham Bar and Grill
12 East 12th Street
New York, NY 10003
212-620-4020

ROSY ROSA PASTA

*Just as good
the second day.*

YIELD: 8-10 SERVINGS

1 pound rosa marina pasta
6 tablespoons butter, divided
10 slices bacon, cooked and
    crumbled
2 medium onions, diced
3 cloves garlic, minced
1/2 cup Parmesan cheese
3 large tomatoes, diced
3 tablespoons chopped fresh
    parsley
1 teaspoon chopped fresh
    thyme leaves

&ed; Cook pasta in boiling salted water until al dente, about 5 minutes. Drain, place in serving bowl and add 3 tablespoons butter. Add bacon to pasta.

Melt remaining butter in a skillet over medium-high heat and sauté onions and garlic until brown, about 10 minutes. Toss into pasta. Add remaining ingredients, toss and serve.

—MARGARET SIMON

WILD MUSHROOM PASTA

YIELD: 4 SERVINGS

1 pound pasta, cooked al dente
5 large shallots, chopped
5 tablespoons extra virgin
    olive oil
1/4 pound pancetta (Italian bacon)
1 pound button mushrooms, sliced
1/4 pound wild mushrooms
    (morels, porcini or shiitake),
    sliced
2 tomatoes, chopped and seeded
1/4 cup white wine
4 tablespoons pine nuts, toasted
1/4 cup chopped parsley
3 tablespoons grated Parmesan
    cheese

&ed; Place cooked pasta in a large serving bowl.

Sauté shallots in oil. Add pancetta and continue sautéing over medium-high heat until cooked through. Add mushrooms and cook until done, about 5 minutes. Add tomatoes and sauté for a minute. Add wine, stirring well.

Pour sauce over pasta and sprinkle with pine nuts, parsley and Parmesan cheese.

Serve with Italian bruschetta and a green salad.

—CAMILLE LaBARRE

ALFRED PORTALE'S
WILD MUSHROOM PASTA
YIELD: 4 SERVINGS

SAUCE
2 cups fresh morels or 24 dried
   morels
2 tablespoons butter
1/2 cup carrots, cut into
   1/8-inch dice
1/2 cup finely diced celery
3/4 cup finely diced onion
1/2 teaspoon finely minced garlic
1 small leek, well trimmed and
   finely diced
3 sprigs fresh parsley
1 bay leaf
3 sprigs fresh thyme
2 cups vegetable stock
2 cups heavy cream
Salt to taste
Freshly ground black pepper

GARNISH
3 cups assorted wild mushrooms*,
   stems partially trimmed
   and discarded
1 tablespoon finely chopped
   shallots
1 tablespoon finely chopped
   parsley
Salt to taste
Freshly ground black pepper

*If dried morels are used, put them
in a bowl and add warm water to
cover. Let stand at least 15 minutes.
Drain and squeeze to extract most of
the excess moisture. Strain water
carefully and use in vegetable stock.
Cut morels, fresh or dried, into
1/2-inch pieces.*

**PASTA AND FINAL SAUCE
PREPARATION**
1/2 pound penne
2 tablespoons finely chopped
   basil
2 tablespoons finely chopped
   parsley
1/2 cup peeled, seeded tomato
   cut into 1/4-inch cubes
4 tablespoons toasted pine nuts

‽ Heat half the butter in a
heavy kettle or oven-proof dish;
add the carrot, celery, onion,
garlic and leek. Cook and stir
about 3 minutes without
browning. Add the morels,
fresh or dried, cook and stir
about 1 minute.

Tie parsley, bay leaf and
thyme into a bundle. Add this
to the kettle. Add the vegetable
stock and cook 15 minutes or
until the liquid has been
reduced to about 1/4 cup. Add
the cream and bring to a boil.
Cook over moderate heat about
15 minutes or until the sauce is
reduced to about 3 cups.

Meanwhile, heat the
remaining tablespoon of butter
in a skillet and add the wild
mushrooms. Cook and stir
about 2 minutes or until the
mushrooms give up their liquid.
Add the shallots, parsley, salt
and pepper and blend well.
Cook about 1 minute and
remove from the heat.

Bring 10 cups of water to a
boil and add salt to taste. Add
the penne and cook 7 to 10
minutes or until the desired
degree of doneness. Drain.

Meanwhile, as the pasta
cooks, sprinkle the morel sauce
with basil and parsley. Add the
wild mushroom mixture and
stir to blend. Add the penne to
this sauce and toss. Spoon
equal portions of the penne
with sauce into each of the four
hot soup plates. Spoon equal
portions of the cubed tomatoes
into the center of each portion
and sprinkle with equal amounts
of pine nuts.

— CHEF ALFRED PORTALE

The Gotham Bar and Grill
12 East 12th Street
New York, NY 10003
212-620-4020

Three-Mushroom Lasagna with Gorgonzola Sauce

Yield: 8-12 servings

2 ounces dried porcini
  mushrooms
1/2 pound (2 sticks) plus
  1 tablespoon unsalted butter
3-1/2 tablespoons olive oil
4 large shallots, minced
2 pounds fresh mushrooms,
  minced
1-1/2 teaspoons salt
1/2 teaspoon freshly ground
  black pepper
1/2 teaspoon tarragon
Cayenne pepper
1/4 cup lemon juice
2 small garlic cloves, minced
3/4 pound fresh shiitake
  mushrooms, stemmed, caps
  sliced 1/4-inch thick
1/2 cup all-purpose flour
2 cups milk
1 cup heavy cream
1/4 pound Gorgonzola
  dolcelatte cheese
1 cup grated Parmesan cheese
Homemade lasagna noodles
  or 1 package (16 ounces)
  lasagna noodles

🦢 Cover the porcini with 3 cups boiling water in a small bowl. Let stand until softened, 20 to 30 minutes. Lift out the mushrooms; reserve the liquid. Coarsely chop the porcini. Strain the liquid through a double layer of cheesecloth and reserve 2 cups.

Melt 2 tablespoons of the butter and 1 tablespoon of the oil in a large heavy skillet over moderately high heat. Add 2 tablespoons of the minced shallots and half the fresh mushrooms. Sauté, stirring frequently, until the mushrooms give up their liquid (it evaporates), and they become lightly browned, 5 to 7 minutes. Season these mushroom duxelles with 1/4 teaspoon each of salt, black pepper and tarragon, a dash or two of cayenne pepper and 1 tablespoon of the lemon juice. Scrape into a bowl. Wipe out the skillet with a paper towel. Repeat with 2 more tablespoons of the butter and 1 tablespoon oil, adding 2 more tablespoons of the shallots and the remaining minced fresh mushrooms. Season as above. Add to the bowl. Wipe out the skillet.

Melt 3 tablespoons of the butter and the remaining 1-1/2 tablespoons oil in the same large skillet over moderately high heat. Add the remaining minced shallots and the garlic, and sauté for 30 seconds. Add the shiitake and porcini mushrooms and sauté, stirring frequently, for 3 minutes. Reduce the heat to moderately low and cook, stirring frequently, for 5 minutes. Add 1 cup of the reserved porcini liquid and simmer, partially covered, for 5 to 10 minutes, until the mushrooms are tender but still slightly chewy. Uncover and cook, stirring frequently, until the remaining liquid evaporates. Season with the remaining 2 tablespoons lemon juice, and salt and pepper to taste. Add to the mushroom duxelles and set aside.

Melt 1 stick of butter in a large skillet over moderate heat. Add the flour and cook, stirring, for 2 to 3 minutes without letting the flour color. Whisk in the remaining 1 cup mushroom liquid, the milk and the cream. Bring to a boil, whisking constantly, until thickened and smooth. Reduce the heat and simmer, whisking frequently, for 5 minutes. Whisk in the Gorgonzola and 1/2 cup of the Parmesan cheese until melted. Season with 1 teaspoon salt and several dashes of cayenne pepper.

Cook the lasagna noodles in a large pot of boiling salted water until just tender. Drain and rinse under cold running water. Place in a bowl of cold water and, one by one, lay the noodles out in a single layer on kitchen towels to dry.

To assemble the lasagna, generously butter two baking pans (14 × 9 × 2-inch). If the sauce has cooled, reheat it slightly over low heat. Arrange a layer of noodles in the bottom of each dish, trimming to fit, if necessary, and overlapping the edges only slightly. Spread a thin layer of mushrooms over the noodles (using one-quarter of the total amount in each pan) and drizzle about 1 cup of sauce over the mushrooms in each pan. Repeat with another layer of noodles, mushrooms and sauce. Top with a final layer of noodles. Spread the remaining sauce over the noodles, dividing evenly, and sprinkle 1/4 cup grated Parmesan cheese over the top of each. Dot each with 1 tablespoon butter. (The lasagnas can be assembled completely and refrigerated, covered, overnight, or frozen for up to 2 weeks.)

Preheat the oven to 375°F. Bake the lasagna (thawed, if frozen) uncovered for 20 to 30 minutes, until heated through and lightly browned on top.

Previously published in *Cooking for a Crowd*, Harmony Books, a division of Crown Publishers, Inc., copyright ©1988, by Susan Wyler, reprinted with permission.

—SUSAN WYLER
COOKBOOK AUTHOR

Five Star
PASTA

CREAMED LASAGNA

A vegetarian treat.

YIELD: 6-8 SERVINGS

8 ounces lasagna noodles
1 egg
1 pound low-fat cottage cheese
1 pound Monterey Jack cheese, shredded
1/2 cup grated Parmesan cheese

SAUCE
6 tablespoons butter
1 pound sliced mushrooms
1 teaspoon lemon juice
1/4 cup plus 3 tablespoons all-purpose flour
1 teaspoon salt
1/8 teaspoon pepper
3 cups milk
2 tablespoons dried parsley

🐦 Cook lasagna noodles in boiling salted water until al dente. Drain and set aside. Beat the egg; add cottage cheese and mix well. Set aside.

For sauce, melt butter in large heavy skillet. Add mushrooms and lemon juice and sauté until mushrooms wilt, about 6 minutes. Add flour, salt and pepper. Gradually stir in milk and cook until thickened, approximately 5 minutes. Stir in parsley and mix well.

Pour 1/2 cup of the sauce into a 9 × 13-inch lasagna pan. Alternate layers of noodles, cottage cheese-egg mixture, Parmesan cheese, Monterey Jack cheese and sauce. Repeat layers, ending with sauce. Bake in 350°F oven for 1 hour. Allow to stand for 20 minutes before serving.

—SHIRLEY CHESSIN

Garden Lasagna

*A variety of vegetables are
highlighted in this lasagna.*

YIELD: 8 SERVINGS

1-1/2 cups sliced mushrooms
1 cup chopped celery
1 cup chopped green pepper
1 medium onion, sliced
3 tablespoons olive oil
1 can (1 pound, 12 ounces)
    whole tomatoes
1 can (8 ounces) tomato sauce
1 can (6 ounces) tomato paste
1 tablespoon chopped parsley
1 teaspoon oregano, basil or
    Italian seasoning
1 teaspoon salt (optional)
1/4 teaspoon pepper
1/2 cup water
2 cups sliced zucchini
1 pound lasagna noodles
1 pound ricotta or cottage cheese
1 egg
1 package (10 ounces) frozen
    chopped spinach, cooked
    and drained
2 cups shredded mozzarella
    cheese
1/2 cup grated Parmesan cheese

Sauté mushrooms, celery, pepper and onion in olive oil over medium-high heat for 15 minutes. Add tomatoes, tomato sauce, tomato paste, seasonings and water. Simmer, covered, for 1 hour. Add zucchini and simmer 20 minutes longer.

Cook lasagna according to package directions.

Mix ricotta cheese, egg and spinach in a small bowl.

Preheat oven to 350°F. Grease a 9 × 13-inch baking dish. Line the pan with one-third of the lasagna noodles, follow with one-third of the sauce, one-half of the cheese mixture and one-third of the mozzarella cheese. Repeat layers, ending with sauce. Sprinkle with the remaining mozzarella and all the Parmesan cheese.

Bake for 45 to 50 minutes. Remove from oven and let stand 15 minutes before serving.

—MARIA BOWERFIND

Five Star
PASTA

VENETIAN RISOTTO
"RISI E BISI"

*A dish made with plump
Italian rice and fresh new peas.*

YIELD: 4 SERVINGS

1 tablespoon minced bacon or
 diced ham
1 onion, sliced
1 tablespoon butter
1 tablespoon olive oil
1-1/2 cups arborio rice
1 cup dry white wine
2-1/2 cups hot chicken broth
1 pound fresh baby peas,
 parboiled in salted water*
1/2 cup chopped parsley
1 to 2 chopped fennel leaves
 (optional)
Freshly ground white pepper
 to taste
Freshly grated Parmesan cheese
 to taste

*A zesty provincial alternative to
boiling the peas: sauté them for a
few minutes in a tablespoon of olive
oil, butter, minced garlic and tomato
sauce. Add homemade broth (or
canned if the top is skimmed) just to
cover and simmer uncovered until
the liquid disappears.*

*One might squeak by with frozen
baby peas but never canned. This
requires constant stirring and
frequent tasting.*

ᘒ Quickly sauté the meat and
onion in butter and oil over
medium-high heat. Add the rice
to this "soffritto" (base) and
sauté until very hot. As soon as
it begins to stick, pour in the
wine. It will be absorbed as
you continue to stir. When the
wine is absorbed, add the
chicken broth, a ladle at a time.
Do not add more liquid until
each addition has been absorbed.
When the rice is half cooked,
about 10 minutes, add the peas,
parsley, fennel and more broth
until the rice is cooked to the
al dente stage.

Remove from heat and flavor
with an additional tablespoon
of butter if desired. Top with
freshly ground pepper and
grated cheese.

—FRANCESCO AND SHERYL
 SCORTEGAGNA

COUSCOUS

YIELD: 4 SERVINGS

1-1/2 cups chicken broth
1/2 cup golden raisins
1/4 cup lemon juice
2 tablespoons minced crystallized
    ginger
2 tablespoons margarine
1/2 teaspoon curry powder
1 cup couscous
1/3 cup chopped celery
1/4 cup chopped scallions
2 tablespoons chopped cilantro
1 teaspoon lime juice
1/2 cup chopped, roasted and
    salted pistachios

᙭ Bring broth to boil and stir in raisins, lemon juice, ginger, margarine, curry powder and couscous. Remove from heat and let stand at least 5 minutes.

Before serving, stir in celery, scallions and cilantro. Add more chicken stock, curry and lime juice, if desired. Sprinkle with pistachios.

A delight with meat and chicken.

— MARY BETH SCHNEIDER

RAISIN AND ALMOND RICE

Excellent with curried dishes.

YIELD: 4-6 SERVINGS

1 tablespoon margarine
1/3 cup finely chopped onion
1/4 cup blanched, slivered
    almonds
1 cup rice
1 tablespoon golden raisins
1 tablespoon raisins
1-1/2 cups low-fat chicken broth
Salt and freshly ground black
    pepper to taste

᙭ Melt margarine in a saucepan. Add onions and almonds and cook over medium-high heat until the onions are limp.

Add rice and raisins, stirring well. Add chicken broth, salt and pepper, and bring to a boil. Cover and simmer until rice is tender and all liquid is absorbed, about 20 minutes.

—VICTORIA MAJORAS

Five Star
GRAINS

BOMBAY KASHI

*A curried grain
side dish.*

YIELD: 6-8 SERVINGS

1 package (6-1/2 ounces) kashi
1 large sweet red pepper, diced
1 large green pepper, diced
1/4 cup sunflower seeds
1/2 cup currants (raisins may
    be substituted)
2 cloves garlic, crushed
1/4 cup orange juice
2 tablespoons curry paste,
    mild or hot

&⤳ Cook kashi according to package directions.

Place peppers in serving bowl. Add sunflower seeds, currants and garlic. Mix well.

Add kashi to bowl while it is hot. Add orange juice and curry paste. Mix thoroughly and allow to stand for 5 minutes. Serve chilled or at room temperature.

This keeps well in the refrigerator for up to 10 days.

—MARSHA RITLEY

WILD RICE FRITTERS

In lieu of potatoes.

YIELD: 8 SERVINGS

1 teaspoon salt
1 tablespoon baking powder
1-1/2 cups all-purpose flour
4 eggs
2 tablespoons molasses
1 carrot, shredded
1 scallion, chopped
1 cup heavy cream
1-1/2 to 2 cups cooked wild rice
Olive oil for frying

&⤳ Sift salt, baking powder and flour in a large bowl.

Beat eggs and molasses in a small bowl; add carrot and scallion. Gradually stir in heavy cream.

Combine wild rice, flour and egg mixtures in a large bowl; cover and allow to sit for 30 minutes.

Heat olive oil in a heavy skillet over medium-high heat. Pour fritter mixture (about 1/4 cup per fritter) into pan. Turn when cooked side is firm and crispy.

Drain on paper towels. Serve immediately.

—CHEF SETH KASPY
CHAGRIN VALLEY HUNT CLUB

SPICY COLD SOBA NOODLES

YIELD: 6 SERVINGS

1/3 cup soy sauce
1 tablespoon molasses
1/4 cup packed brown sugar
1/4 cup tahini
1/4 cup sesame oil
1/4 cup chili oil
3 tablespoons balsamic or red
    wine vinegar
1/2 bunch scallions, white and
    green part, thinly sliced
Salt to taste
1/2 pound Soba or Japanese
    buckwheat noodles*

Available in Japanese and health food markets.

Heat soy sauce in small saucepan over high heat; cook until soy is reduced by half. Reduce heat to low.

Stir in molasses and warm through; remove from heat and place in medium-size mixing bowl. Whisk in brown sugar, tahini, sesame oil, chili oil, vinegar and scallions. Season to taste with salt, if desired.

Bring a large pot of salted water to a rapid boil. Add noodles, return water to a boil and cook, stirring occasionally, about 3 minutes or just until noodles begin to soften. (Watch carefully; soba noodles can overcook very quickly.)

Pour noodles into a colander, drain and plunge immediately into a large bowl of ice water. Drain again and rinse well under cold running water.

Combine noodles and sauce; toss well and chill.

Previously published in *CITY Cuisine*, William Morrow & Co., copyright ©1989, by Susan Feniger and Mary Sue Milliken, reprinted with permission.

— CHEF SUSAN FENIGER
— CHEF MARY SUE MILLIKEN

Five Star
GRAINS

CITY Restaurant
180 South La Brea
Los Angeles, CA 90036
213-938-2155

Border Grill
1445 4th Street
Santa Monica, CA 90401
213-451-1655

The cover: Carrot and Dill Soup on page 76
Lettuce Salad with Roquefort and Beets on page 89
Carrots with Grapes on page 117

Mushroom Lover's Soup

A strong mushroom flavor.
Best prepared a day or two ahead.
YIELD: 6 SERVINGS

4 to 6 dried black mushrooms*
2 tablespoons olive oil
2 medium shallots, finely
 chopped
2 scallions, finely sliced,
 including some green
12 ounces fresh white
 mushrooms, sliced
4 cups low-salt chicken broth;
 or stock
1 tablespoon oyster sauce*
1 cup half and half
Salt and pepper to taste
Enoki mushrooms* and cilantro
 leaves for garnish
Available in Oriental food stores

ॐ Soak black mushrooms in small bowl in just enough hot water to cover for approximately 30 minutes. Drain, reserving liquid, and slice thinly, discarding stems.

Heat oil in wok or saucepan and stir-fry shallots and onions approximately 5 minutes or until soft. Add black and white sliced mushrooms; stir-fry over medium heat until soft and liquid has evaporated, approximately 10 minutes. Add chicken broth, oyster sauce and reserved black-mushroom liquid and simmer 5 minutes.

Strain solids from broth and purée in food processor or blender until smooth, adding some half and half, if necessary. Return purée to broth and add remaining half and half. Heat through.

Serve hot, at room temperature or cold with garnishes. Refrigerate unused portions.

—BECKY DUNN

Sharrow Bay Watercress Soup

Creamy, delicate flavor.
YIELD: 6 SERVINGS

6 tablespoons butter
1 medium onion, chopped
1/4 cup all-purpose flour
3 bunches (about 4 cups)
 watercress, trimmed
4-1/2 cups chicken stock
 (preferably homemade)
 or chicken broth
1 cup half and half
1/2 cup heavy cream
Salt and freshly ground pepper
 to taste

ॐ Melt butter in heavy saucepan over medium-low heat. Add onion and cook until translucent, stirring occasionally, approximately 10 minutes. Do not brown.

Add flour, stir and cook another 3 minutes. Add watercress and cook 2 minutes. Stir in stock and bring to a boil. Reduce heat and simmer 5 minutes. Transfer mixture to container of food processor and purée. (Can be made ahead to this point.)

Return to saucepan. Add half and half and cream and heat through. Season with salt and pepper and serve immediately.

—CAROL SHERWIN

WILD RICE SOUP
A rich first course.
YIELD: 8 SERVINGS

2/3 cup wild rice
2 cups salted water
3 medium leeks, including
    some green, diced
6 medium mushrooms, diced
1/2 cup (1 stick) butter or
    margarine
1 cup all-purpose flour
8 cups chicken broth
1 cup half and half
3 tablespoons dry sherry
Salt and white pepper to taste

ॐ Wash wild rice thoroughly. Place in a heavy saucepan with salted water and bring to a boil. Cover, reduce heat and simmer for 45 minutes until tender but not mushy. Drain excess liquid and set aside.

Sauté leeks and mushrooms in butter over medium-high heat until soft, about 10 minutes. Sprinkle in flour, stirring until flour is cooked but not brown.

Slowly whisk in chicken broth, stirring until flour mixture is well blended. Continue cooking until soup thickens.

Add cooked rice, half and half, sherry, salt and pepper. Heat gently over medium-high heat and stir, being careful not to boil.

— KATHY GROVES
— PAMELA LaMANTIA

Five Star
SIDE DISHES

SOUPS

Sweet Red Pepper Soup en Crôute

*A special soup to start
an elegant meal.*

YIELD: 4 SERVINGS

4 red peppers, halved, seeded
    and coarsely chopped
6 shallots, finely chopped
1 cup dry white wine
2 cups chicken stock
Salt and pepper to taste
4 tablespoons sour cream
2 teaspoons chopped fresh
    basil (about 1/2 teaspoon
    per bowl)
1 box phyllo dough
Melted butter or margarine
    (about 2 ounces)

🐟 Place red peppers, shallots and wine in a saucepan and simmer until soft. Purée in blender and add enough chicken stock to make the consistency you like. Add salt, pepper and sour cream and place in 4 oven-proof bowls. Sprinkle basil in each bowl and add 3 drops of olive oil.

Lay one piece of phyllo dough on a table, brush with melted butter or margarine and repeat, using a total of 4 sheets on top of each other. Brush final layer with butter. Cut four circles and cover the soup bowls. Refrigerate.

Preheat oven to 375°F. Place soup bowls in oven and cook for approximately 18 minutes until phyllo is golden brown and puffed. Serve immediately.

—PAMELA GROSSCUP

Prawn Bisque

*From Winston's Restaurant
in London, with the
compliments of the chef.*

YIELD: 4-6 SERVINGS

2 ounces rice flour
3-1/2 pints chicken stock
6 tablespoons butter or
    margarine
1 small carrot, finely diced
1 small onion, finely diced
2 shallots, finely diced
6 sprigs parsley, chopped
12 prawns or 24 shrimp,
    shelled and deveined
1 sprig fresh thyme, chopped
    or 1/4 teaspoon dried
1/2 bay leaf
1/4 cup whiskey
1/4 cup plus 2 tablespoons dry
    white wine
1/4 cup cream

🐟 Add rice flour to chicken stock, bring to a boil, reduce heat and simmer 20 minutes.

Sauté diced vegetables in butter in a large skillet over medium-high heat. Add cleaned shellfish, thyme and bay leaf to vegetables and sauté with whiskey and wine for 6 to 8 minutes. Cool.

Place vegetable/shellfish mixture into container of food processor and purée.

Add purée to hot stock and warm through. Whisk in cream and serve immediately.

Garnish with a swirl of chopped parsley.

—DR. MICHAEL MAGUIRE

Roasted Red Pepper Soup

Yield: 12 servings

13 large sweet red peppers,
  roasted
2 to 4 tablespoons olive oil
1 bunch scallions, trimmed and
  thinly sliced
3 shallots, minced
1 small poblano pepper, or half
  of a large one, diced
4 tomatoes, blanched, peeled,
  seeded and diced
1 canned chipotle pepper in
  adobo sauce, seeds removed
  and minced fine
1/8 teaspoon each dried thyme
  and basil
3 quarts chicken stock
1 to 2 tablespoons fish sauce
  (Vietnamese nuac mam)
1 to 2 tablespoons rice vinegar
1 to 2 teaspoons fine sugar
24 fresh shrimp, shelled and
  deveined
1 cup yellow summer squash,
  julienned
Fresh basil and cilantro

   To prepare roasted peppers, cut off top and remove seeds, roast near hot fire to blister skins, then seal in plastic to cool. Remove skins, then purée.

Heat about 2 tablespoons of olive oil in a heavy-bottomed stockpot. Add and sauté the poblano peppers, scallions and shallots over medium-high heat until they begin to brown. Stir in the diced tomatoes and the chipotle pepper.

Add the thyme, basil, chicken stock, fish sauce, rice vinegar and sugar. Bring to a boil, reduce heat and simmer 15 minutes (or longer to develop flavor).

Prepare shrimp by shelling, deveining and grilling while soup simmers.

Add puréed peppers and julienned squash to soup; adjust seasoning.

To serve, place 2 shrimp in each bowl. Top with a sprinkle of basil and cilantro. Cover with 8 ounces of hot soup.

—Chef Ralph DiOrio

Five Star
SIDE DISHES
SOUPS

Sammy's
1400 West 10th Street
Cleveland, OH 44113
216-523-1177

CARROT AND DILL SOUP
YIELD: 6-8 SERVINGS

1 pound potatoes (may use combination of sweet and baking potatoes)
1-3/4 pounds carrots
2 medium onions, chopped
2 tablespoons butter
1-1/2 teaspoons salt
1/2 teaspoon white pepper
2 tablespoons chopped fresh dill (can increase amount if desired)
5 cups chicken or vegetable stock
Sour cream or yogurt for garnish

This recipe is featured on the color cover of the Side Dishes section tab.

&> Bake potatoes in a conventional or microwave oven until soft.

Scrub carrots but do not peel. Slice and steam until soft; drain.

Sauté onions in butter over medium-high heat until golden. Place onions in container of food processor. Deglaze pan over high heat with 1/4 cup stock and add to food processor, blending well. Add carrots to food processor and purée. Scoop out potato pulp and add to processor along with salt and pepper. Process until nicely puréed.

Pour purée into saucepan and add dill and stock. Simmer for 15 minutes or until heated through. Thin with chicken stock, milk or cream, if necessary.

To serve, pour in bowls and garnish with sour cream or yogurt.

—TERRI KLINE

CURRIED CREAM OF BROCCOLI SOUP
YIELD: 8 SERVINGS

1 tablespoon butter or margarine
1 large onion, chopped
2 cloves garlic, minced
2 teaspoons curry powder, or more to taste
Salt and freshly ground black pepper to taste
3 cups chicken stock
1 large bunch (1 pound) broccoli, chopped, upper stems included
1 large potato, peeled and cubed
1 cup whole or low-fat milk

&> Melt the butter over medium-high heat in a large saucepan and sauté the onion and garlic for approximately 5 minutes. Add the curry powder, salt, pepper and chicken broth and bring to a boil. Add broccoli and potato. Reduce heat, cover and simmer for 20 minutes.

When the vegetables are tender, purée the soup in a food processor or blender. Return to saucepan, stir in milk and reheat, being careful not to boil. Serve hot.

—ANNA ROSTAFINSKI, RD

CORN-TOMATO CHOWDER
YIELD: 6 SERVINGS

1/4 pound slab bacon, cut into
    1/4-inch dice
3 tablespoons unsalted butter
2 large onions, cut into 3/8-inch
    dice
2 tablespoons all-purpose flour
2 large ripe tomatoes, peeled,
    seeded and coarsely chopped
1 quart milk
1 teaspoon salt
1/4 teaspoon freshly ground
    pepper
1/4 teaspoon crumbled sage
1/8 teaspoon grated nutmeg
1 small bay leaf
2 medium red potatoes, peeled
    and cut into 3/8-inch dice
2 cups corn kernels (from 2 to
    3 ears of corn)
3/4 teaspoon fresh lemon juice
Dash of cayenne pepper

↋ Blanch the bacon in a saucepan of boiling water for 5 minutes. Drain and rinse briefly; drain well. Pat dry on paper towels.

Melt the butter over moderate heat in a large flameproof casserole. Add the onions and cook, stirring occasionally, until softened and translucent, about 5 minutes. Sprinkle on the flour and cook, stirring, for about 2 minutes without letting the flour color. Add the tomatoes. (If they are very juicy, cook, stirring, until most of the moisture evaporates, 2 to 3 minutes.)

Gradually whisk in the milk. Season with the salt, pepper, sage, nutmeg and bay leaf. Bring to a boil and add the potatoes. Reduce the heat and simmer, partially covered, stirring occasionally for 10 minutes.

Add the corn and continue to simmer, partially covered, until the corn and potatoes are tender, about 10 minutes longer. Add the lemon juice and cayenne. Season with additional salt and pepper to taste. Serve hot.

Previously published in *Tailgate Parties*, Harmony Books, a division of Crown Publishers, Inc., copyright ©1984, by Susan Wyler, reprinted with permission.

—SUSAN WYLER
COOKBOOK AUTHOR

Five Star
SIDE DISHES
SOUPS

JAN'S GAZPACHO

Fresh garden flavors.

YIELD: 8-12 SERVINGS

1 can (29 ounces) tomato purée
1/2 cup olive oil
8 tablespoons wine vinegar
2 teaspoons salt
Freshly ground pepper to taste
2 teaspoons cumin
1/8 teaspoon cayenne pepper
2 cloves garlic, peeled
1 bottle (32 ounces) Clamato juice
3 cucumbers
3 green peppers
1 red pepper
1 large onion
2 carrots
1 to 2 chopped fresh jalapeño peppers (optional)
1 or 2 sprigs chopped cilantro (optional)

❧ Place tomato purée in large bowl and slowly whisk in olive oil, vinegar, salt, pepper, cumin and cayenne.

Mince garlic in container of food processor. Add one-fourth bottle of Clamato juice. Peel cucumber lengthwise, leaving on some skin. Cut into chunks. Seed peppers and cut into chunks. Peel onion and cut into chunks. Finely mince carrots in processor container and set aside to be added last.

Place one-third of the vegetables and one-fourth bottle of Clamato juice in container of food processor and pulse until finely chopped. Add to tomato purée.

Place one-fourth bottle of Clamato juice in container of processor with another one-third of the vegetables and pulse until medium coarse. Add to purée.

Place remaining Clamato juice and vegetables in processor container and coarsely chop. Add to purée. Add carrots to purée.

Refrigerate for 24 hours before serving. Stir and adjust seasonings.

Serve in chilled bowls and pass croutons if desired. For variety, try adding salad shrimp to the chilled salad bowls before you add soup. Additional vegetables may be used for a thicker soup.

—JAN CHAPMAN

QUICK TOMATO SOUP

Extends the tomato season.

YIELD: 6-8 SERVINGS

2 cans (6 ounces each)
  tomato paste
1 can (29 ounces) whole
  tomatoes, or 6 medium
  fresh tomatoes
2 cans (29 ounces each)
  tomato sauce
6 carrots, sliced
1 stalk celery, sliced
3 white onions, cut into wedges
2 bay leaves
1 teaspoon basil
Salt and pepper to taste
Swiss cheese, grated

  Mix all ingredients, except cheese, in a large pot and simmer for at least 3 hours.

Serve in bowls and sprinkle with cheese.

—ANN GELEHRTER

STRAWBERRY RHUBARB SOUP

A light, refreshing summer soup.

YIELD: 4-6 SERVINGS

1 pint strawberries, hulled
  and sliced
1 pound rhubarb
1-1/2 cups orange juice
4 tablespoons sugar
1/4 cup chopped orange sections

  Hull and slice strawberries. Set aside 4 of the best slices for garnish.

Trim rhubarb and cut stalks into bite-size chunks.

Heat fruit and orange juice to boiling in a saucepan over medium heat. Reduce heat and simmer 10 minutes.

Remove from heat and place mixture in container of blender. Add sugar and blend until smooth. Add orange sections, cover and refrigerate.

To serve, pour chilled soup into goblets and garnish with strawberry slices.

—ALICE CRONQUIST

Five Star
SIDE DISHES
SOUPS

Grandpa Tubaugh's Potato Soup
YIELD: 8-12 SERVINGS

5 pounds (about 8 large) red
    potatoes, peeled and diced
7-1/2 cups chicken broth*
6 medium onions, diced
6 stalks celery with leaves, diced
1 carrot, finely chopped
1/4 pound (1 stick) butter
6 slices bacon plus 4
    tablespoons drippings
6 cups half and half
1 jar (4 ounces) pimiento,
    drained and chopped
Salt and freshly ground pepper
    to taste
1-1/2 teaspoons minced fresh
    dillweed
1 pound longhorn cheese

For thicker soup, use only 4 cups chicken broth.

Put diced potatoes and chicken broth in a stockpot and cook over medium heat until potatoes are almost tender.

Partially mash the potatoes in broth with a potato masher. The result should be partially mashed, pea-sized chunks of potato. Set aside.

Sauté onions, carrots and celery in butter over medium-high heat until soft but firm.

Fry bacon in skillet until crisp. Crumble and add to potatoes along with drippings. Add vegetables and stir in half and half. (Soup should be quite thick.) Add pimiento, salt, pepper and dillweed. Heat through but do not boil.

To serve, coarsely grate cheese in bottom of bowls before ladling soup.

Leftovers make a great clam chowder if you add 1 can (6 ounces) chopped clams to every cup of potato soup.

—Jan Chapman

Kenneth Mahall Family Ham and Sauerkraut Soup
YIELD: 10 SERVINGS

1 ham bone
3/4 pound ham, cubed
1 teaspoon peppercorns
1 bay leaf
2 tablespoons vegetable oil
    or butter
1 large onion, chopped
2 cups any fresh or leftover
    vegetables (beans, carrots,
    asparagus, celery)
Several sprigs of parsley
Butter or olive oil for sautéing
3 to 4 medium potatoes, peeled,
    cooked and cubed
1 can (14 ounces) sauerkraut,
    drained and rinsed
1 to 2 teaspoons cider vinegar
    to taste

Place ham bone, ham, peppercorns and bay leaf in a large kettle with about 1-1/2 to 2 quarts of water. Bring to a boil. Reduce heat and simmer for 1-1/2 to 2 hours.

Sauté onion, vegetables and parsley in butter or oil over medium-high heat until onion is limp. Reduce heat, simmer and steam for approximately 6 to 7 minutes.

Remove ham bone from soup. Add steamed vegetables, cooked potatoes and sauerkraut.

Add vinegar and simmer the soup for another 10 to 15 minutes.

—Pat DeFabio-Shimrak

Cabbage Borscht

*From Russia to Cleveland
with rave reviews!*

YIELD: 12 SERVINGS

4 pounds chuck steak, with bone
1/2 cup dried baby lima beans
3 russet potatoes, peeled
  and diced
2 to 4 carrots, thickly sliced
1 to 2 stalks celery, sliced,
  including leafy tops
1 large onion, sliced
2 cans (16 ounces each)
  tomatoes, diced
1/2 cup firmly packed brown
  sugar
2 tablespoons lemon juice
3 to 4 cloves garlic, minced
Salt and pepper to taste
1 medium cabbage, cut in
  wedges

&ep; Cover lima beans with
water and soak overnight.

Cover chuck steak with
cold water and bring to a boil.

Skim off foam, reduce heat
and cook until meat is tender.
Remove meat and refrigerate
both stock and meat.

Skim the fat from the beef
stock and add stock to beans
and water. Bring to a rolling
boil.

Add potatoes, carrots,
celery and onion. Reduce heat,
cover and simmer for about
20 minutes.

Add tomatoes and season-
ings. Cover and simmer 2 hours.

Add beef and cabbage
wedges and simmer until cabbage
is tender and meat is hot.

Serve in heated bowls.

— DR. LINDA W. SHUCK

Cabbage Soup

Great for Sunday supper.

YIELD: 8-10 SERVINGS

2 pounds beef (short ribs,
  brisket, etc.)
1 (2-pound) cabbage, shredded
1 large onion, chopped
1 can (28 ounces) tomatoes
1 can (8 ounces) tomato sauce
1 can (6 ounces) tomato paste
3 tablespoons brown sugar
Juice of 1 lemon
2 tablespoons golden raisins

&ep; Place 2 quarts of lightly
salted water in a large kettle or
pot. Cut beef into cubes and
add to kettle. Add cabbage and
bring to a boil. Reduce heat
and simmer for 10 minutes.

Skim foam from top of kettle.
Add onion, tomatoes, tomato
sauce and tomato paste; continue cooking over medium-
high heat, partially covered,
for 1-1/2 hours.

Add brown sugar, lemon
juice and raisins; simmer,
covered, for another hour.

Serve with French bread.

— MARY KLEIN

Five Star
SIDE DISHES
SOUPS

Italian Soup

Sausage and tortellini
make this special.

1 pound Italian sausage
1 cup chopped onion
2 cloves garlic, minced
1-1/2 to 2 cups water
5 cups beef broth
1/2 to 1 cup red wine
2 cups chopped tomatoes or
    1 can (16 ounces) stewed
    tomatoes
1 cup sliced carrots
1/2 teaspoon crushed basil
    leaves
1/2 teaspoon oregano
8 ounces tomato sauce
1 to 2 cups chopped celery
8 ounces frozen tortellini
    (meat or cheese)
3 tablespoons chopped parsley
1 medium green pepper,
    chopped
Grated Parmesan cheese

➤ Remove sausage from casing and roll into bite-size balls. Brown in a 5-quart Dutch oven over medium-high heat. Remove meat from Dutch oven and drain all but 1 tablespoon of drippings.

Add onion and garlic to the reserved drippings and sauté over medium-high heat until tender, about 5 minutes.

Add water, broth, wine, tomatoes, carrots, basil, oregano, tomato sauce, celery and sausage and bring to a boil. Reduce heat and simmer, uncovered, for 30 to 45 minutes.

Add tortellini, parsley and green pepper and simmer, uncovered, another 35 to 40 minutes until the tortellini are tender.

Serve in bowls and garnish with grated Parmesan cheese.

For a little added spice, try sprinkling dried red peppers in the soup when ready to serve.

— LARRY FERRONE

Minestrone

Italian classic.

1/4 cup olive oil
1 medium onion, sliced
2 cloves garlic, minced
1 can (28 ounces) plum
    tomatoes, including juice
4 cups chicken stock or
    chicken broth
1 tablespoon parsley
2 teaspoons basil
1 teaspoon oregano
1 leek, chopped
2 carrots, sliced
2 ribs celery, sliced
Salt and pepper to taste
2 cans (15 ounces each)
    cannellini beans or white
    kidney beans
2 cups shredded cabbage
1 medium zucchini, sliced
1/4 cup elbow or small shell
    macaroni
Parmesan cheese, for garnish

➤ Heat oil in 4-quart pot. Add onion and garlic and sauté over medium-high heat until soft.

Add tomatoes and juice. Stir in chicken stock, herbs, leek, carrots, celery, salt and pepper. Bring to a boil. Reduce heat, cover and simmer 20 minutes.

Stir in beans and cabbage. Cover and simmer 10 minutes.

Stir in zucchini and macaroni. Simmer, uncovered, 10 minutes or until macaroni is cooked. Serve with Parmesan cheese.

— ANNA P. OSBORNE

Soupe au Pistou

A hearty bean and vegetable soup with pesto.

Yield: 4-6 servings

2 tablespoons finely chopped
garlic
Olive oil for sautéing
1 cup diced zucchini
1 cup diced yellow squash
1/2 cup diced skinless, seedless
tomatoes
1/4 cup fava or lima beans
1/2 cup chopped leek,
white part only
1/2 cup presoaked white beans
5 cups chicken stock
Salt and pepper to taste
1/4 cup cooked pasta
per serving

PESTO
1 cup cleaned basil leaves
1/2 cup extra virgin olive oil
1/8 cup pine nuts
1/8 cup Parmesan cheese
2 cloves garlic, lightly mashed
1 teaspoon salt
1/4 teaspoon pepper

Sauté chopped garlic in olive oil over moderate heat. Add all vegetables, and chicken stock to cover. Cook until the beans and vegetables are tender, about 45 minutes. Season to taste.

To make pesto, place ingredients in container of food processor or blender and process to a smooth paste. Do not over-process or the basil will become too dark.

Add the cooked pasta to vegetables and heat through. Add 1 full tablespoon of the pesto to each serving of soup. Adjust seasoning if necessary.

—Chef Debra Ponzek

Montrachet
239 West Broadway
New York, NY 10013
212-219-2777

BLACK BEAN CHILI

Hearty and spicy.

YIELD: 4 SERVINGS

1 cup black beans
1 bay leaf
2 teaspoons cumin seeds
2 teaspoons oregano
2 teaspoons paprika
1/2 teaspoon cayenne pepper
2 tablespoons corn oil
2 medium onions, diced
2 cloves garlic, chopped
1/2 teaspoon salt
2 tablespoons chili powder
1 can (28 ounces) chopped
    tomatoes
1 teaspoon chopped red chili
    pepper, roasted
1/2 teaspoon rice vinegar
2 tablespoons chopped fresh
    cilantro

GARNISHES
1/2 cup grated Cheddar cheese
1/2 cup sour cream or yogurt
1/2 cup cilantro sprigs

ô► Sort through beans, rinse and soak overnight.

Drain; cover with water to a level of 2 inches above the beans. Add bay leaf; bring to a boil. Reduce heat; simmer while preparing remaining ingredients.

Toast cumin seeds in a frying pan until fragrant. Add oregano for a few seconds. Remove from heat. Stir in paprika and cayenne. Remove from pan; grind to make a coarse powder and set aside.

Heat oil and sauté onion until soft. Add garlic, salt, herb mixture and chili powder and cook 5 minutes. Add tomatoes and chopped chili peppers. Simmer for 15 minutes. Add onion-tomato-herb mixture to beans. Cover and simmer approximately 1 hour. Add rice vinegar and cilantro.

Garnish with cheese, sour cream and additional cilantro.

Serve with brown rice. This chili can also be served in soft tortillas.

—LAURIE ELMETS

BLACK BEAN STEW
YIELD: 10 SERVINGS

1 package (12 ounces) black beans,
   washed and picked over
No-stick cooking spray
1-3/4 cups chopped scallions,
   including tops
3 cloves garlic, minced
2 cans (15 ounces each) tomato
   purée or 1 large can tomatoes
1 cup fresh or canned unseasoned
   pumpkin purée
1-1/2 cups beef stock
1 tablespoon cumin
1-1/2 tablespoons balsamic
   vinegar
8 ounces fat-free ham, cut into
   small squares or 12 ounces
   chicken or turkey, cooked
   and ground
Freshly ground black pepper
1 cup dry sherry
Salt to taste
1 cup plain low-fat yogurt,
   strained
2 limes, sliced into 10 slices

Place the beans in a large saucepan and cover with boiling water to a level of 3 inches above the beans. Simmer until the beans are tender, about 3 hours. Drain.

Spray the large saucepan thoroughly with no-stick cooking spray. Sauté 1-1/2 cups scallions and garlic until just soft. Add the tomato purée, pumpkin, beef stock, cumin, vinegar and black beans. Simmer for 25 minutes. Add the meat, black pepper, and sherry and heat through. Salt to taste. Blend yogurt with 1/4 cup scallions.

To serve, ladle into large bowls and top with a dollop of yogurt and a slice of lime.

A version of this recipe appears in **Count Out Cholesterol Cookbook** *and was voted one of* **The Plain Dealer**'s *10 favorite recipes of 1989! At 175 calories per serving, we think that's quite a compliment.*

— MARY WARD
COOKBOOK AUTHOR

Five Star
SIDE DISHES
SOUPS

Red Lentil Soup

An authentic Scottish soup.

Yield: 6 servings

1/2 cup red lentils
1/8 cup vegetable oil
1/2 cup diced carrots
1/4 cup diced turnips
1 onion, diced
1 large potato, peeled and diced
5 cups water
Ham bone or ham hock
Salt and pepper to taste

☙ Wash lentils and drain. Combine vegetables and simmer in saucepan with oil until tender, approximately 20 minutes.

Add water, ham bone and lentils and bring to a boil. Reduce heat, cover and simmer gently for 2 to 2-1/2 hours. Add salt and pepper to taste.

To serve, remove ham bone and ladle into serving bowls.

*Red lentils are **always** used in this Scottish soup. They can be purchased in some Middle Eastern stores and Gaelic import shops. The original Scottish recipe called for "a teacup full of lentils and a walnut of drippings."*

— Gillian Graham

Split Pea Soup

Yield: 8 servings

1-1/2 cups dry green split peas
2 carrots
1 large baking potato
1 onion, chopped
3 quarts chicken stock, defatted
2 bay leaves
Salt and freshly ground pepper to taste
1/2 pound veal sausage, thinly sliced (optional)

☙ Soak peas several hours in water to cover.

Peel carrots and leave whole. Peel and cube potato and onion.

Combine chicken stock, drained peas, carrots, onion, bay leaves and potato in large pot and bring to a boil.

Reduce heat and simmer 30 minutes. Remove carrots and continue to simmer until peas are very tender and partly dissolved, about 1 hour.

Strain into clean pot. Discard bay leaves and place solid vegetables in container of food processor and purée. Return to pot. Slice carrots and add. Season to taste.

Sauté thinly sliced veal sausage (optional). Drain on paper towels and add to soup.

Serve in preheated bowls with tossed green salad and French bread. Flavor improves if made ahead. If frozen, heat and thin with chicken stock or water.

— Joan Kekst

Nopalito Chorizo Esopa

CACTUS SAUSAGE SOUP

Hot, hot, hot!

Yield: 6 servings

1 pound chorizo*, crumbled
1 medium onion, chopped
1 poblano chili, seeded and chopped or 1/4 teaspoon cayenne pepper
4 cups chicken broth
1 jar (15 ounces) cooked nopalito* (cactus), rinsed in cold water
1 cup sour cream
1 cup tomatoes, chopped
Chopped cilantro for garnish

*Spanish sausage and cactus are available in specialty food stores.

☙ Brown the chorizo in a large pot over medium-high heat.

Add the chili and onion and cook until soft. Drain all the fat. Pour in the broth and nopalito and simmer approximately 30 minutes. Add tomatoes and cook for approximately 5 minutes.

Ladle into bowls and spoon on a dollop of sour cream. Sprinkle cilantro on top and pass additional sour cream.

Serve with flour tortillas and brown rice.

— Carole Ubinger

Five Star

SIDE DISHES

SALADS

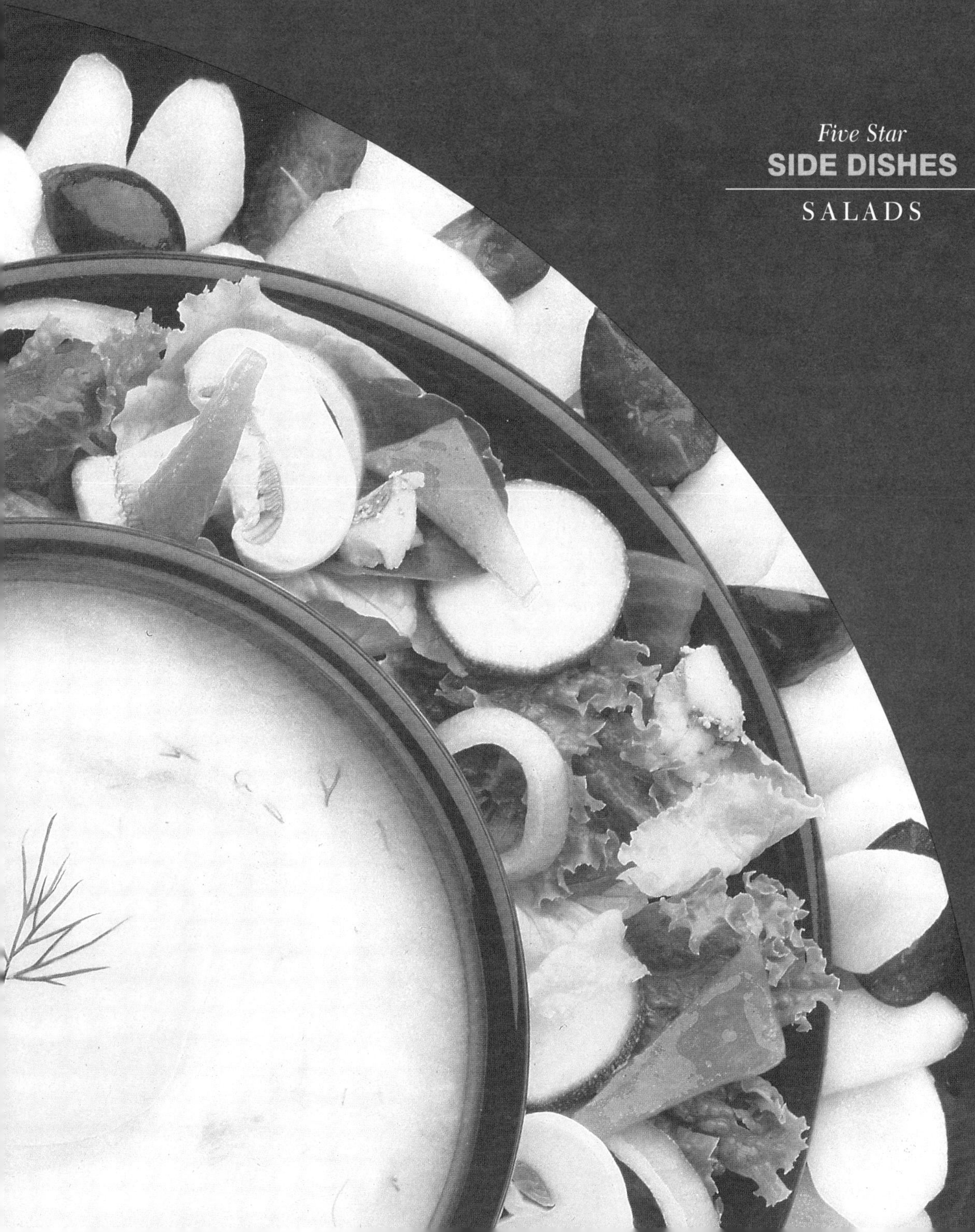

Apple Spinach Salad

*Rich in iron, high in fiber
and only 130 calories per serving!*

Yield: 4 servings

4 cups spinach leaves
2 tablespoons vegetable oil
2 tablespoons cider vinegar
1/4 teaspoon salt
1/8 teaspoon sugar
1 medium tart apple, cut in
 thin slices
1/4 cup chopped red onion
1/4 cup chopped raisins

🦢 Wash and dry spinach.
Tear into bite-size pieces and
set aside in a salad bowl.

Combine oil, vinegar, salt
and sugar in a medium-size
bowl. Whisk ingredients. Add
apple, onions and raisins. Toss
to coat with dressing and let
stand at least 15 minutes.

To serve, stir apple mixture
into salad bowl and toss with
spinach until well coated.

— Cindy Carr

Spinach Salad

Yield: 8-10 servings

2 pounds fresh spinach,
 stems removed
2 heads red leaf lettuce
1 small red onion, sliced
 into rings
1 pound bacon, cooked crisp
 and crumbled

DRESSING
1 tablespoon minced onion
1/4 cup sugar
1 teaspoon dry mustard
1 tablespoon poppy seed
1/3 cup cider vinegar
1 cup vegetable oil
1-1/2 cups crumbled feta cheese

🦢 Wash and drain stemmed
spinach and leaf lettuce. Tear
greens into bite-size pieces.
Add red onion and bacon.

To make dressing, combine
onion, sugar, mustard, poppy
seed, vinegar and oil in a separate bowl. Pour half of dressing
over the salad greens and toss.

Add feta cheese to the
remaining half of the dressing.
To serve, pour remaining dressing with cheese over the salad
and toss well.

— Pamela LaMantia

Country Greek Salad

Yield: 8 servings

1 medium head of lettuce,
 finely cut
2 medium cucumbers, peeled
 and thinly sliced
4 medium tomatoes, sliced
1 medium onion, sliced
1 medium green pepper, sliced
Salt and pepper
10 whole black olives
1/2 pound feta cheese, crumbled

DRESSING
5 tablespoons olive oil
5 tablespoons vinegar
2 tablespoons oregano

🦢 Mix all of the vegetables in
a large bowl. Salt and pepper
to taste.

Mix dressing, pour over
salad and toss well. Top salad
with olives and crumbled feta
cheese and serve.

— Pat George

LETTUCE SALAD
WITH ROQUEFORT AND BEETS
YIELD: 8 SERVINGS

2 heads leaf lettuce (1/2 pound
    spinach may be substituted
    for one of the heads)
1 bunch watercress
1/4 pound zucchini, thinly sliced
1 medium red onion,
    sliced into thin rings
1/2 cup sliced mushrooms
1 cup sliced and drained
    pickled beets

DRESSING
1/2 cup vegetable or olive oil
2 tablespoons wine vinegar
2 tablespoons lemon juice
1/3 cup crumbled Roquefort
    cheese
1/2 teaspoon salt
1/2 teaspoon sugar
1/2 teaspoon paprika
1/2 teaspoon celery seed
1/4 teaspoon pepper

ℝ Wash salad greens and tear
into bite-size pieces in a large
salad bowl. Wash and stem
watercress and add to salad.

To make dressing, combine
all ingredients in a jar, shake
vigorously, and refrigerate at
least 4 hours for flavors to mingle.
Shake well before serving.

Add remaining salad ingredients and toss with dressing
before serving.

*This sauce may be stored for
several months in the refrigerator.*

— DR. LINDA W. SHUCK

This recipe is featured on the color
cover of the Side Dishes section tab.

Five Star
SIDE DISHES
SALADS

Balsamic Vinegar Dressing

A tasty combination of flavors.

Yield: 2/3 cup (8 servings)

1/3 cup olive oil
1/3 cup balsamic vinegar
1 teaspoon Dijon-style mustard
1/2 teaspoon salt
1/2 teaspoon sugar
1 clove garlic, crushed

❧ Whisk all ingredients in a large glass bowl. Use immediately.

— Laura Thomson

Best Ahead Salad

Yield: 8 servings

1 head romaine lettuce
2 small heads Boston lettuce
3/4 cup grated fresh Parmesan cheese
3/4 cup croutons

DRESSING
3/4 cup vegetable oil
1/2 cup wine vinegar
3 cloves garlic, minced
3 tablespoons Worcestershire sauce
1 teaspoon salt
1 tablespoon lemon juice
1/2 teaspoon pepper

❧ Clean, dry and tear lettuce into bite-size pieces.

Mix dressing ingredients, and whisk well.

To serve, sprinkle lettuce with cheese, add dressing and toss. Add croutons and toss again.

Dressing is best prepared ahead of time.

— Ann Gelehrter

Mixed Greens and Slivered Grapes
with Dijon Vinaigrette Dressing

Yield: 12 servings

1 head radicchio
1 head romaine
1 bunch watercress
1 bunch arugula
3 cups red seedless grapes
Salt and pepper to taste

DRESSING
1/2 cup balsamic vinegar
8 teaspoons Dijon-style mustard
1-1/2 cups extra virgin olive oil
1 teaspoon pepper
1 tablespoon chopped parsley
1 tablespoon minced garlic

❧ Wash and dry salad greens and tear into bite-size pieces in a large salad bowl.

Wash and dry grapes. Slice into halves lengthwise and add to greens. Salt and pepper to taste and toss.

Mix vinegar and mustard in a small bowl. Whisk in olive oil by droplets until combined, being careful not to whisk too quickly or the dressing will separate. Add pepper, parsley and garlic.

Toss with dressing and serve.

Make sure the lettuce is completely dry before tossing with dressing. Serve with muffins or fresh bread. Dressing can be made ahead and chilled for one week.

— Douglas Katz

WATERCRESS SALAD
WITH LEMON DRESSING
YIELD: 8-10 SERVINGS

1 clove garlic, crushed
1/4 cup lemon juice
2 tablespoons sour cream
1 tablespoon sugar
1/2 cup safflower oil
1/2 pound watercress, washed and stemmed
1/2 cup grated Monterey Jack cheese
1/2 cup fresh fruit (berries or grapes)
1/4 cup chopped and toasted pecans

&> Combine garlic, lemon juice, sour cream and sugar in blender. Slowly add oil while the blender is running.

Arrange watercress on chilled plates. Drizzle with lemon dressing. Top with cheese, fruit and pecans.

—TERRI KLINE

SALAD WITH ARTICHOKES AND GRAPEFRUIT
YIELD: 8 SERVINGS

1 can (15 ounces) artichoke hearts
1/4 cup vegetable oil
2 tablespoons white wine vinegar
1 teaspoon Worcestershire sauce
1/2 teaspoon salt
1/8 teaspoon pepper
1 tablespoon snipped parsley
3 cups torn iceberg lettuce
2 cups torn romaine lettuce
1 cup torn endive
2 pink grapefruits, peeled, halved and sectioned

&> Cut each artichoke heart in half.

Combine oil, vinegar, Worcestershire sauce, salt, pepper and parsley; mix well. Pour dressing over artichoke hearts. Cover and chill 3 to 4 hours or overnight.

To serve, combine lettuce, endive and grapefruit sections in a large bowl. Add artichokes with dressing and toss.

—KITTY UNGER

Five Star
SIDE DISHES
SALADS

TOMATO SALAD
YIELD: 4 SERVINGS

2 tomatoes, sliced
1/2 cup vegetable oil
3 tablespoons white vinegar
2 tablespoons chopped scallions
1 tablespoon sugar
1 teaspoon Worcestershire sauce
1 teaspoon sweet basil
3/4 teaspoon salt
1/2 clove garlic, minced
1/8 teaspoon pepper
1/8 teaspoon thyme
1 head leaf lettuce

&❧ Slice tomatoes and place in a medium-size bowl.

Combine remaining ingredients and pour over tomatoes. Refrigerate for 1 hour and serve on a bed of greens.

—BARBARA GIBBS

MUSHROOM GARDEN SALAD
YIELD: 6-8 SERVINGS

1 pound mushrooms
1 green pepper, cut in chunks
2 tomatoes, cut in wedges
Leaf lettuce

DRESSING
1/4 cup vegetable oil
3 tablespoons lemon juice
1/4 cup sliced scallions,
    including green tops
1 tablespoon crushed basil
    leaves
1 teaspoon salt
1/4 teaspoon ground cumin
1/8 teaspoon pepper

&❧ Combine dressing ingredients in a large bowl and whisk. Let stand for 1 hour at room temperature.

Slice mushrooms in half. Pour dressing over mushrooms and let stand 15 minutes. Add green pepper and tomatoes and mix gently.

Line a bowl or platter with lettuce. Arrange mushroom mixture on top of the lettuce just before serving.

—CINDY CARR

CUCUMBERS WITH TOMATOES AND YOGURT
YIELD: 8 SERVINGS

2 medium cucumbers
2-1/2 tablespoons minced onion
1-1/2 teaspoons salt
2 firm ripe tomatoes, coarsely
    chopped
3 tablespoons chopped fresh
    coriander
2 teaspoons ground cumin
2 cups plain low-fat yogurt
2 to 3 tablespoons fresh
    chopped mint leaves
    (optional)

&❧ Peel cucumbers and slice in half lengthwise. Scoop out the seeds and slice once again lengthwise, then crosswise, making the pieces about 1/8 to 1/4-inch thick. Put cucumbers and onion in a small bowl. Mix with salt and let stand 5 minutes. Put mixture in a sieve and press out any juice. Combine cucumbers, onion, tomato and coriander in a larger bowl.

Heat cumin until fragrant by putting in foil over heat for about 30 seconds. Mix with yogurt and pour over vegetables. Cover and chill before serving. Garnish with mint.

Excellent with Lamb Curry; see page 197.

—COOKBOOK COMMITTEE

SUMMER PESTO SALAD
YIELD: 4 SERVINGS

PESTO DRESSING
2 cups packed fresh basil leaves
1 cup grated Romano cheese
1/4 cup pine nuts
1 clove garlic
1/3 cup olive oil
1/4 cup red wine vinegar

SALAD
4 lettuce leaves (red leaf
    preferred)
2 large ripe tomatoes, sliced
1 large red onion, sliced
4 balls buffalo-milk mozzarella
    cheese*

*Buffalo-milk mozzarella cheese, a
delicate soft cheese, can be purchased
at Italian markets or delicatessens.*

❧ Combine basil leaves, Romano cheese, pine nuts and garlic in container of food processor with a metal blade. Process with on-off pulses until finely chopped, about 10 seconds.

Slowly drizzle the oil, in a thin stream, into the processor while the motor is running. Add vinegar and pulse until blended.

To serve, arrange lettuce leaves on four individual salad plates, alternating slices of tomato, red onion and mozzarella cheese. Top each salad with a generous serving of the Pesto Dressing and serve.

—PAMELA LaMANTIA

Five Star
SIDE DISHES
SALADS

93

SALADE NIÇOISE

YIELD: 4 SERVINGS

1/2 pound fresh green beans
4 to 6 small new potatoes
1 medium red onion, thinly
    sliced
10 cherry tomatoes, halved
1/4 pound Niçoise olives or
    black olives
3 hard-cooked eggs, quartered
1 can (6-1/2 ounces) solid white
    albacore tuna, drained and
    flaked
1 tablespoon chopped fresh
    tarragon
1 tablespoon chopped fresh
    parsley
1 lemon, thinly sliced

DRESSING
1 large egg yolk
1/4 cup tarragon vinegar or
    white wine vinegar
1 tablespoon Dijon-style
    mustard
1 tablespoon minced shallot
Freshly ground white pepper
3/4 cup olive oil

&❧ Wash and trim green beans. Steam until they are barely tender. Boil new potatoes until tender. Quarter potatoes; set aside. Separate onion slices into rings.

Arrange beans, potatoes, onion rings, tomatoes, olives, eggs and tuna on a platter. Garnish with fresh herbs and thin lemon slices and chill.

Combine egg yolk, vinegar, mustard, shallot and pepper in container of food processor or blender; blend until well combined. With motor on low, add olive oil in a thin stream until mixture emulsifies.

Serve salad with dressing on the side and accompany with a chilled French Chardonnay.

—LAURA STERKEL GRANT

CHARRED RARE PEPPER TUNA WITH RADISH SALAD
AND SOY-GINGER VINAIGRETTE
YIELD: 4 SERVINGS

8 ounces sashimi grade
    yellowfin tuna (desired
    weight after trimming)
3 tablespoons freshly ground
    coarse black pepper
1 tablespoon finely chopped
    fresh ginger
1-1/2 cups julienned carrots
1/2 cup julienned leeks
1 cup thinly sliced red onions
1 cup julienned daikon
    (Japanese radish)
1/4 cup thinly sliced radishes
1/4 cup finely chopped cilantro
1/2 cup soy sauce
1/2 cup freshly-squeezed
    lime juice
1 tablespoon finely chopped
    shallots
1 teaspoon *each* finely chopped
    ginger and garlic
1 cup peanut oil
1-1/2 tablespoons sesame oil
Salt and fresh pepper to taste

❦ Combine pepper and ginger on a sheet of waxed paper. Carefully roll the trimmed tuna in the mixture so that the surface is coated evenly.

Heat a large skillet over high heat; carefully sear the tuna on each side for approximately 30-45 seconds. (You may also grill it quickly on each side.) Keep refrigerated until ready for plate presentation.

In medium bowl, combine carrots, leeks, red onions, daikon, radishes and cilantro. Set aside.

For vinaigrette, place shallots, ginger, garlic, soy sauce and lime juice in the bowl of blender or food processor. Process for 1 minute. Strain mixture into a bowl. Slowly whisk in oils. Season to taste with salt and pepper.

Plate presentation: Toss radish salad with some of the dressing. Evenly divide the salad between four plates, mounding them in the center of each plate. Using a very sharp knife, slice the charred tuna into 16 slices (about 1/8″ thick). Fan four slices around the radish salad, and ladle vinaigrette over tuna.

— CHEFS DAVID AND
ANNE GINGRASS

Five Star
SIDE DISHES
SALADS

Postrio
545 Post Street
San Francisco, CA
94102
415-776-7825

CAESAR SALAD WITH BACON
YIELD: 4-6 SERVINGS

1 large head romaine lettuce
2 cloves garlic, halved
3/4 cup vegetable oil
6 to 8 slices bacon
1 bunch scallions
2 tablespoons extra virgin olive oil
2 cloves garlic, minced
1 cup French bread cubes,
    crusts removed
1 egg, coddled*
Juice of 1 lemon
1 teaspoon freshly ground
    black pepper
1/2 teaspoon salt
1/2 cup grated Parmesan cheese

To coddle egg, bring water to a boil, turn off heat and add egg for one minute.

❧ Wash and dry romaine. Tear into bite-size pieces in salad bowl. Cover and refrigerate until ready to serve.

Add 2 cloves garlic to vegetable oil and allow to stand for several hours.

Fry bacon until crisp; drain and crumble.

Chop scallions, including tops, and set aside.

Heat 2 tablespoons olive oil with 2 cloves minced garlic in a medium skillet. Add bread cubes and sauté until lightly browned and crisp. Set aside.

Remove garlic cloves from salad oil. Whisk in coddled egg, lemon juice, salt and pepper.

Add scallions, bacon, bread cubes and Parmesan cheese to romaine. Stir in just enough dressing to coat salad.

Serve remaining dressing at table.

—NANCY SIMPSON

COBB SALAD
WITH BUTTERMILK HERB DRESSING
Light, pretty salad with an excellent dressing.
YIELD: 6 SERVINGS

1/2 head iceberg lettuce
1/2 head red leaf lettuce
1/2 bunch watercress, chopped
2 medium tomatoes, diced
1/2 cup crumbled bleu cheese
6 slices bacon, cooked and
    crumbled
4 scallions, chopped
2 hard-cooked eggs, chopped
2 whole chicken breasts,
    cooked and cubed
1 large avocado, diced
Chopped parsley for garnish

**BUTTERMILK HERB
DRESSING***
1/2 cup buttermilk
1/2 cup mayonnaise
1 large shallot, minced
1 large clove garlic, minced
1/2 teaspoon coarse salt
1/2 teaspoon freshly ground
    pepper
1 tablespoon minced chives
1/2 teaspoon ground thyme
1 teaspoon minced parsley

*Best made at least 24 hours
before serving.*

❦ To make Buttermilk Herb Dressing, whisk the buttermilk, mayonnaise, shallot and garlic in a medium bowl. Add the salt, pepper, chives, thyme and parsley, blending well.

Cut lettuce into small pieces. Toss lightly in a bowl with watercress and arrange on a serving platter.

Arrange tomatoes, bleu cheese, bacon, scallions, eggs, chicken and avocado in rows across lettuce. Garnish with parsley and chill.

To serve, pass the salad with dressing on the side.

—LAURA STERKEL GRANT

Five Star
SIDE DISHES
SALADS

ORANGE SHRIMP SALAD

Attractive luncheon dish.
YIELD: 8-10 SERVINGS

3 pounds cleaned, cooked shrimp
1 red onion, thinly sliced
6 large oranges, peeled
　　and sectioned
1-1/2 cups apple cider vinegar
1 cup vegetable oil
1/2 cup ketchup
2/3 cup fresh lemon juice
1 clove garlic, minced
1/4 cup sugar
1/2 teaspoon pepper
1/2 teaspoon salt
2 teaspoons mustard seed
1 teaspoon celery seed
5 teaspoons dried sweet
　　pepper flakes
2 tablespoons chopped fresh
　　parsley
1/2 teaspoon dried crushed
　　red pepper

᠃ Combine all ingredients in a large bowl. Cover and refrigerate for 24 to 48 hours. Serve on a bed of lettuce.

—SHIRLEY LINKOW

CHICKEN SESAME SALAD

This could also be served as an appetizer.
YIELD: 8 SERVINGS

1 cup teriyaki sauce
1/2 cup soy sauce
2 cups pineapple juice
1 cup sesame oil
1 cup vegetable oil
2 tablespoons sesame seed
1/4 cup honey
2-1/2 to 3 pounds skinless,
　　boneless chicken breasts
Mixed salad greens (to serve 8)
2 apples, peeled and sliced
　　right before serving

᠃ Combine teriyaki sauce, soy sauce, pineapple juice, sesame oil, vegetable oil, sesame seed and honey. Whisk to blend and set aside.

Grill chicken breasts over hot coals, approximately 10 minutes, being careful not to overcook. Refrigerate in just enough dressing to cover and marinate 45 minutes.

To serve, slice chicken breasts lengthwise and fan over mixed salad greens. Arrange apple slices on chicken and top with some of the dressing.

—CHEF RICHARD TAYLOR
WEMBLEY CLUB

Duck, Endive and Arugula Salad
with beets and walnut
vinaigrette
Yield: 4 servings

4 duck thighs
1 tablespoon oil
2 beets, cooked, peeled and
    thinly sliced into rounds
2 to 3 heads Belgian endive
1 bunch baby arugula
2 shallots, finely minced
1 tablespoon chopped parsley
1/2 cup excellent quality
    walnut oil
3 tablespoons sherry vinegar
Salt and freshly ground
    white pepper
12 toasted walnut halves

ఈ Season duck with salt and pepper. Heat oil in heavy-bottomed sauté pan over medium-high heat. Add duck, skin-side down. Cook approximately 6 minutes before turning. (Skin should be crisp.) Continue cooking until duck is medium cooked, approximately 12 minutes. Keep warm.

To serve, remove bones from duck and cut into thin slices. Arrange sliced beets in center of four large salad plates. Combine endive, arugula, shallots and chopped parsley in a large bowl and toss with oil and vinegar. Season with salt and pepper. Arrange salad over beets, garnish with sliced duck and toasted walnut pieces.

— Chef Alfred Portale

The Gotham Bar and Grill
12 East 12th Street
New York, NY 10003
212-620-4020

Five Star
SIDE DISHES

SALADS

RICE SALAD WITH SHRIMP

YIELD: 6-8 SERVINGS

2 cups rice*
3 cups chicken stock
20 large cooked shrimp, whole
   or chopped
2 cups chopped walnuts
1/2 cup chopped raisins
2 tablespoons chopped parsley
1/2 cup chopped scallions
1/2 cup chopped celery
1/2 cup chopped carrots
1/2 cup chopped green pepper
Parsley or watercress for garnish

LEMON FRENCH DRESSING
4 tablespoons lemon juice
1/2 cup vegetable oil
1/2 cup olive oil
1/2 teaspoon lemon peel
Salt and freshly ground pepper

*If using brown rice in this recipe, be
sure to adjust the cooking time to
40 to 45 minutes.*

&❧ Wash rice in sieve until water is clear.

Place rice and chicken stock in heavy saucepan and bring to a boil for 2 to 3 minutes. Lower heat, cover and simmer for 15 minutes or until all the stock is absorbed. Fluff with a fork and let cool.

To make Lemon French Dressing, combine the oils and the lemon juice with a wire whisk. Add lemon peel, salt and pepper and whisk again.

Combine cooled cooked rice, cooked shrimp and all the remaining ingredients in large salad bowl. Toss with Lemon French Dressing and serve on bed of lettuce. Garnish with fresh parsley or watercress.

—MADELYN ALVAREZ
—DINAH VINCE

CURRIED RICE

*Delicious curry flavor
contrasted with
sweet raisins and
crunchy peppers.*

YIELD: 4 SERVINGS

1 cup cooked brown rice
1 cup cooked basmati rice
1 green pepper, chopped
1 red pepper, chopped
5 scallions, chopped
1/4 cup raisins
2 tablespoons chopped parsley
1/4 cup slivered almonds
   (optional)

DRESSING
1/3 cup plain yogurt
2 tablespoons mayonnaise
1 tablespoon lemon juice
1 to 3 teaspoons curry powder
1 clove garlic, minced
1 tablespoon soy sauce

&❧ Cool rice and toss with other ingredients. Mix dressing well, pour over salad and toss. Chill for at least 2 hours.

—JANE TEMPLE

*When similar recipes were submitted,
acknowledgement was given to each contributor.*

THAI BEEF SALAD
YIELD: 4 SERVINGS

1 head romaine
2 scallions, diced
1 head radicchio
1 cup extra virgin olive oil
1/3 cup fresh lemon juice
1/4 cup Thai fish sauce*
2 shallots, minced
1/2 jalapeño pepper, diced
1 pound flank steak

Can by purchased at specialty food stores.

❧ Clean all of the greens. Shred romaine with knife and place in bowl with scallions. Arrange radicchio leaves on four plates. Combine olive oil, lemon juice, fish sauce, shallots and jalapeño in bowl and whisk.

Grill flank steak until rare to medium rare. Allow to stand for 5 minutes. Julienne steak and place in bowl of lettuce and scallions. Pour vinaigrette and toss lightly. Arrange on top of radicchio.

— CHEF ZACHARY BRUELL

*Z-Contemporary Cuisine
Eton Collection
28601 Chagrin Boulevard
Woodmere, OH 44122*

Five Star
SIDE DISHES

SALADS

TORTILLA SALAD

Edible shell is attractive and easy to make.

YIELD: 6 SERVINGS

6 large (9-inch) flour tortillas
Vegetable oil
1 pound lean ground beef
1 can (15-3/4 ounces) chili
    hot beans
1 can (4 ounces) chopped
    green chilies
1/2 cup water
2 tablespoons red salsa
4 cups shredded iceberg lettuce
4 ounces Cheddar cheese,
    shredded
4 scallions, chopped
2 tomatoes, chopped
1 small avocado, peeled and
    chopped
1/2 cup sour cream
Salsa

Preheat oven to 375°F. Lightly brush both sides of tortillas with oil. Place each tortilla over a narrow-bottom baking bowl (1 to 1-1/2 quarts). Bake in oven for about 8 minutes or until tortillas hold shape. Carefully remove from oven and cool.

Lightly brown ground beef until pink color disappears. Drain fat. Stir in beans, green chilies, 1/2 cup water and 2 tablespoons of salsa. Simmer until thoroughly heated, stirring occasionally.

Divide lettuce among tortilla bowls. Spoon hot bean mixture over lettuce and top with cheese, scallions, tomatoes and avocado.

To serve, add a dollop of sour cream to each salad and pass the salsa.

—BARBARA BRATEL COLLIER
FOOD CONSULTANT
HOME ECONOMIST

Antipasto and Cavatelli Salad
WITH SUN-DRIED TOMATOES
YIELD: 12 SERVINGS

2 packages of sun-dried tomatoes
1/3 pound Swiss cheese
1/3 pound mozzarella cheese
1/3 pound hard salami
1/3 pound cooked ham
1/3 pound cooked turkey breast
1 cup pitted black olives
1 cup pitted green olives
1 red pepper
1 green pepper
1 yellow pepper
1 pound cavatelli pasta
Salt and pepper to taste

DRESSING
4 cloves garlic
1/2 cup fresh basil
1/2 cup fresh oregano
2 tablespoons chopped shallots
1 cup extra virgin olive oil
1/4 cup balsamic vinegar

Soak the sun-dried tomatoes in 1 cup boiling water for 2 minutes. Drain and chop into small, bite-size pieces; set aside.

Cut the cheese, meats and peppers into 1/2-inch cubes. Add olives and set aside.

Cook the cavatelli pasta in boiling salted water until al dente; drain.

To prepare dressing, place garlic, basil (reserving some for garnish), oregano, shallots, olive oil and vinegar in container of food processor and process until finely chopped and well blended.

Combine all ingredients in a large serving bowl. Drizzle with dressing. Add salt and pepper and toss well.

—RUSSELL VERNON
WEST POINT MARKET
AKRON, OHIO

Five Star
SIDE DISHES
SALADS

Black Bean and Corn Salad
with cumin dressing
Yield: 10 servings

8 cups water
1/2 pound dried black beans
1 teaspoon salt
1/2 teaspoon dried oregano
1/4 teaspoon ground cumin
1 clove garlic, minced
1-1/2 cups yellow or white corn, blanched for 3 minutes, drained and chilled
1/2 cup chopped red pepper
3/4 cup chopped red onion

DRESSING
1/3 cup olive oil
1 teaspoon balsamic vinegar
1 teaspoon cider vinegar
1 tablespoon red wine vinegar
1/4 to 1/2 teaspoon sugar
1/4 to 1/2 teaspoon salt
1/2 teaspoon ground cumin
1/8 teaspoon cayenne pepper

Bring water to a boil and add beans. Cover, remove from heat and soak 1 hour. Return to heat, add salt, oregano, cumin and garlic. Simmer until beans are tender but not mushy (about 35 to 45 minutes) or soak beans overnight in cold water to cover.

The next day, if soaking overnight, simmer in the same water until tender, adding salt, oregano, cumin and garlic.

To make dressing, combine oil and vinegars, and whisk in sugar, salt, cumin and pepper.

Drain beans completely. Toss with dressing and refrigerate for at least 6 hours, stirring occasionally.

Drain the dressing from beans, saving it in a small jar. Most will be absorbed. Toss in corn, pepper and onion and chill for 4 to 6 hours before serving. Add remaining dressing, only if necessary.

Beans and dressing can be made up to 3 days ahead, and corn can be blanched the day before serving.

— Linda Y. Turner

Fanalucia
Corn relish.
Yield: 8 servings

6 ears or 1 can (2 pounds) corn, drained
1/2 medium green pepper
5 stalks celery
1 large onion
2-1/2 tablespoons pimiento
2/3 cup vegetable oil
2-1/2 tablespoons wine vinegar
2-1/2 teaspoons salt
1-1/4 teaspoons pepper
1/4 teaspoon dry mustard
Parsley sprigs

Cut corn from cob. Finely chop vegetables and mix with corn. Pour oil, vinegar and seasonings over vegetables and let stand for several hours. Garnish with parsley sprigs.

This relish was concocted by Mr. Joseph's grandmother, Fanny Joseph, who named it for herself and her two daughters, Alice and Lucy.

— Bill Joseph

INSALATA DI TRI COLORE
Great colors.
YIELD: 4-6 SERVINGS

3 large sweet red peppers
1-1/4 cups extra virgin olive oil
1/3 cup red wine vinegar
2 cloves garlic, minced
8 slices (1/2-inch thick)
       baguette-style bread
1 clove garlic
6 cups torn arugula
1/4 pound Asiago cheese, cut in
       1/2-inch slices
1/4 cup chopped Italian parsley
Freshly ground pepper

❧ Charbroil peppers over a
gas flame until blackened. Place
in paper bag for 10 minutes.
Peel and remove seeds; rinse and
pat dry. Cut in 1/2-inch strips
and marinate in 1/2 cup oil.

Mix vinegar and garlic
in a bowl. Gradually whisk in
2/3 cup oil.

Preheat broiler. Rub bread
with garlic and brush with
2 tablespoons oil. Toast bread
on both sides. Cut in half and
set aside.

Toss arugula lightly with
dressing and arrange on platter.
Place peppers, then cheese on
top. Garnish with parsley and
season with pepper. Serve with
bread.

—LAURA STERKEL GRANT

PASTA PUTTANESCA SALAD WITH WILD MUSHROOMS
Perfect picnic pasta.
YIELD: 25 SERVINGS

3 pounds bow tie pasta
3 shallots, minced
1/2 pound shiitake mushrooms,
       sliced
1/3 cup peas
1/3 cup sliced Kalamata olives
1/3 cup sliced sun-dried tomatoes
1/3 cup minced parsley
1/3 cup tiny capers
1/4 cup balsamic vinegar
3/4 cup extra virgin olive oil
1/4 cup minced basil leaves
Salt and pepper to taste

❧ Cook pasta in boiling salted
water until tender; cool.

Sauté shallots and shiitake
mushrooms in 2 tablespoons
of olive oil. Add peas, olives,
tomatoes, parsley and capers
and mix well.

Whisk vinegar, remaining
oil and basil. Set aside.

Mix pasta with vegetables
and toss with vinaigrette. Season
with salt and pepper.

—JOHN L. PISTONE II

Five Star
SIDE DISHES

SALADS

Broccoli Salad

YIELD: 6 SERVINGS

1 bunch broccoli
1 small red onion, chopped
1 pound bacon, fried crisp
      and crumbled
1/2 cup grated Cheddar cheese

DRESSING
1/2 cup mayonnaise
1 tablespoon red wine vinegar
1/4 cup sugar

  Clean and cut broccoli, using flowerets and tender stalk. Add onion, bacon and Cheddar cheese; mix well.

  Whisk mayonnaise, red wine vinegar and sugar; pour over salad. Toss and refrigerate for 3 to 4 hours before serving.

—JOAN A. CONRAD

Calypso Broccoli Salad

YIELD: 8 SERVINGS

3/4 cup mayonnaise
2 tablespoons cider vinegar
1/8 cup sugar
1 bunch broccoli, washed and
      finely diced
1/2 cup diced celery
1/2 cup minced onion
1/2 cup diced jicama
1/2 cup golden raisins
1/2 cup diced sweet red pepper
1 pound bacon, cooked crisp
      and crumbled
Dry roasted peanuts (optional)

  Mix mayonnaise, vinegar and sugar in a large bowl. Add remaining ingredients and toss. Chill for at least 1 hour.

—HOUGH CATERERS, INC.

Cauliflower Layer Salad

An easy do-ahead salad.

YIELD: 8-10 SERVINGS

1 head cauliflower
1 head iceberg lettuce
1 red onion, chopped
Salt to taste
1 to 1-1/2 cups mayonnaise
1/4 cup sugar
1/2 cup grated Parmesan cheese
1/2 pound bacon, cooked crisp
      and crumbled

  Wash and break cauliflower and lettuce into bite-size pieces.

  Layer salad ingredients in an oblong glass dish or bowl in this order: lettuce, cauliflower and onion.

  Spread mayonnaise over top layer. Sprinkle with sugar and cheese and top with bacon.

  Cover and refrigerate at least 12 hours.

—NANCY SHENKER

CURRIED POTATO SALAD

YIELD: 6 SERVINGS

2 pounds small red skinned
    potatoes
1 sweet red pepper, cored,
    seeded and chopped
1 bunch scallions, sliced
1 tablespoon chopped fresh
    thyme
1 tablespoon Dijon-style mustard
1 tablespoon curry powder
2/3 cup plain yogurt
Salt and pepper to taste

৯ Boil potatoes until tender.
Cool; cut into quarters. Mix
potatoes, scallions and thyme.

    Combine mustard, curry
powder, yogurt, salt and pepper; mix well. Pour mixture
over potatoes and toss lightly.
Adjust seasonings to taste. Chill.

— MERLENE TREUHAFT

WISCONSIN TRUE BLEU POTATO SALAD

Zippy flavor.

YIELD: 6 SERVINGS

4 cups peeled and cubed
    cooked potatoes
1/2 cup diced celery
1/2 cup sliced scallions
1/2 cup sliced water chestnuts

DRESSING
1-1/4 cups sour cream
2 tablespoons minced parsley
2 tablespoons white wine
    vinegar with tarragon
1/2 teaspoon celery seed
1/2 teaspoon salt
1/8 teaspoon pepper
3/4 cup (3 ounces) Wisconsin
    bleu cheese, crumbled

৯ Combine potatoes, celery,
scallions and water chestnuts
in a large bowl.

    Combine sour cream,
parsley, vinegar and seasonings;
mix well. Stir in bleu cheese.
Pour over salad ingredients and
toss lightly.

— CAROL MOORE
WEST POINT MARKET
AKRON, OHIO

Five Star
SIDE DISHES
SALADS

Warm Couscous Salad

Yield: 8-10 servings

2/3 cup dried currants
1-1/2 cups diced celery
3 tablespoons margarine or butter
1-1/2 cups vegetable stock or chicken stock
1-1/2 cups couscous
1/3 cup thinly sliced scallions
1/3 cup lightly toasted pine nuts
1/4 cup lemon juice
1/2 cup olive or vegetable oil
1/4 cup minced parsley leaves
1/4 teaspoon cinnamon

Soak currants in enough hot water to cover for 15 minutes. Drain and set aside.

Sauté celery in margarine in a large skillet. Add stock and bring to a boil. Stir in couscous, cover skillet and remove from heat. Let stand for approximately 4 minutes. Add remaining ingredients and serve.

—JoAnn Singer

Tabbouleh

Bulgur wheat salad.

Yield: 4 servings

1/2 cup bulgur wheat
2 cups water
1/2 cup chopped scallions
1 cup chopped parsley
1 cup chopped mint leaves
1/4 cup chopped sun-dried tomatoes
1 to 2 ripe tomatoes

DRESSING
Juice of 1 lemon
Juice of 1 lime
1/4 teaspoon salt
1/8 teaspoon freshly ground pepper

Soak wheat in water for at least 2 hours. Drain and discard water.

Mix wheat, scallions, parsley, mint and sun-dried tomatoes in a bowl.

Whisk dressing ingredients and pour over salad. Cover and chill for at least 3 hours before serving. To serve, garnish with fresh tomatoes.

—Cookbook Committee

Barley Salad

Yield: 8 servings

1 quart water
1 teaspoon beef stock or bouillon
Salt and pepper to taste
1/2 pound dry barley
1/4 cup diced tomato
1/4 cup diced gourmet (seedless) cucumber
1/4 cup diced red pepper
1/4 cup diced red onion
1/4 cup shredded carrot
1/4 cup diced yellow squash
1/8 cup chopped fresh parsley
1/8 cup chopped fresh mint

DRESSING
2 teaspoons olive oil
1/2 cup red wine vinegar
1 clove garlic, crushed

Bring water to a rolling boil. Add beef stock, salt, pepper and barley and cook for 30 minutes or until barley is done. Chill for at least 1 hour.

Combine tomato, cucumber, pepper, onion, carrots, squash, parsley and mint in a large serving bowl. Add barley to serving bowl and mix thoroughly.

Whisk oil, vinegar and garlic in a small bowl. Drizzle over salad and toss.

—Cleaven Smith, Jr.

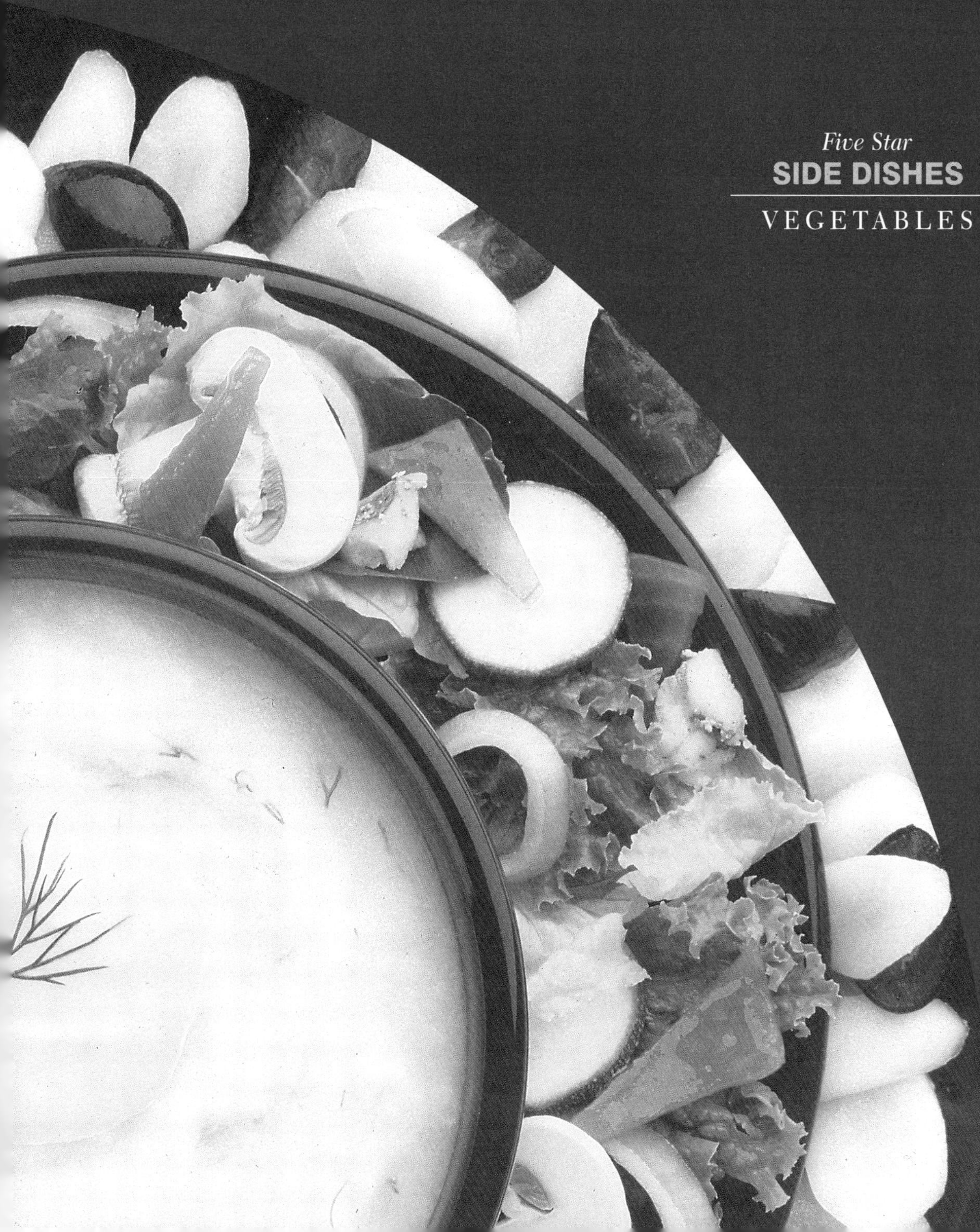

Five Star

SIDE DISHES

VEGETABLES

SHARON'S ZUCCHINI MEDLEY

YIELD: 3 SERVINGS

`1 tablespoon margarine
2 medium unpeeled zucchini, cut into 1/4-inch slices
1 tablespoon chopped onion
1 teaspoon basil
1 clove garlic, minced
2 large tomatoes, peeled and cut into wedges
3 tablespoons grated Parmesan cheese

❧ Melt margarine in a non-stick skillet. Add zucchini, onion, basil and garlic, stirring to blend. Cook over medium heat until zucchini is tender. Add tomatoes and stir to heat through. Sprinkle with Parmesan cheese and serve.

Great with grilled meats or as a topping for pasta.
— SHARON KEYS

ZUCCHINI-TOMATO BAKE WITH BASIL

Easily triples or quadruples to serve larger groups.

YIELD: 4-6 SERVINGS

2 to 3 (about 3/4 pound) small zucchini
4 large slices whole-wheat bread
Salt and pepper to taste
4 tablespoons butter, melted
2 to 3 (about 1 pound) medium tomatoes, peeled and sliced
1 tablespoon chopped fresh basil
Sugar to taste
1/4 to 1/2 pound mozzarella cheese, sliced

❧ Preheat oven to 375°F. Slice unpeeled zucchini very thin; sprinkle with salt. Set aside for 30 minutes; rinse and pat dry.

Toast bread lightly, cut into cubes and drizzle with melted butter.

Lightly grease a 2-quart oven-proof dish; place half the zucchini in the bottom. Season with pepper. Place tomatoes on zucchini and sprinkle with half the basil and sugar. Top with half of the cheese slices and half of the bread. Repeat layers, ending with bread cubes. Bake for 1 hour.
— DR. KAREN SZAUTER

RATATOUILLE

YIELD: 8-10 SERVINGS

1 cup olive oil
1 medium eggplant (1 pound), unpeeled, cut into 1-inch cubes
2 large green peppers (about 2-1/2 to 3 cups), cubed
2 large onions, chopped
2 cloves garlic, minced
1 can (28 ounces) whole tomatoes, chopped, with liquid
1/3 cup red wine vinegar
2 tablespoons sugar
2 tablespoons capers
2 tablespoons tomato paste
1 tablespoon salt
1/2 cup chopped fresh parsley
1/2 cup pimiento-stuffed olives, sliced in thirds
2 teaspoons dried basil
1/2 cup pine nuts

❧ Combine oil, eggplant, green pepper, onions, garlic and tomatoes in a large saucepan or kettle. Cook over medium-high heat until almost tender, approximately 20 minutes.

Add vinegar, sugar, capers, tomato paste, salt, parsley, olives and basil. Cover and simmer approximately 15 minutes.

Just before serving, add pine nuts. If desired, some of the liquid may be drained before serving.

— MARG WILLIAMS

When similar recipes were submitted, acknowledgement was given to each contributor.

Eggplant Parmigiana
Yield: 4-6 servings

1 large eggplant
1 cup all-purpose flour
1 cup Italian-seasoned bread
   crumbs
1/4 cup grated Romano cheese
2 cloves garlic, minced
Salt and pepper to taste
3 eggs, lightly beaten
2 tablespoons vegetable oil
3/4 pound provolone cheese,
   sliced
1 jar (32 ounces) prepared
   spaghetti sauce
Grated Parmesan cheese

❧ Mix bread crumbs, Romano cheese, garlic, salt and pepper in a shallow bowl.

Pour beaten eggs into a shallow dish or plate.

Peel and slice eggplant. Dredge sliced eggplant in flour.

Dip both sides of flour-dredged eggplant into egg mixture, then coat with bread-crumb mixture. Heat vegetable oil in a large skillet over medium-high heat. Panfry eggplant in skillet over medium-high heat until lightly browned, approximately 5 minutes each side.

Remove from skillet, drain on paper towels and place on cookie sheet. Cover each slice of eggplant with a slice of provolone cheese. Broil for 2 minutes or until cheese melts.

Serve eggplant with warm spaghetti sauce and Parmesan cheese.
—Alice Cronquist
—Angela McDougal

Five Star
SIDE DISHES
VEGETABLES

Caponata

Excellent with pita toasts.

YIELD: 8-12 SERVINGS

1 large eggplant
1 large green bell pepper
1/3 cup extra virgin olive oil
2 large onions, cut into 1/2-inch
    squares
3 celery ribs with leafy tops,
    cut into 1/4-inch pieces
2 large cloves garlic, minced
1/4 teaspoon freshly ground black
    pepper, or more to taste
1 can (28 ounces) Italian-style
    peeled tomatoes, seeded,
    drained and coarsely
    chopped
2 tablespoons tomato paste
1/4 cup chopped green brine-
    cured olives
2-1/2 tablespoons chopped capers
2 tablespoons red wine vinegar
2 teaspoons sugar
2 teaspoons salt
3/4 teaspoon oregano
1/8 teaspoon crushed hot
    red pepper
1 tablespoon chopped flatleaf
    parsley

◈ Punch a few holes in the eggplant with a fork or knife. If you have a gas stove, cook the eggplant and pepper directly on the flame, turning until charred all over. If not, broil the vegetables as close to the heat as possible to achieve the same results. The eggplant will soften, but don't let it get completely mushy. Remove the top from the eggplant and peel off the skin. If it doesn't come off easily, scrape the flesh from the skin with a knife. Rub the charred skin off the pepper. Cut the vegetables roughly into 1/2-inch pieces.

Heat the oil in a large, non-aluminum, flameproof dish.

Add the onions and sauté over moderately high heat until they begin to brown, 3 to 5 minutes. Add the celery, reduce heat and cook until softened, about 5 minutes longer. Add half the garlic and cook for 1 minute.

Add the eggplant, green pepper, tomatoes, tomato paste, olives, capers, vinegar, sugar, salt, oregano and hot pepper. Cook, partially covered, for about 20 minutes, or until most of the liquid is evaporated. Stir in the parsley, black pepper, and remaining garlic.

Serve as a vegetable or salad, or as a spread for an hors d'oeuvre.

As with many highly seasoned tomato dishes, this dish improves overnight in the refrigerator. It's best served at room temperature.

Previously published in *Tailgate Parties*, Harmony Books, a division of Crown Publishers, Inc., copyright ©1984, by Susan Wyler, reprinted with permission.

—SUSAN WYLER
COOKBOOK AUTHOR

When similar recipes were submitted, acknowledgement was given to each contributor.

GRILLED VEGETABLES

*A vegetable medley
to complement any cookout!*

YIELD: 8 SERVINGS

4 small zucchini
4 small yellow squash
4 small eggplant
3 tomatoes
3 onions
2 tablespoons olive oil
Salt and pepper to taste
1/4 cup balsamic vinegar
1/4 cup chopped fresh Italian
    parsley

∾ Heat grill and brush with vegetable oil.

Cut zucchini, squash and eggplant lengthwise, leaving them intact at stem. Slice tomatoes and onions in half. Brush vegetables with olive oil and sprinkle with salt and pepper.

Spread vegetables on grill and cook over medium-high heat until brown, approximately 5 minutes. Turn vegetables and grill another 5 minutes or until lightly charred. Remove from grill; cut from stems and mix. Sprinkle with balsamic vinegar and parsley. Serve immediately.

— SUSIE HELLER
— CAMILLE LABARRE

ZUCCHINI FRITTATA

YIELD: 6 SERVINGS

8 zucchini, peeled and cut into
    thin rounds
3 tablespoons olive oil
9 eggs, discard 3 yolks
3/4 cup Italian seasoned bread
    crumbs
1/2 cup grated Romano cheese
3/4 teaspoon baking powder
1/2 cup butter or olive oil
4 cups béchamel sauce or Italian
    tomato sauce to serve over
    frittata, if desired

∾ Preheat oven to 400°F. Sauté zucchini in olive oil in a large skillet until limp; set aside.

Beat eggs in large bowl until frothy. Add bread crumbs, cheese and baking powder, mixing well. Add zucchini to mixture.

Melt butter and pour into a large 2-inch deep fluted quiche dish or a 10-1/2-inch oven-proof omelet pan. Pour in egg-zucchini mixture and bake for approximately 25 minutes, until eggs are set and frittata is golden.

To serve, cut the frittata into wedges. Pass sauce if desired.

— DIANN G. SCARAVILLI

Five Star
SIDE DISHES
VEGETABLES

Vegetable Crêpes
with Parmesan Cheese Sauce

For special occasions.

Yield: 6 servings

CRÊPES
1 cup all-purpose flour
1/2 teaspoon salt
6 eggs, beaten
3 cups milk
3 tablespoons butter or
    margarine, melted
1/2 cup grated Parmesan cheese

VEGETABLES
3 to 4 cups each cubed carrots,
    small cauliflower and
    broccoli flowerets or
    60 asparagus spears

PARMESAN CHEESE SAUCE
1 cup plus 2 tablespoons butter
    or margarine
1 cup plus 2 tablespoons
    all-purpose flour
3 teaspoons salt
1/2 teaspoon white pepper
6 cups milk, scalded
1-1/2 cups grated Parmesan cheese
1-1/2 cups canned fried onions
    (optional)

❦ Sift flour and salt into a bowl. Stir in beaten eggs. Add milk slowly, beating with a wire whisk. Add melted butter and Parmesan cheese. Refrigerate mixture for 1 to 2 hours.

Heat crêpe pan and add butter. When pan is nearly smoking, add 2 to 3 tablespoons of batter and swirl to coat pan. Cook crêpes about 1 minute per side. Continue cooking crêpes, adding butter between each, until all batter is used. This makes approximately 20 crêpes.

Stack crêpes on plate and cover with a clean, dry cloth. Set aside and continue with recipe, or refrigerate crêpes up to two days.

Steam vegetables until just tender; combine broccoli, cauliflower and carrots. This can be done ahead of time and refrigerated, or it can be cooked while crêpe batter is standing.

To make Parmesan Cheese Sauce, melt butter in a saucepan and add flour, stirring to blend with a wire whisk. Do not brown. Add salt and pepper and gradually add the scalded milk. Add Parmesan cheese, stirring constantly with a wire whisk over low heat until sauce begins to boil. Reduce heat and simmer for 5 minutes. Sauce can also be made ahead and refrigerated.

To assemble crêpes, place approximately 1/3 cup of mixed vegetables or 3 asparagus spears in the center of crêpe. Spoon 2 tablespoons of sauce over vegetables and fold over sides of crêpe. Place, seam side down, in a greased oven-proof dish.

Cover all crêpes with remaining sauce and heat covered in a 325°F oven for approximately 30 minutes.

To serve, top with optional fried onions.

This versatile recipe can be used as a main course or as a side dish.

—Lloyd Taplin

VEGETABLE TERRINE WITH HERBES DE PROVENCE

YIELD: 8 SERVINGS

2 zucchini
2 yellow squash
1 small eggplant
Salt and pepper to taste
1 large onion, thinly sliced
Olive oil for frying
1-1/2 teaspoons chopped fresh
    thyme
3 roasted red peppers
12 ounces goat cheese, crumbled

RED PEPPER SAUCE
1 roasted red pepper
1/2 cup olive oil
Salt and pepper to taste

HERBES DE PROVENCE
2 teaspoons chopped fresh thyme
2 teaspoons chopped fresh parsley
2 teaspoons chopped fresh savory

๛ Thinly slice the zucchini, squash and eggplant lengthwise, by hand or with a mandoline. Keep the vegetables separate. Lay the zucchini on a baking sheet so that the strips do not overlap. Season with salt and pepper. Broil the zucchini for 2 to 3 minutes. Repeat for squash and eggplant. Reserve.

Sauté the onion in olive oil until translucent. Season with salt, pepper and thyme. Allow to cool.

Peel the roasted red peppers, remove the seeds and split in half. Reserve 3 for the terrine and 1 to make the sauce.

Begin layering the eggplant in a 10 × 4-inch terrine mold or shallow pan until it is about 1/2-inch deep on the bottom. Cut to fit so that the pieces lie flat. Lay peppers flat over eggplant.

Place crumbled goat cheese on top of the peppers, spreading the cheese as evenly as possible and filling in any gaps in the layers.

Add the yellow squash, keeping the layers even. Then add the onions, spreading them evenly over the yellow squash. Finish the terrine with a layer of zucchini.

Cut a piece of cardboard the same size as the terrine mold. Place on top of the terrine and press with a 2-pound weight (e.g. 2 pounds butter). Refrigerate overnight.

To serve, turn terrine upside down and remove from mold. Slice the terrine about 1/2-inch thick. Place slices on pieces of aluminum foil and heat in the oven before serving.

To make sauce, place the roasted peppers in container of food processor and process until smooth. Continue processing and slowly drizzle in the olive oil until smooth. Season with salt and pepper. Strain through a fine sieve.

Serve terrine with Red Pepper Sauce and sprinkle with the Herbes de Provence.

—CHEF DEBRA PONZEK

Five Star
SIDE DISHES
VEGETABLES

Montrachet
239 West Broadway
New York, NY 10013
212-219-2777

BRAISED SPINACH
YIELD: 4 SERVINGS

1-1/2 pounds spinach (escarole
    or Swiss chard may be
    substituted)
1/4 cup olive oil
1 large clove garlic, minced
1/4 teaspoon salt

⇛ Rinse spinach thoroughly
and remove tough stems. Heat
olive oil and garlic in a 10-inch
skillet over low heat. Add spinach,
cover and braise 8 minutes,
stirring occasionally with a fork.
Sprinkle with salt and serve.

—LINDA Y. TURNER

MINTED CARROTS
YIELD: 6 SERVINGS

6 medium carrots, sliced
3 tablespoons butter
1 tablespoon chopped fresh mint
    leaves or 1/2 teaspoon
    dried mint
2 tablespoons light brown sugar
1 tablespoon honey
Salt and pepper

⇛ Steam carrots in a medium
saucepan until tender; drain.
Add butter, mint leaves, brown
sugar and honey. Cook over low
heat until heated through. Season
to taste and serve.

—MARG WILLIAMS

BABY SPRING TURNIPS

If baby turnips are unavailable,
try pearl onions or baby carrots.

YIELD: 6 SERVINGS

4 bunches small, early white
    turnips, with green tops
1/2 teaspoon salt
6 tablespoons sweet butter or
    margarine
Salt and pepper to taste

❧ Trim the leafy section of
the tops of the turnips to
within 1 inch of the turnip,
leaving bright green stems.
Trim the bottom of turnips to
remove rough root ends.

Place washed turnips in a
sauté pan large enough to hold
turnips in single layer. Cover
with just enough cold water to
submerge turnips. Add salt and
simmer over medium-high heat
until turnips are tender but not
too soft. (The water will evaporate
toward the end of the cooking
process.)

Gradually add the butter,
gently stirring to glaze the
turnips. Season with salt and
pepper to taste.

— JEAN BINGAY

CARROTS WITH GRAPES

YIELD: 12 SERVINGS

2 pounds carrots, peeled and cut
    into thick, diagonal slices
2 tablespoons butter or margarine
1/8 teaspoon sugar
1/2 cup water
1 tablespoon vodka
1-1/2 cups seeded and halved
    dark purple grapes
Salt to taste

❧ Sauté sliced carrots in butter
or margarine in a large skillet for
2 minutes. Sprinkle sugar over
carrots and continue cooking
2 to 3 minutes. Add water and
vodka and cook until carrots
are almost tender. Add grapes,
cover pan and cook until carrots
and grapes are tender, approximately 5 minutes. Salt to taste.

— DR. TENA TARLER ROSNER

This recipe is featured on the color
cover of the Side Dishes section tab.

Five Star
SIDE DISHES
VEGETABLES

Purée of Potatoes and Root Vegetables

Yield: 6-8 servings

6 potatoes, peeled
6 parsnips or 2 celery roots
    or 6 carrots or 4 turnips,
    peeled (proportions and
    combinations can vary)
4 tablespoons butter
1/2 cup milk (more or less,
    depending on consistency
    preferred)
Salt and pepper to taste
Freshly grated nutmeg to taste

ॐ Simmer potatoes and other vegetables in salted water until soft enough to put through a ricer or food mill. Add butter, milk, salt, pepper and nutmeg. Serve immediately or keep warm in top of double boiler.

— Maynard Thomson

Potato Pancakes

Yield: 6-8 servings

2-1/2 cups peeled, grated potatoes
1 onion, grated
3 eggs
3 tablespoons all-purpose flour
Salt and pepper to taste
Vegetable oil for frying
Applesauce
Sour cream

ॐ Place grated potatoes in a bowl of cold water.

Drain potatoes well, squeezing out all excess water. Place in mixing bowl with onion, eggs, flour, salt and pepper and mix well.

Cover the bottom of a heavy skillet with vegetable oil and heat. Drop spoonfuls of potato mixture into the hot oil, forming patties 1/4-inch thick and 3 inches in diameter. Cook over medium heat until brown. Turn and brown other side until crisp.

Serve hot with applesauce and sour cream as accompaniments.

To keep pancakes warm, place them on a rack over a baking sheet in a 200°F oven.

— Peggy Ratcheson

Greenleaf Potatoes

Easy and different.

Yield: 4-8 servings

1/3 cup corn oil
1 teaspoon dillweed
1/2 teaspoon crumbled rosemary
1/2 teaspoon thyme
1/8 teaspoon garlic powder
Salt and pepper to taste
4 large baking potatoes

ॐ Preheat oven to 350°F. Pour corn oil into a shallow 13 × 9-inch baking pan; sprinkle dillweed, rosemary, thyme, garlic powder, salt and pepper on top of oil.

Wash, scrub and dry potatoes. Cut in half lengthwise and place, cut-side down, in a single layer on top of oil and seasonings. Bake for approximately 45 to 60 minutes or until potatoes are tender.

Serve alone or with sour cream and chives.

— Helen B. Greenleaf

ROASTED GARLIC POTATOES

YIELD: 4 SERVINGS

2 pounds baking potatoes,
    peeled and cubed
1 tablespoon peanut oil
8 cloves garlic, peeled
Leaves from 1 small bunch thyme
    (3 or 4 sprigs), minced
1/4 cup heavy cream
Juice of one lemon
3 tablespoons butter
Salt to taste

෫ Preheat oven to 350°F. Cover potatoes with cold water and bring to a boil. Cook about 20 minutes until soft; drain.

Heat peanut oil in sauté pan over medium-high heat and lightly brown whole garlic cloves. Place sauté pan with garlic in oven and roast garlic until soft, about 12 minutes. Turn garlic occasionally, being careful not to burn.

Place garlic in container of blender or food processor with thyme, cream and lemon juice; blend until smooth and reserve.

Beat potatoes with electric mixer until almost smooth. Add roast garlic mixture and beat until smooth. Add butter and season to taste with salt. Keep warm.

Previously published in *The Mansion on Turtle Creek Cookbook*, Grove/Weidenfeld, copyright ©1987, by Dean Fearing, reprinted with permission.

— CHEF DEAN FEARING

Five Star
SIDE DISHES

VEGETABLES

*The Mansion on Turtle Creek
2821 Turtle Creek Boulevard
Dallas, TX 75219
214-559-2100*

CORN PUDDING

YIELD: 8-10 SERVINGS

1/4 cup butter
1/4 cup all-purpose flour
1 tablespoon sugar
4 eggs
1 cup half and half
1/2 pound sharp Cheddar
    cheese, grated
1 red pepper, finely chopped
1 green pepper, finely chopped
1-1/2 packages (10 ounces each)
    frozen corn, thawed
Salt and pepper to taste

❧ Preheat oven to 350°F.
Lightly grease a 1-1/2-quart
oven-proof dish.
    Melt butter in a large
saucepan. Stir in flour and
sugar until smooth. Add eggs
and stir. Add half and half,
cheese, peppers and corn. Add
salt and pepper to taste.
    Spoon into oven-proof dish
and bake for 40 minutes or
until bubbly.

—MRS. DONALD RITTER

SWEET POTATO AND APPLE CASSEROLE

*Served during Passover
in many Cleveland homes.*

YIELD: 10-12 SERVINGS

1-1/2 cups (3 medium) peeled
    and grated sweet potatoes
1-1/2 cups peeled and grated
    carrots
1-1/2 cups peeled and grated
    Granny Smith apples
3/4 cup raisins
3/4 cup prunes
1/2 cup diced dried apricots
    (optional)
3/4 cup matzo meal
1/2 cup sugar
3/4 teaspoon ground cinnamon
3/4 cup margarine, melted
1/2 cup fresh lemon juice

❧ Preheat oven to 350°F.
Mix all ingredients in a large
oven-proof dish and bake,
covered, for 45 minutes.
Remove cover and continue
baking for 10 to 15 minutes,
until the top is crusty.

—TOBIE KOGAN

SWEET POTATO BAKE

*Wonderful with
Thanksgiving dinner.*

YIELD: 10-12 SERVINGS

6 large sweet potatoes, boiled,
    peeled and mashed
1-1/2 cups sugar
2 tablespoons all-purpose flour
1/2 teaspoon baking powder
1/8 teaspoon ground nutmeg
1/2 cup (1 stick) margarine, melted
4 eggs
1/2 cup milk
1 tablespoon lemon juice
2 teaspoons vanilla
Ground cinnamon

❧ Preheat oven to 350°F.
Combine all ingredients, except
cinnamon, in a large bowl. Spoon
mixture into a greased 2-quart
oven-proof dish. Sprinkle
cinnamon over the top.
    Bake for 30 to 45 minutes
or until firm.

—SHEILA JACOBS

HOLIDAY ACORN SQUASH

Attractive autumn fare.

YIELD: 8 SERVINGS

4 acorn squash
1 bag (1 pound) fresh cranberries,
    washed and picked over
3 tablespoons butter
3/4 cup sauterne or other
    white wine
1/2 teaspoon freshly grated
    nutmeg
3/4 cup honey

⅋ Preheat oven to 350°F. Bake whole squash for approximately 45 minutes.

While squash is baking, sauté cranberries in butter in a heavy skillet over medium-high heat. Reduce heat, add sauterne and simmer for 10 minutes, stirring frequently to prevent burning.

Sprinkle nutmeg over the berries; add honey and simmer an additional 5 minutes.

Remove squash from oven and cut in half lengthwise. Scoop out seeds and any fiber that clings to them.

Fill cavities of squash with cranberry mixture. Return filled squash halves to the oven for 10 minutes.

—MOLLY BARTLETT
SILVER CREEK FARM

BARBECUE BLACK-EYES

A Southern New Year's tradition.

YIELD: 12 SERVINGS

8 slices bacon
2 large onions, chopped
2 stalks celery, diced
2 carrots, diced
7 cups cooked or canned black-
    eyed peas, reserving liquid
1/2 cup barbecue sauce
2 teaspoons prepared mustard
1 cup diced green pepper
    (optional)

⅋ Cook bacon until crisp; drain and crumble. Reserve drippings.

Sauté onions, celery and carrots in bacon drippings. Add peas, 2 cups reserved liquid, barbecue sauce and mustard; simmer for 45 minutes. Add additional liquid as needed, stirring frequently. Stir in green pepper and heat through. Top with crumbled bacon and serve.

The flavor in this recipe is enhanced the longer it cooks.

—MARY SUSAN LYON

Five Star
SIDE DISHES
VEGETABLES

HOME-STYLE TOFU
Aromatic and delicious.
YIELD: 4 SERVINGS

4 squares (2 ounces each) tofu
Vegetable oil for frying and
    sautéing
1/2 sweet red pepper, sliced
1/2 green bell pepper, sliced
1/2 cup bamboo shoots
1/2 cup sliced water chestnuts
1/2 cup sliced mushrooms
1 cup Kung Pao Sauce
2 tablespoons hoisin sauce*
1/2 cup chicken stock or water
2 tablespoons chopped scallions
1/2 teaspoon sliced ginger root
1/2 teaspoon chopped garlic
2 teaspoons cornstarch (optional)
1 tablespoon sesame oil

KUNG PAO SAUCE
1 tablespoon hoisin sauce
1 tablespoon oyster sauce*
Light and dark soy sauce for taste
    and color
2 tablespoons sesame oil
2 to 3 tablespoons cooking wine
1 teaspoon sugar
Available at Oriental markets

⁂ Mix King Pao Sauce ingredients and set aside for later use.

Cut each piece of tofu diagonally into four triangles. Heat oil in wok and deep fry tofu until golden brown. Remove to a platter and drain oil, reserving 2 tablespoons in wok. Stir-fry red and green peppers for 1 minute; set aside. Stir-fry bamboo shoots, water chestnuts and mushrooms for 1 minute; set aside.

Mix Kung Pao Sauce, hoisin sauce and chicken stock; place in heated wok. Cook over high heat, stirring often, until sauce is reduced and coats the back of a spoon. Add chopped scallions, ginger root and garlic. Mix well and cook for one minute. Add cornstarch, if desired, and stir to combine.

Combine all sautéed ingredients in wok and stir-fry until heated through and sauce covers all ingredients. Sprinkle sesame oil over mixture and serve warm.

Serve with rice or noodles and chicken or beef.

—ROSE WONG
    PEARL OF THE ORIENT RESTAURANT
    SHAKER HEIGHTS, OHIO

GRILLED MARINATED TOFU
YIELD: 6 SERVINGS

1 pound tofu, cut in 2-inch × 1-inch
    rectangles
1 cup dried shiitake mushrooms
1 cup water
1/2 cup soy sauce
1/2 cup red wine vinegar
1/2 cup sherry
1/2 cup olive oil
1 tablespoon chopped fresh
    oregano
1-1/2 teaspoons chopped garlic
1/2 teaspoon black peppercorns
1/2 teaspoon kosher salt

🐦 Place tofu rectangles between 2 towels with a plate on top. Set aside, draining, for 2 to 3 hours.

Simmer mushrooms in water in a medium-size saucepan for 20 minutes. Add remaining ingredients, except tofu, and simmer 5 minutes longer.

Place tofu in a single layer in a shallow pan. Pour marinade mixture over the tofu. Marinate in the refrigerator a minimum of 8 hours or up to 24 hours.

Strain marinade and reserve. Thinly slice shiitake mushrooms and reserve for garnish.

Grill marinated tofu over medium-high heat until dark brown and crunchy on all sides.

Serve topped with reserved marinade and garnished with the sliced shiitake mushrooms.

Excellent with Spicy Pickled Vegetables and Soba Noodles. See pages 127, 69.

— CHEF SUSAN FENIGER
— CHEF MARY SUE MILLIKEN

Five Star
SIDE DISHES
VEGETABLES

CITY Restaurant
180 South La Brea
Los Angeles, CA 90036
213-938-2155

Border Grill
1445 4th Street
Santa Monica, CA 90401
213-451-1655

CRANBERRY ONION CONFIT

Wonderful jewel-like quality.

YIELD: 6 CUPS

2 medium onions (red or white),
    sliced
1/2 cup butter
Zest of 3 oranges
2 bags (1 pound each) cranberries
2 cups sugar
3 cups cranberry juice
1 cup orange juice or 1/4 cup
    vinegar
1 teaspoon ground cinnamon
1/2 teaspoon ground ginger
1/8 teaspoon ground nutmeg
1/8 teaspoon ground cardamom
1/8 teaspoon ground coriander
1 cup fresh basil

➤ Sauté onion in butter over medium to low heat until caramelized, approximately 20 to 25 minutes. Set aside.

Boil 1/2 cup water and add the orange zest. Let sit for 2 to 3 minutes; drain and set aside.

Combine the cranberries, sugar, cranberry juice, orange juice, cinnamon, ginger, nutmeg, cardamom and coriander in a large saucepan and bring to a rolling boil. Reduce heat and simmer for 40 to 50 minutes. Cool and add sautéed onions, basil and orange zest.

For a change of pace, use this recipe in place of applesauce.

—JOANN SINGER

PEACH AND BELL PEPPER SALSA

A nice accompaniment for pork chops or pork roast.

YIELD: 8 SERVINGS

4 fresh peaches, peeled and
    diced into 1/4-inch pieces
2 tablespoons finely chopped
    scallions
1 tablespoon diced red pepper
1 tablespoon diced green pepper
1 tablespoon lime juice
1 tablespoon chopped fresh
    cilantro
1 tablespoon chopped fresh
    Italian parsley
1 tablespoon olive oil
1 teaspoon chopped jalapeño
    chilies
1/2 teaspoon cumin
1/2 teaspoon salt
1/8 teaspoon pepper
1/2 cup (4 ounces) peach jam

➤ Mix all ingredients, except peach jam, in a large bowl. Cover and refrigerate for at least 30 minutes.

Melt the peach jam in a saucepan, stirring constantly. Remove from heat and add to salsa, stirring to combine.

—MARY ANN LANG

Pineapple Chutney
Yield: 2 cups

3/4 cup fresh orange juice

1/4 cup passion fruit purée or juice (if unavailable, use an additional 1/4 cup orange juice)

1 scallion, trimmed and chopped

1 shallot, chopped

1 clove garlic, chopped

1 jalapeño chili, seeded and chopped

1 tablespoon grated fresh ginger, with juice

1 teaspoon chili powder

1 teaspoon curry powder

1/2 ripe fresh pineapple, peeled, cored, and cut into small cubes

1/4 red pepper, seeded and cut into julienne strips

1/2 tablespoon finely chopped fresh mint

1/2 tablespoon finely chopped fresh basil

❧ Place orange juice, passion fruit purée, scallion, shallot, garlic, jalapeño, ginger, chili powder and curry powder in a medium saucepan and cook over medium-high heat for approximately 10 minutes. Bring to a boil and cook, stirring frequently, until liquid is reduced to 1/4 cup.

Remove saucepan from heat and strain liquid into a medium bowl. Add pineapple, red pepper, mint and basil; mix well. Cool slightly, cover, and refrigerate several hours to chill before serving.

Serve as an accompaniment to grilled meats and seafood. This recipe may be prepared up to 3 days in advance. Cover tightly and refrigerate.

Previously published in *The Mansion on Turtle Creek Cookbook*, Grove/Weidenfeld, copyright ©1987, by Dean Fearing, reprinted with permission.

— Chef Dean Fearing

Five Star
SIDE DISHES
SAUCES

The Mansion on Turtle Creek
2821 Turtle Creek Boulevard
Dallas, TX 75219
214-559-2100

Judy's Bread and Butter Pickles

YIELD: 8 HALF-PINTS

8 cups unpeeled, sliced
    cucumbers
2 cups sliced onion
3 small green peppers, seeded
    and chopped
1/3 cup salt
2 cups apple cider vinegar
3 cups sugar
2 teaspoons ground turmeric
2 teaspoons celery seed
2 teaspoons mustard seed

Combine cucumbers, onions, green peppers and salt. Let stand 1 hour. Drain and rinse with cold water.

Boil remaining ingredients for 10 minutes. Mix vegetables and juices together and heat for 5 minutes.

Pack into sterilized jars; seal and refrigerate.

— DIANE GASIOR HIENTON

Hren Horseradish and Beet Relish

A traditional Easter relish served with ham.

YIELD: 1 PINT

6 large or 2 cans (16-1/2 ounces
    each) beets
1/2 cup grated horseradish or
    1/4 cup pure bottled
    horseradish
1/3 cup sugar
1/2 teaspoon salt
1/8 teaspoon pepper
1/4 cup vinegar

Wash beets and trim, leaving 1-inch stem. Cook in water to cover, approximately 1 hour or until tender. Drain, slip off skins and cool.

Grate beets and horseradish; place in medium bowl. Add sugar, salt, pepper and vinegar; mix well.

Refrigerate at least 24 hours before serving.

This keeps well in the refrigerator for at least a month.

— MARY FEDAK
UKRAINIAN NATIONAL WOMEN'S
LEAGUE OF AMERICA

Spicy Pickled Vegetables

Yield: 2 quarts

8 cups assorted sliced vegetables:
   carrots, jalapeño peppers,
   Napa cabbage, daikon
   radish, red pepper, onions,
   cucumber
1 quart white wine vinegar
1 quart plus 1 cup water
1/2 cup salt
1 cup sugar
1 tablespoon black peppercorns
1 teaspoon crushed red chili
   pepper

ৎ❧ Slice vegetables into approximately 2-inch × 1-inch × 1/8-inch pieces; place in large mixing bowl and set aside.

Combine remaining ingredients in a medium-size saucepan and bring to a boil; remove from heat and pour over vegetables. Allow vegetables to marinate in the refrigerator several hours or overnight before serving.

Drain vegetables and serve with Spicy Soba Noodles or Grilled Marinated Tofu (see pages 69, 123).

—Chef Susan Feniger
—Chef Mary Sue Milliken

CITY Restaurant
180 South La Brea
Los Angeles, CA 90036
213-938-2155

Border Grill
1445 4th Street
Santa Monica, CA 90401
213-451-1655

Five Star
SIDE DISHES

S A U C E S

Roasted Salmon
with Couscous and Leeks
Yield: 4-6 servings

2-1/2 pounds Norwegian
    salmon fillet, skin intact

MARINADE
2 tablespoons balsamic vinegar
2 tablespoons honey
1 tablespoon grainy mustard
2 teaspoons minced garlic
Salt and pepper to taste

COUSCOUS
1 cup chicken stock or broth
2 tablespoons olive oil
2 tablespoons butter
2-1/2 tablespoons cinnamon
1 tablespoon allspice
1/2 cup pine nuts
1 cup couscous

LEEKS
8 leeks, washed, dried and
    julienned
Vegetable oil for deep-frying

‽ Check salmon for bones and remove. Combine marinade ingredients and pour over salmon. Sprinkle salmon with salt and pepper to taste. Refrigerate for at least 20 minutes.

Combine all ingredients for couscous, except the couscous, in a large pot.

Bring all ingredients to a boil; add couscous, stirring well. Cover and remove from heat. Do not remove cover or stir until couscous is thoroughly steamed, about 8 minutes.

Remove green from leeks. Julienne the white part as thin as possible. Heat vegetable oil and deep-fry leeks until brown and crispy. Drain on paper towels.

Drain marinade from salmon and bake in 475°F oven for approximately 7 minutes per inch of thickness or until fish flakes.

To serve, place couscous on serving platter, follow with salmon and top with leeks.

—Bonnie Davis Catering
BEACHWOOD, OHIO

SALMON AND SNAPPER
WITH AVOCADO AND TOMATILLO SAUCE
YIELD: 4 SERVINGS

2 salmon fillets, 8 ounces each
2 snapper fillets, 8 ounces each

SAUCE
5 tomatillos
1 shallot, peeled
1 clove garlic
1 jalapeño, stem removed
1 ripe avocado (California)
1 bunch cilantro, chopped
1/2 cup olive oil
1 cup fish or chicken stock
1/2 cup (1 stick) butter, room
    temperature
Salt and pepper to taste

TOMATO RICE
1 cup uncooked rice
4 ripe plum tomatoes, stemmed
    and roughly chopped
1/2 yellow onion, chopped
2 tablespoons butter
Salt and pepper to taste

Five Star
ENTRÉES

SALMON

❧ To make tomato rice, cook the rice according to package directions. Place the tomatoes and onion in a blender and purée (add a little water if necessary). Stir the butter into the warm rice and add the puréed tomato-onion mixture. Bring the rice to a boil and allow the liquid to reduce. When the liquid has evaporated but the rice is still very moist, remove from the heat and keep warm. Season to taste.

Lightly oil the tomatillos, shallot, garlic and jalapeño in a small pan. Roast the ingredients at 350°F for approximately 1 hour or until the ingredients have softened. Transfer the roasted ingredients to a blender.

Remove the skin and seed from the avocado. Add the avocado, cilantro, 1/4 cup olive oil and the stock to the blender. Blend the ingredients for about 30 seconds or until just smooth. Do not over-blend. Transfer the sauce to a pan and heat until warm. Stir in the butter and salt and pepper to taste.

Cut the fillets of salmon and snapper into 2-ounce squares. It is desirable to cut the fillets into pieces of equal thickness and shape. Drizzle the remaining olive oil over the pieces of fish.

Lightly salt and pepper the pieces of fish. Sauté the pieces of fish in a non-stick skillet over high heat, turning them frequently until the fish is just heated through but still translucent at the center.

To serve, spoon some of the warm sauce onto four dinner plates. Spoon some of the tomato rice into the center of the plate. Lay the pieces of fish in the sauce around the rice.

—CHEF ROBERT DEL GRANDE

Cafe Annie
1728 Post Oak Boulevard
Houston, TX 77056
713-840-1111

SALMON WITH SHIITAKES

Easy and elegant.

YIELD: 4 SERVINGS

4 shallots, chopped
Olive oil for sautéing
1/2 pound shiitake mushrooms
3 to 4 tablespoons Madeira
Salt and pepper to taste
Chopped fresh tarragon to taste
4 salmon fillets (6 ounces each),
    skinned and boned

❧ Heat skillet over medium-high heat and sauté shallots in olive oil until translucent. Add shiitakes and sauté until soft.

Add Madeira and cook 2 minutes. Add salt, pepper and fresh tarragon and cook 2 minutes; set aside.

Heat a heavy cast-iron skillet over medium-high heat and add enough oil to cover bottom of pan. Place salmon fillets in pan and cook over high heat for 2 to 3 minutes or until a crust forms. Turn and continue cooking another 3 to 4 minutes until salmon is slightly pink in the middle.

To serve, place salmon fillets on plates and spoon sauce over each fillet.

For variation: Use chopped scallions, shallots, plum tomatoes and tarragon. Cook with shiitakes. Add Madeira and 1/4 cup heavy cream.

— PAMELA GROSSCUP

BARBECUED POACHED SALMON

Prepared in foil.
No clean-up.

YIELD: 6-10 SERVINGS

CUCUMBER SAUCE
2 cucumbers
1 pint sour cream or yogurt
1 tablespoon chopped fresh dill

1 whole fresh salmon (approx-
    imately 6 to 8 pounds),
    scaled with gills removed
Juice of 2 fresh lemons
1 cup white wine

❧ To prepare sauce, peel and seed cucumbers; place in container of food processor and chop. Blend in sour cream or yogurt and dill; chill.

Cut two layers of heavy-duty aluminum foil and place salmon in the center. Sprinkle fish with the lemon juice and wine. Wrap the foil securely around the fish, making sure there is a tight seal at both ends.

Bake on a closed barbecue grill at medium-high setting for approximately 20 minutes. Turn and cook an additional 20 minutes.

Bone salmon and serve with cucumber sauce.

— GINNA HERMANN

SALMON STEAK
WITH CURRY-LEMON
CREAM SAUCE AND MINT RICE
YIELD: 6 SERVINGS

6 salmon steaks, 1-inch thick
Salt and pepper to taste

CURRY-LEMON CREAM SAUCE
1 teaspoon turmeric
1 teaspoon ground coriander
    seed
1 teaspoon ground cumin seed
1/2 teaspoon freshly ground
    black pepper
1/2 teaspoon cayenne or Indian
    red pepper
1 to 2 tablespoons olive oil
1 teaspoon minced fresh ginger
1 teaspoon minced garlic
1 shallot, minced
2 cups heavy cream
1/2 cup chicken stock
Juice of 1 lemon
2 bunches of cilantro
Salt and pepper to taste

MINT RICE
1 shallot, minced
2 tablespoons olive oil
2 cups basmati or arborio rice
4 cups chicken stock
2 bunches fresh mint
Salt and pepper to taste

෪ Salt and pepper both sides of salmon steaks. Place in 400°F oven and bake for approximately 7 minutes for medium-rare salmon.

To make Curry-Lemon Cream Sauce, grind first 5 ingredients and blend together.

Pour the olive oil in a small skillet and sauté the ginger, garlic and shallot for 2 minutes. Add the heavy cream, stock and dry ingredients; simmer until reduced by one-third.

Add lemon juice and 1 bunch of cilantro, unchopped, and continue to reduce sauce to half of original volume, about 5 to 7 minutes. Remove unchopped cilantro. Chop remaining cilantro and use for garnish for salmon steaks.

To make Mint Rice, sauté the shallot in olive oil for 2 minutes. Add the rice and mix well.

Add chicken stock, mint, salt and pepper and bring to a boil. Place in a 350°F oven for approximately 18 minutes or until liquid is absorbed and rice is dry.

—MIKE SYMON
PLAYERS PIZZA
LAKEWOOD, OHIO

GRILLED MARINATED SWORDFISH

YIELD: 2 SERVINGS

2 swordfish steaks, 8 ounces each

MARINADE
1/2 cup olive oil
1/4 cup teriyaki sauce
2 to 3 tablespoons dry sherry
2 scallions, chopped

TOPPING
1/4 cup olive oil
1 clove garlic, minced
1 green pepper, sliced
1 small onion, sliced
6 to 8 mushrooms, sliced
1 roasted red pepper*
1 tablespoon dry sherry
Salt and pepper to taste

Roasted red peppers can be purchased in jars at most supermarkets.

&c Mix marinade ingredients and add swordfish. Marinate for a minimum of 1 hour. Turn fish frequently, basting with marinade.

Preheat grill. Grill fish over high heat, 5 to 6 minutes each side. While fish is grilling, sauté garlic, green pepper and onion in olive oil until soft. Add fresh mushrooms and continue cooking. Add red pepper and sherry and cook through. Salt and pepper to taste.

To serve, arrange fish on platter and top with vegetables.

— MARY RYDZEL

SKEWERED GRILLED SEAFOOD

YIELD: 8 SERVINGS

8 bamboo skewers, soaked in cold water
1 pound swordfish, cut into large squares
1 pound large shrimp, uncooked with shells removed
1-1/2 pounds sea scallops
1-1/2 pounds tuna, cut in large squares
2 tablespoons soy sauce
1 tablespoon lemon juice
1/3 cup extra virgin olive oil
Salt and pepper to taste

&c Alternate seafood on skewers.
Mix soy sauce, lemon juice, olive oil, salt and pepper. Brush onto seafood and cook over a hot fire for about 4 minutes, or marinate skewered seafood in soy mixture in refrigerator for 30 minutes before grilling.

Serve with brown rice and grilled vegetables.

— CAMILLE LaBARRE

BAKED RED SNAPPER
WITH GARLIC, MUSHROOMS AND TOMATOES

A treat from Provence.

YIELD: 4 SERVINGS

4 red snapper fillets (3/4 pound each) or 1 whole red snapper (4 pounds)
1/2 large onion, cut into 4 to 5 slices
Juice of 1/2 lemon
1/2 cup (1 stick) margarine or butter
6 large cloves garlic, peeled and thinly sliced
12 large fresh mushrooms, sliced
1/2 large onion, diced
1 can (28 ounces) Italian tomatoes with liquid
1 bay leaf
1 teaspoon chopped fresh leaf oregano
1 teaspoon sugar
Salt and freshly ground pepper to taste
1/2 cup dry white wine

&c Rinse fish and pat dry. Place fish in lightly greased baking dish. Put slices of onion on top of fillets and sprinkle with lemon juice.

Heat skillet over medium-high heat and sauté garlic, mushrooms and onion in margarine or butter until just soft. Add tomatoes, bay leaf, oregano, sugar, salt and pepper. Simmer uncovered for 15 minutes. Add wine.

Spoon two-thirds of vegetable sauce on top of fillets. Reserve remaining one-third for basting. Bake, uncovered, in 400°F oven for 30 to 40 minutes (50 minutes for one large fish), basting frequently.

— DR. JERRY M. SHUCK

STUFFED SWORDFISH

YIELD: 4 SERVINGS

4 swordfish steaks, 1-inch thick
8 ounces mozzarella cheese,
    cut into 4 slices

STUFFING
2 tablespoons butter
1 cup julienned leeks
2 tablespoons diced yellow squash
2 tablespoons diced zucchini
1 tablespoon minced fresh basil
1 tablespoon minced fresh parsley
1 tablespoon minced fresh
    tarragon
Salt and pepper to taste

To make stuffing, sauté leeks in butter over medium heat until soft and translucent, about 5 minutes. Add yellow squash and zucchini and cook an additional minute. Remove from heat and add basil, parsley and tarragon. Add salt and pepper to taste and set aside to cool.

Dry the fish and slice partially through to form a pocket. Place 1 tablespoon of stuffing and one slice of mozzarella into each pocket. Close swordfish with toothpicks.

Broil swordfish 5 minutes each side. Serve immediately.

—CHEF RALPH DIORIO

Sammy's
1400 West 10th Street
Cleveland, OH 44113
216-523-1177

MARINATED TUNA
YIELD: 4-6 SERVINGS

1 tuna steak (approximately
    1-1/2 pounds)
2 tablespoons garlic juice
1/2 cup chopped fennel
6 tablespoons coarse sea salt
2 tablespoons ground black
    pepper
1 teaspoon wasabi powder
2 bay leaves, crushed

GARLIC VINAIGRETTE
1-1/4 cups canola oil
1/2 cup extra virgin olive oil
1/4 cup plus 2 tablespoons
    lemon juice
2 tablespoons garlic juice
2 tablespoons fennel juice
1 teaspoon Szechwan oil

₨ Line 15-inch × 10-inch jelly-roll pan with parchment paper. Brush tuna on all sides with garlic juice.

Combine fennel, pepper, wasabi powder and bay leaves; place one half of the mixture on the parchment paper. Top with tuna and cover with remaining fennel mixture.

Cover tuna with parchment paper and press down with a weighted baking sheet. Refrigerate and marinate 12 hours.

Combine ingredients for the Garlic Vinaigrette and mix well.

Remove tuna from refrigerator and brush off excess fennel mixture. Cut tuna into rectangles and slice crosswise.

To serve, arrange tuna on plate with salad dressed in Garlic Vinaigrette.

— CHEF THOMAS KELLER

Checkers Restaurant
535 South Grand Avenue
Los Angeles, CA 90071
213-624-0000

Lobster Pipirana

Yield: 2 servings

2 live lobsters, 1 pound each
1/2 cup olive oil
1/4 cup sherry vinegar
Salt and pepper to taste
1/2 cucumber, seeded, peeled
    and sliced
2 plum tomatoes, diced
1/2 small red onion, thinly sliced
1/4 red pepper, thinly sliced
1/4 yellow pepper, thinly sliced
1/4 green pepper, thinly sliced
2 cloves garlic, minced
2 tablespoons chopped fresh
    tarragon
2 tablespoons chopped fresh basil

ᔑᕈ Cook and cool lobster; cut lobster meat into medallions and place in bowl. Reserve the claws.

Combine oil, vinegar, salt and pepper and whisk. Toss with lobster. Add cucumber, onion, peppers, tomatoes, garlic and fresh herbs to lobster, mixing well.

To serve, arrange on a platter and garnish with lobster claws.

— Chef Emilio Manuel Gervilla

Emilio's
4100 West Roosevelt Road
Hillside, IL 60162
708-547-7177

Five Star
ENTRÉES
FISH & SEAFOOD

STIR-FRY SCALLOPS
WITH VEGETABLES
YIELD: 3 SERVINGS

1 pound sea scallops
3 tablespoons vegetable oil
2 slices fresh ginger root, minced
1 large clove garlic, minced
1/4 pound snow peas
1/4 cup sliced water chestnuts
1/2 cup chopped celery
2 scallions, cut in 1/2-inch pieces
1/2 cup chicken stock
1/2 teaspoon salt
1/2 teaspoon sugar
Dash of black pepper
1 medium tomato, cut in quarters

SEASONING SAUCE
1 tablespoon cornstarch
2 teaspoons soy sauce
2 tablespoons sherry
Water to make 1/4 cup
2 drops sesame oil

❧ To prepare Seasoning Sauce, combine all ingredients in a measuring cup and whisk. Set aside.

Wash scallops to remove any sand particles and pat dry; cut in half.

Heat oil in wok or large skillet over medium-high heat. Add ginger root and garlic and cook until golden. Add scallops, stirring to coat with oil. Add vegetables, except tomato, and stir-fry approximately 2 minutes. Add chicken stock, salt, sugar and pepper and heat quickly. Continue cooking until vegetables are tender crisp.

Add Seasoning Sauce and tomato and mix well. Serve warm.

Serve over steamed rice.

— DR. IRVING BERGER

SCALLOPONÉE
MEUNIÈRE
YIELD: 4 SERVINGS

8 large sea scallops
Salt and pepper to taste
1 tablespoon flour
2 eggs, beaten
1/4 cup butter, divided
1 teaspoon chopped parsley
1 teaspoon capers
Juice of 2 lemons

❧ Pound scallops with a wooden mallet to break down the fibers until about 1/4-inch thick.

Season with salt and pepper and dredge in flour on both sides.

Heat 2 tablespoons of the butter in a skillet until light brown. Dip scallops in beaten eggs and sauté on both sides until golden. Remove from heat and place in serving dish.

Add the remaining 2 tablespoons of butter to the skillet and let it brown. Add parsley, capers and lemon juice and heat through.

Pour over scallops and serve piping hot.

Serve with rice and a green vegetable.

— CHARLOTTE RILEY

CRISPY SAUTÉED SCALLOPS
WITH BLACK OLIVE VINAIGRETTE
YIELD: 4 SERVINGS

BLACK OLIVE VINAIGRETTE
1 cup pitted black olives
  (preferably Niçoise)
1 cup extra virgin olive oil
2 large cloves garlic, chopped
2 anchovy fillets
2 tablespoons fresh lemon juice
2 tablespoons chopped basil

SHERRY WINE VINAIGRETTE
1/4 cup sherry wine vinegar
1 teaspoon Dijon-style mustard
2 shallots, minced
1/2 cup virgin olive oil
Salt and pepper to taste

1 pound sea scallops
Olive oil
6 cups lettuce greens
8 large radicchio leaves

❧ Combine all ingredients for Black Olive Vinaigrette in a blender; blend until almost smooth. It should be fairly chunky. Vinaigrette will separate slightly if allowed to sit; this is normal.

For Sherry Wine Vinaigrette, mix vinegar, mustard and shallots in a small bowl and whisk in oil. Season to taste.

Slice scallops 1/4-inch thick across grain. Lay on a flat plate (do not overlap) and season well with salt and pepper. Set aside.

Ladle Black Olive Vinaigrette around rim of each serving plate and place 2 radicchio leaves in the center. Toss the greens with Sherry Wine Vinaigrette and spoon onto each radicchio leaf.

Heat a large sauté pan until very hot. Add just enough olive oil to coat bottom of pan and place scallops, seasoned-side down (being careful not to overlap), in pan. Cook until crispy on one side, but still rare on the other side. Remove scallops from pan and place on the greens, crispy side up. Serve immediately.

— CHEF DEBRA PONZEK

Five Star
ENTRÉES
SCALLOPS

Montrachet
239 West Broadway
New York, NY 10013
212-219-2777

HUNAN SHRIMP
YIELD: 2 SERVINGS

1 teaspoon minced garlic
1 teaspoon minced ginger
1 tablespoon ketchup
2 teaspoons sugar
1 teaspoon white wine
1/2 teaspoon white wine vinegar
1 cup vegetable oil for frying
2/3 pound large raw shrimp,
    peeled and deveined
1/2 medium onion, chopped
2 small scallions, chopped
1 tablespoon cornstarch dissolved
    in 1 tablespoon water
1/2 teaspoon sesame oil

৯ৣ Combine garlic, ginger, ketchup, sugar, wine and vinegar in a small bowl and set aside.

Add oil to wok and heat. When oil is hot, add shrimp and stir-fry until shrimp are just cooked. Remove shrimp from wok and drain oil. Add onions to wok and stir-fry 1 minute. Add garlic mixture and cornstarch dissolved in water. Stir-fry until sauce thickens.

Add shrimp and sesame oil and heat through, about 2 minutes.

— SZECHWAN HOUSE
BEACHWOOD, OHIO

SAUTÉED SHRIMP
WITH ROSEMARY
YIELD: 4 SERVINGS

1 pound pasta (rotini or small
    shells), cooked and drained
2 large cloves garlic, minced
1 medium shallot, minced
2 tablespoons fresh rosemary or
    1 tablespoon dried
    rosemary, ground to a
    coarse powder
Fresh ground pepper to taste
2 tablespoons olive oil, butter
    or margarine
1 pound shrimp, shelled
    and rinsed
2 tablespoons brandy or
    vermouth
2 small tomatoes, peeled,
    seeded and diced
8 ounces fresh mushrooms,
    sliced (optional)
1/3 cup chopped fresh parsley

৯ৣ Place warm pasta in serving bowl.

Sauté garlic, shallot, rosemary and pepper in oil over medium-high heat. Add shrimp and sauté another 3 minutes. Add brandy, tomatoes and mushrooms and cook for 1 minute.

To serve, pour over pasta, toss and garnish with parsley.

— DR. MICHAEL MAGUIRE
— TOM PEPKA
— CHARLOTTE RILEY

When similar recipes were submitted, acknowledgement was given to each contributor.

Sautéed Shrimp with Sweet Potato and Carrot Pancakes, Crystallized Pecans and Bourbon Sauce

Yield: 8 servings

SWEET POTATO AND CARROT PANCAKES
2 large sweet potatoes, peeled
1 large carrot, peeled
6 scallions, finely sliced
1/2 cup finely ground pecans
2 eggs
1/2 cup all-purpose flour
Salt and white pepper to taste
1/4 cup vegetable oil

CRYSTALLIZED PECANS
1 tablespoon vegetable oil
1-1/2 cups toasted pecan halves
1/4 cup sugar
1/8 teaspoon ground cayenne
      pepper

SAUTÉED SHRIMP WITH BOURBON SAUCE
2 cups fish stock
1 onion, finely diced
1 leek, finely diced
1 bay leaf
1/2 cup bourbon
24 shrimp, shelled and deveined
Salt, white pepper and cayenne
      pepper to taste
3 tablespoons clarified butter
6 shallots, finely chopped
1 cup butter

☙ To prepare pancakes, shred potatoes and carrots. Rinse under cool water; squeeze and towel dry. Place mixture in a medium-size bowl and add scallions, ground pecans, eggs, flour, salt and pepper; stir. (If mixture is too dry, add an egg.)

Heat vegetable oil in a large skillet until hot. Spoon batter into hot pan, making 2-1/2-inch pancakes. Cook until brown on both sides (about 4 minutes). Keep warm in a 200°F oven.

To prepare Crystallized Pecans, heat oil in a medium-size skillet over medium heat. Add pecans, sugar and cayenne pepper. Stir constantly until sugar crystallizes. When mixture begins to carmelize, remove from heat. Pour, in single layer, on baking sheet and let cool. May be made ahead.

To prepare Sautéed Shrimp with Bourbon Sauce, combine fish stock, onion, leek and bay leaf. Simmer in a medium-size saucepan over medium-high heat until stock is reduced by half; strain. Add 1/4 cup bourbon to fish stock; set aside.

Season shrimp with salt, white pepper and cayenne pepper.

Heat the clarified butter in a medium-size skillet; add shrimp and shallots. Sauté over medium heat 2 minutes or until shrimp begin to turn pink. Add remaining 1/4 cup bourbon and flambé. Immediately remove shrimp from skillet.

Deglaze pan with the reserved fish stock mixture. Reduce sauce by half; gently whisk in butter.

To serve, place pancakes in center of plate with shrimp and crystallized pecans as the border. Top with the butter bourbon sauce.

—Chef Paul Minnillo
THE BARICELLI INN
CLEVELAND, OHIO

BREADED CATFISH
WITH BACON BUTTER
YIELD: 4 SERVINGS

1 can (6 ounces) hickory-smoked
   almonds
2 cups white bread crumbs
1 egg
3 tablespoons water
1 cup all-purpose flour
4 to 6 catfish fillets (8 ounces each)
Butter for sautéing
Lemon slices for garnish

BACON BUTTER
2 cups (4 sticks) butter, softened
6 slices bacon, cooked and
   chopped
1/4 teaspoon smoke flavoring
1 scallion, chopped
1/4 cup fresh chopped parsley
Juice of 1/2 lemon
1 tablespoon chopped garlic
1 tablespoon chopped shallots

꙳ Combine all ingredients for Bacon Butter and mix well. Roll into a log and freeze.

Place almonds and bread crumbs in container of food processor or blender and process until finely ground. Set aside.

Whisk egg and water in a shallow bowl. Dip catfish fillets in flour, then egg mixture, then bread-crumb mixture. Sauté in a buttered skillet over medium-high heat until brown. Transfer to 400°F oven and continue cooking until fish flakes, approximately 10 minutes.

Top with a slice of Bacon Butter and garnish with lemon slices.

—CHEF SETH KASPY
CHAGRIN VALLEY HUNT CLUB

SOFT SHELL CRAB
YIELD: 4 SERVINGS

1 bunch of basil
8 live soft shell crabs
1 cup olive oil, divided
2 Vidalia onions
1 cup (2 sticks) of butter
Assorted herbs in bunches
Yellow plum tomatoes
Red plum tomatoes
1/4 cup cassis vinegar
Salt and pepper

🐟 Clean crabs by removing "dead men fingers" and any sharp extensions.

Make marinade of 1/4 cup plus 2 tablespoons olive oil and fresh herbs. Place crabs in marinade for 20 to 30 minutes.

Peel Vidalia onions, slice in rondelles and place in a pan with a little olive oil, salt and pepper.

Make a vinaigrette by grilling tomatoes gently over mesquite grill. Remove and gently chop tomatoes, add to a bowl with vinegar and remaining olive oil.

Grill onions and chop. Add to vinaigrette. Season with salt, pepper and chopped basil.

Grill crabs for approximately 5 to 6 minutes.

To serve, pour a small amount of vinaigrette on individual plates. Add the crabs and top with the remaining vinaigrette.

— CHEF JONATHAN WAXMAN

Five Star
ENTRÉES

FISH & SEAFOOD

Table 29
4110 St. Helena Highway
Napa, CA 94558
707-224-3300

Calamar el Ajo

For garlic lovers.

YIELD: 4 SERVINGS

1/4 cup vegetable oil
1 tablespoon butter
4 cloves garlic, minced*
1 pound calamari, cleaned and
    cut in rings
1/3 cup dry white wine
8 ounces whole button mushrooms
2 cans (8 ounces each) no-salt
    tomato sauce
1 tablespoon basil
Parsley for garnish

*For a stronger version, double
amount of garlic.*

೨ Heat oil, butter and garlic in
a cast-iron skillet. Sauté calamari
approximately 3 minutes. Remove
calamari and set aside.

Add wine to skillet and
simmer for 2 minutes. Add mushrooms, tomato sauce and basil.
Simmer for 15 minutes, stirring
occasionally. Return calamari to
skillet and heat through, about
2 minutes.

Serve over pasta of your choice.

—PEGGY J. VAN BUSKIRK

Cioppino

A savory seafood stew.

YIELD: 8-10 SERVINGS

1/3 cup olive oil
1 large fennel bulb, coarsely
    chopped
1 large onion, coarsely chopped
2 cloves garlic, minced
4 celery stalks, sliced
2 large carrots, sliced
2 cups sliced fresh mushrooms
2 cups chopped red, yellow
    and green peppers
2 teaspoons fennel seed
1 teaspoon crumbled thyme
1 teaspoon crumbled oregano
1/2 teaspoon dill seed
1/8 teaspoon ground bay leaf or
    1 bay leaf
2 cups white wine
2 cans (28 ounces each) Italian-
    style tomatoes
1 can (6 ounces) tomato paste
1 bottle (8 ounces) clam juice
1/2 pound raw shrimp, shelled
    and deveined
1/2 pound scallops
2 pounds fish fillets (halibut,
    orange roughy or cod), cut
    into 1-inch pieces
2 tablespoons lemon juice
2 tablespoons Pernod
1/2 cup minced fresh parsley

೨ Heat oil in a large soup
pot over medium-high heat.
Add fennel, onion and garlic.
Cook until softened, about
5 minutes, stirring occasionally.

Add celery, carrots, mushrooms and peppers. Sauté lightly,
about 3 minutes.

Add fennel seed, thyme,
oregano, dill, bay leaf, wine,
tomatoes, tomato paste and
clam juice. Reduce heat and
simmer for 45 minutes. (Can
be made ahead and refrigerated
at this point.)

Just before serving, bring
stew to a rolling boil. Add shrimp,
scallops and fish and simmer
until fish is just cooked and
scallops are whitened, about
3 to 5 minutes.

Stir in lemon juice and
Pernod.

Serve garnished with parsley.

*Serve with saffron rice and
crusted bread.*

—JANET STERRETT

CREOLE JAMBALAYA
YIELD: 6-8 SERVINGS

2 tablespoons butter
3/4 cup chopped scallions
4 cloves garlic, minced
1/3 pound boiled ham, cubed
1/2 pound sliced hot sausage
2 cups chicken stock or low-salt
    chicken broth, divided
1 can (28 ounces) tomatoes
    with liquid
2 tablespoons parsley
2 bay leaves
1 tablespoon chervil
1-1/2 teaspoons thyme
3/4 teaspoon hot sauce or more
    to taste
1 teaspoon salt
1/2 teaspoon black pepper
1 package (1 gram) powdered
    saffron
1-1/2 pounds raw shrimp,
    cleaned and deveined
1-1/4 cups raw long grain rice

∾ Melt butter in a large kettle. Add onion, garlic, ham and sausage and sauté until brown over medium-high heat.

Add 1 cup of chicken stock, tomatoes and seasonings and bring to a boil.

Add shrimp. Place rice on top of mixture and cover with remaining cup of chicken stock. Do not stir.

Reduce heat, cover and simmer slowly for 30 minutes or until rice is done. This can also be baked in a 350°F oven for approximately 35 minutes.

Remove bay leaves, toss and serve.

—JOHN EDWARDS

Five Star
ENTRÉES
FISH & SEAFOOD

Seafood and Chicken Newburg

Yield: 8 servings

1/2 cup (1 stick) butter, divided
1/3 cup all-purpose flour
1 teaspoon salt
Pepper to taste
Cayenne pepper to taste
1 can (13-3/4 ounces) chicken broth
1 cup heavy cream
1/4 cup dry sherry
3 whole skinless, boneless chicken
    breasts, cooked and chopped
2 cups tiny cooked shrimp,
    rinsed and drained
2 cans (6 ounces each) crab meat,
    rinsed, drained and
    picked over
1/4 cup chopped onion
8 ounces fresh mushrooms,
    chopped
1/4 cup chopped parsley
1/2 cup chopped chives

Melt 3 tablespoons of butter in a heavy skillet. Stir in flour, salt, pepper and cayenne and cook over medium heat until smooth.

Stir in chicken broth and cream and bring to a slow boil, stirring constantly. Continue cooking until mixture is thick and smooth. Stir in sherry, chicken, shrimp and crab.

Heat remaining 5 tablespoons butter in a skillet over medium-high heat and sauté onion, mushrooms, parsley and chives until tender.

Combine seafood and mushroom mixture in a chafing dish. Serve over toast points or puff pastry.

— Diane Welsh

Paella Valenciana

Yield: 8 servings

1 chicken (2 pounds), cut into
  small pieces with bones
1/2 pound pork butt, cut into
  1-inch pieces
2 red peppers, diced
2 green peppers, diced
3 tomatoes, diced
1 onion, diced
2 tablespoons tomato paste
6 cloves garlic
2 lobsters (1 pound each),
  cut into 8 pieces
12 mussels
8 clams
8 large shrimp

1-1/2 cups chicken stock
1-1/2 cups fish stock or clam juice
1-1/2 teaspoons saffron
Salt and pepper to taste
1-1/2 cups rice
Olive oil for sautéing

GARNISHES
1/4 cup diced red peppers
1/2 cup cooked peas
2 hard-cooked eggs, finely
  chopped

&⋗ Clean seafood, saving shrimp shells. Put chicken stock, fish stock, shrimp shells, saffron, salt and pepper in a large pot and bring to a boil. Reduce heat.

Heat large skillet with olive oil and sauté onions, peppers and garlic. Add tomatoes, then tomato paste. Salt and pepper to taste.

Sauté chicken pieces in olive oil in another pan. Season and set aside.

Reheat skillet and sauté pork pieces. Mix chicken, pork and vegetables. Set aside.

Place the rice on the bottom of a large paella pan, then the meat and vegetable mixture. Spoon, do not pour, the stock over the rice mixture and bring to a boil.

Preheat oven to 500°F. Add seafood to paella pan and cook until all liquid is absorbed, about 30 to 45 minutes.

To serve, garnish with diced hard-cooked eggs, peas and red peppers.

— CHEF GABINO SOTELINO

Five Star
ENTRÉES
FISH & SEAFOOD

Ambria
2300 North Lincoln Park West
Chicago, IL 60614
312-472-5959

TROUT TRIUMPH
YIELD: 4 SERVINGS

1 pound trout fillets
3 tablespoons olive oil
2 cloves garlic, minced
1/4 teaspoon freshly ground
    pepper
Oat flake cereal crumbs
Lemon slices for garnish
Parsley for garnish

⁏   Rinse trout fillets in cold water and pat dry.

Pour 1 tablespoon olive oil in a 12 × 8 × 2-inch baking dish. Rub the trout with the remaining oil.

Lay fillets in the pan and sprinkle with garlic, freshly ground pepper and oat cereal crumbs.

Bake, uncovered, at 500°F for 10 minutes. Remove carefully.

Garnish with lemon slices and parsley. Serve immediately.

— MARY B. TRACY

RED PEPPER COULIS
Great with grilled or fried fish!
YIELD: 5-6 SERVINGS

1 tablespoon butter
1/2 medium onion, diced
2 sweet red peppers, seeded
    and diced
Salt and pepper to taste
1 cup chicken broth
3 tablespoons extra virgin olive oil

⁏   Melt butter in a heavy skillet. Add onions and sauté approximately 5 minutes. Add red peppers, salt and pepper and continue cooking. Add chicken broth and bring mixture to a boil. Reduce heat and simmer for 20 minutes.

Place mixture in container of food processor and blend until smooth. Return mixture to skillet and cook over medium-high heat until mixture reaches the texture of heavy cream, approximately 5 minutes. Stir in olive oil and mix well.

Coulis is a liquid purée of cooled, seasoned vegetables or seafood. It may be used as a sauce, sauce enhancer or as a soup ingredient.

— CAMILLE LaBARRE

Native Cod Cheeks with Boston Bean Cakes

Yield: 4 servings

2 cups presoaked, white
    pea beans
1/4 cup firmly packed brown
    sugar
1/4 cup molasses
1/2 teaspoon dry mustard
1 sprig fresh thyme
1 teaspoon salt
1 small onion studded with
    3 cloves
1 piece (4 ounces) salt pork
1 pound cod cheeks or scallops
Salt and pepper to taste
Clarified butter
1 lemon, cut into wedges

∾ Cover beans with fresh water, bring to a boil and simmer 20 minutes.

Place beans with their cooking liquid in an oven-proof dish. Add sugar, molasses, mustard, thyme and salt. Press the onion and salt pork into the center of the beans. Cover and place in a 250°F oven.

Check beans after 2 hours and add more water if needed. Continue baking 6 more hours or until beans are tender. When beans are cooked, drain and reserve excess liquid.

Purée two-thirds of beans in food processor, adding 3 tablespoons of cooking liquid. Mix purée with remaining beans and adjust seasoning. Allow to cool and form into little cakes 2 inches in diameter.

Pat dry cod cheeks in a paper towel. Season with salt and pepper.

Sauté cheeks over high heat in clarified butter until golden. Brown bean cakes in non-stick pan with 1 teaspoon of whole butter. Serve with a lemon wedge.

Serve with your favorite coleslaw.

—Chef William Poirier

Biba
272 Boylston Street
Boston, MA 02116
617-426-5684

Basting Sauce for Salmon

Yield: 2 servings

3/4 pound salmon fillet
1/3 cup mayonnaise
1/3 cup margarine or butter,
    melted
1 tablespoon white vinegar
1 tablespoon honey
1 tablespoon fresh lemon juice
2 tablespoons fresh dill

❧ Mix all ingredients and brush top of salmon fillet.

Broil, basting often, until fish starts to flake, approximately 10 to 12 minutes.

Serve remaining sauce on the side.

— Sue Sherwin

Swordfish Marinade

Yield: 2 servings

1 pound swordfish
2 tablespoons soy sauce
2 tablespoons fresh orange juice
1 tablespoon olive oil
2 tablespoons tomato paste
1 tablespoon minced fresh
    parsley
1 clove garlic, minced
1 tablespoon lemon juice
1 teaspoon oregano

❧ Mix all of the ingredients and marinate fish for at least 1 hour. Grill or bake as desired.

— Sue Sherwin

Summer Grill Marinade

*Quick, easy
and oil-free.*

Yield: 2-4 servings

2 pieces of cold-water fish
    (tuna, salmon or swordfish),
    5 ounces each

MARINADE
1/4 cup lemon juice
2 tablespoons soy sauce
1 teaspoon grated ginger
1 tablespoon Dijon-style mustard

❧ Mix all ingredients and marinate fish for 2 to 4 hours. Grill until done, basting with marinade.

— Jane Temple

SAUCE
FOR GRILLED FISH
YIELD: 6 SERVINGS

6 fish fillets (tuna, halibut,
    swordfish or salmon)
36 arugula leaves

SAUCE
3/4 cup olive oil, divided
1 red onion, thinly sliced
3 cloves garlic, minced
1 yellow squash, thinly sliced
    and quartered
1 zucchini, thinly sliced and
    quartered
1/4 cup chopped fresh parsley
1/4 cup cassis or raspberry
    vinegar*
1 tomato, thinly sliced and
    quartered
Salt and pepper to taste
1 tablespoon basil
*Available in specialty stores.

❧ Reserve 2 tablespoons olive oil. Sauté onion and garlic in remaining olive oil over medium-high heat. Add squash and zucchini. Add parsley, vinegar and tomatoes and toss. Simmer for about 8 minutes.

Brush fish fillets with remaining olive oil. Season with salt, pepper and basil and grill over medium-high heat on both sides.

To serve, place fish fillets on top of arugula and spoon sauce over each fillet.

—JOHN EDWARDS

Five Star
ENTRÉES

FISH & SEAFOOD
SAUCES

Five Star
ENTRÉES

POULTRY

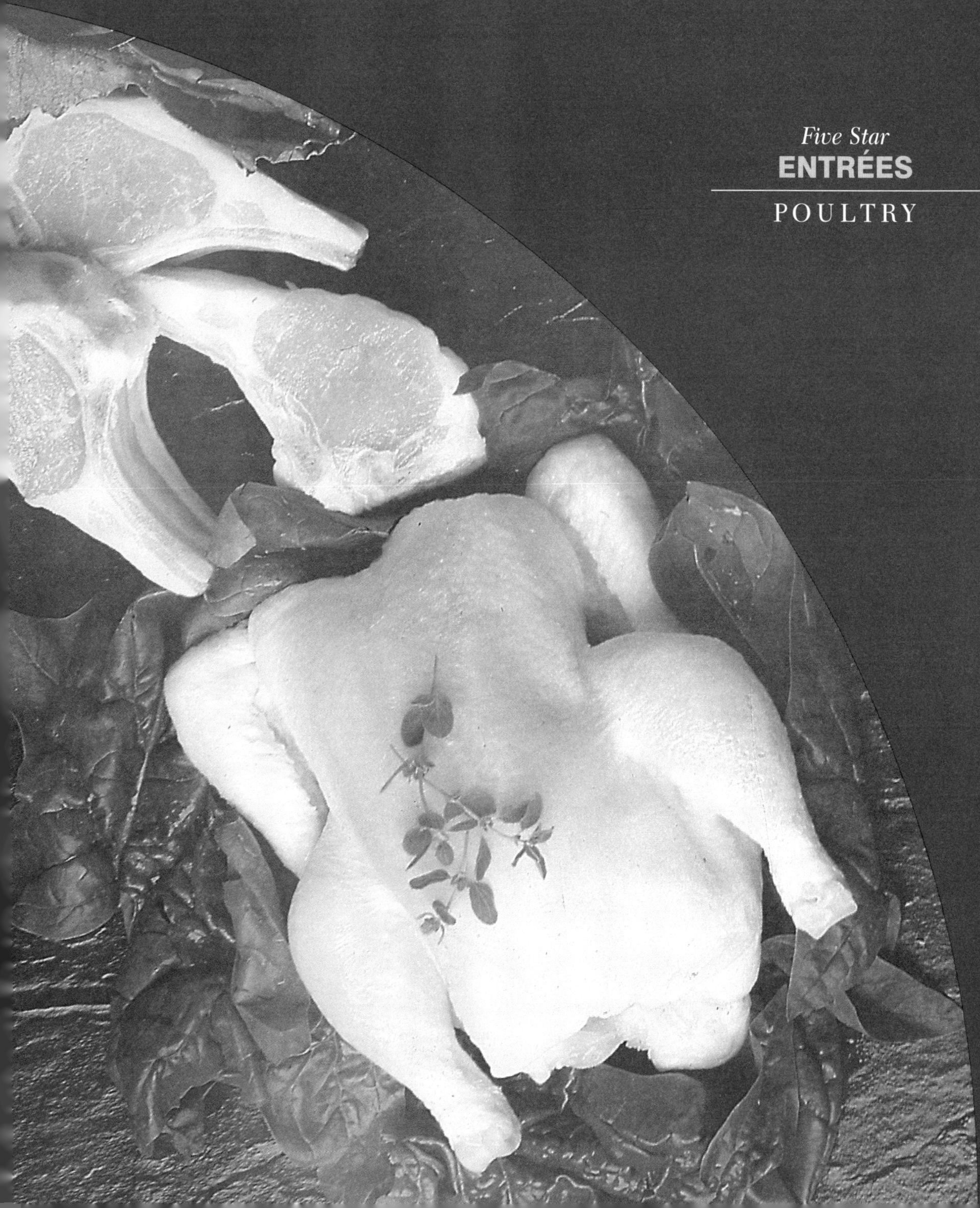

CHICKEN BREASTS
IN BRANDY MUSHROOM SAUCE
YIELD: 2 SERVINGS

2 whole skinless, boneless
    chicken breasts
3 tablespoons butter
2 teaspoons vegetable oil
4 shallots, minced
1 cup sliced shiitake
    or cremini mushrooms
1/2 cup brandy
1/2 cup chicken stock
    (not bouillon)
1/3 cup sour cream or yogurt
Salt and white pepper to taste
2 tablespoons chopped fresh
    parsley

᠅ Lightly pound chicken breasts between two sheets of waxed paper until they are of uniform thickness. Separate into 4 "supremes" and remove any tendons.

Add 1-1/3 tablespoons of butter and 1 teaspoon of vegetable oil to a large skillet and sauté the shallots and mushrooms until softened and golden, approximately 5 minutes. Remove from pan and place on serving platter.

Add remaining butter and oil to skillet and sauté the chicken over medium-high heat until well browned and cooked through, approximately 5 minutes per side. **Do not overcook**. Remove from skillet and set aside.

Pour brandy and stock into skillet, scraping up any browned bits. Heat to boiling. Carefully flame brandy. When flame dies down, stir in sour cream and simmer for 2 to 3 minutes. **Do not overheat,** as sauce will separate.

Return mushrooms and shallots to skillet and simmer slowly. Season with salt and pepper.

To serve, pour sauce over chicken supremes and garnish with parsley.

Serve with fresh asparagus and red skinned potatoes.

— NINA NEUDORFER

ORANGE CHICKEN
YIELD: 2-3 SERVINGS

1 pound skinless, boneless chicken
    breast, cut in 2-inch pieces
1 orange
1/4 cup cornstarch
Vegetable oil for deep frying

MARINADE
1 teaspoon sesame oil
1 teaspoon soy sauce
1 tablespoon white wine
1/2 teaspoon sugar
Salt and pepper to taste
1/2 egg yolk (optional)

ORANGE SAUCE
2 tablespoons white wine
1 tablespoon hoisin sauce
1 tablespoon oyster sauce
1 tablespoon sesame oil
4 tablespoons orange juice
    concentrate
1 teaspoon chopped ginger
1 teaspoon chopped scallions
1 teaspoon chopped garlic
2 tablespoons sugar

∾ Mix ingredients for marinade in glass dish. Add chicken pieces and marinate for at least 1 hour.

Peel half the orange and cut the peel into 1/4-inch strips. Save the other half for garnish.

Mix orange sauce ingredients in a small bowl and stir until sugar dissolves. Set aside.

Remove chicken pieces from marinade and lightly coat with cornstarch. Heat oil in wok or large skillet and deep-fry chicken over medium-high heat for 2 minutes. Remove chicken and set aside.

Reheat oil until smoking. Fry chicken until crisp, approximately 1 minute. Set aside.

Drain oil and rinse wok or skillet. Heat wok and add 1 tablespoon oil. Fry orange peel until crispy.

Add orange sauce to wok and stir until sauce thickens. Add fried chicken and stir quickly to coat all chicken. Sprinkle with sesame oil and serve.

—ROSE WONG
PEARL OF THE ORIENT
SHAKER HEIGHTS, OHIO

Five Star
ENTRÉES
POULTRY

Chicken with Artichoke Hearts

Yield: 4 servings

4 whole skinless, boneless
    chicken breasts
1 can chicken broth
1 can artichoke hearts, drained
2 tablespoons butter
1/4 cup all-purpose flour
3/4 cup half and half
Salt and pepper to taste
3/4 cup grated Parmesan cheese
3 tablespoons dry white wine
1/2 pound fresh mushrooms,
    sliced

➤ Preheat oven to 325°F. Lightly grease a 12 × 9-inch oven-proof dish.

Poach chicken in broth in a large skillet for about 15 minutes. Remove chicken and save broth.

Overlap chicken breasts in prepared dish. Cut artichoke hearts in quarters and place them on top of chicken.

Melt 1 tablespoon butter in a small saucepan and add flour. Pour in reserved chicken broth and half and half. Season with salt and pepper. Continue cooking until sauce is thickened. Stir in Parmesan cheese and wine. Pour sauce over chicken and artichokes.

Sauté sliced mushrooms in remaining tablespoon of butter and arrange on top of chicken mixture.

Bake, uncovered, for 30 minutes.

— Barb Woodburn

Pesto-Stuffed Chicken Breasts

Yield: 6 servings

4 to 6 skinless, boneless
    chicken breasts, pounded

MARINADE
1/2 cup olive oil
2 to 3 sun-dried tomatoes,
    finely chopped
2 garlic cloves, minced

PESTO
1 cup basil leaves
2 garlic cloves, quartered
1/2 cup pine nuts
1/2 cup extra virgin olive oil
1/4 cup grated Parmesan cheese
1/4 cup grated Romano cheese
Freshly ground black pepper
    to taste

➤ Mix ingredients for marinade in a shallow dish. Place chicken breasts in marinade for 1 hour.

To make pesto, put basil leaves in blender or food processor and process for 30 seconds. Add garlic and pine nuts and process until mixed. While the processor is running, slowly add the oil in a steady stream and process until thickened. Add Parmesan and Romano cheeses and pepper; mix well.

Remove chicken breasts from marinade and place a tablespoon of pesto on each breast. Roll up and secure with toothpicks. Grill over a hot fire about 5 to 10 minutes per side.

— Kathy Pavlish

CHICKEN IN ROSÉ SAUCE
YIELD: 6-8 SERVINGS

4 skinless, boneless chicken
    breasts, halved
4 tablespoons margarine
2 tablespoons all-purpose flour
3/4 cup chicken broth
1/2 cup rosé
1/4 cup thinly sliced scallions
1/2 cup thinly sliced mushrooms
1 can (14 ounces) artichoke
    hearts packed in water,
    drained and halved
    horizontally

➤ Preheat oven to 350°F.
Melt 2 tablespoons margarine
in a 12 × 9 × 2-inch baking dish.
Add chicken breasts and bake
20 to 30 minutes.

Melt remaining 2 table-
spoons margarine in a medium
saucepan. Add flour, mix well
and cook over medium-high
heat briefly. Add chicken broth
and rosé wine, stirring constantly,
until sauce is thick and smooth.

Remove chicken from the
oven. Turn each piece and cover
with scallions, mushrooms and
artichoke hearts. Pour sauce
over all and return to oven for
another 30 minutes.

Serve warm.

— PAT McMANAMON

BREAST OF CHICKEN PARISIENNE
YIELD: 6 SERVINGS

4 whole skinless, boneless
    chicken breasts
All-purpose flour
1/4 cup butter
2 tablespoons sherry
1/2 teaspoon tomato paste
1/2 cup beef stock
1 cup sour cream
1 tablespoon Parmesan cheese
1 tablespoon currant jelly
Salt and pepper to taste
2 cups sliced mushrooms

➤ Halve chicken breasts,
dredge in flour and sauté in
butter until nicely browned.
Pour sherry over chicken and
remove from pan.

Add tomato paste, 1 tablespoon flour and beef stock. Stir
until mixture thickens. Whisk
in sour cream. Add cheese,
jelly, salt and pepper. Return
chicken to pan and add mushrooms. Cover and cook for
30 minutes or until chicken
is cooked.

Serve with rice or buttered noodles.

— BEA ZIMMERMAN

CHICKEN KIEV

YIELD: 6 SERVINGS

3 whole skinless, boneless
    chicken breasts
Salt and pepper to taste
1 egg
All-purpose flour
Bread crumbs
1/4 cup margarine

ONION BUTTER
3/4 cup butter, softened
1 tablespoon chopped parsley
1 tablespoon chopped chives
1 tablespoon chopped shallots
    or scallions
1/2 teaspoon salt
1/4 teaspoon pepper

∾ To make Onion Butter, mix butter, parsley, chives, shallots or scallions, salt and pepper; form into six small balls. Freeze.

Cut chicken breasts in half and pound to 1/4-inch thickness. Place frozen onion-butter balls in center of chicken, roll up and secure edges with toothpicks. Sprinkle with salt and pepper.

Beat egg with a little water in a flat dish. Dredge chicken roll-ups in flour, dip in egg, and roll in bread crumbs.

Heat margarine in skillet and brown chicken on all sides. Remove from skillet and place in a baking dish. Bake in a 400°F oven for 15 to 20 minutes.

— MARGARET FORD

CHICKEN
WITH AVOCADO AND OLIVES

YIELD: 6 SERVINGS

4 whole skinless, boneless
    chicken breasts, halved
1/2 cup plain low-fat yogurt
1 medium avocado
2 tablespoons mayonnaise
1/2 cup chopped black olives
1/2 cup chopped pecans
1 tablespoon chopped pimiento
1 teaspoon chopped fresh basil
Freshly ground black pepper
    to taste
1 cup grated Monterey Jack
    cheese

∾ Preheat oven to 350°F. Pound each chicken breast half until slightly flattened and place in an oven-proof baking dish. Spread each piece with yogurt and bake for approximately 20 minutes.

Peel and seed avocado. Mash pulp and add mayonnaise, blending until the mixture is smooth. Add chopped olives, pecans, pimiento, basil and pepper. Stir well.

Spread avocado mixture over cooked chicken breasts and top with grated cheese. Place under broiler until cheese melts. Serve immediately.

— AL SENGER

LIME CHICKEN
WITH FIESTA RICE

*A low-fat, low-salt
Mexican dish.*

YIELD: 4 SERVINGS

1 lime
4 cloves garlic, minced
4 skinless, boneless chicken
    breasts
1-1/4 cups salt-free, fat-free
    chicken broth
1 cup fast-cooking brown rice
Hot pepper sauce to taste
1/2 cup diced celery
1/2 cup diced red pepper
1/2 cup diced yellow pepper
1/4 cup sliced scallions

∾ Grate lime peel and set aside.

Juice lime, add garlic. Pour over chicken breasts in a small dish. Bring broth to a boil, add rice, simmer for 10 minutes. Add hot pepper sauce to taste. Add celery and peppers. Cover, remove from heat; set aside.

Sauté chicken breasts in a non-stick pan over medium-high heat until done.

To serve, place rice in the center of a platter, and top with sliced scallions. Sprinkle lime peel on chicken and arrange around edge of the rice.

— MARY LOU GAFFNEY

MEXICAN CHICKEN BREASTS
YIELD: 6-8 SERVINGS

4 whole skinless, boneless
    chicken breasts
1 cup (7 ounce can) diced
    green chilies
4 ounces Monterey Jack
    cheese, cut into 8 strips
1/2 cup corn flakes, crumbled
1/4 cup Parmesan cheese
1 tablespoon chili powder
1/2 teaspoon salt
1/4 teaspoon cumin
1/4 teaspoon black pepper
1/4 cup melted butter, to which
    1 minced clove garlic has
    been added

➥ Preheat oven to 400°F. Cut chicken breasts in half and pound each to 1/4-inch thickness. Place 2 tablespoons of the diced chilies and 1 strip of cheese in the center of each breast. Roll up and tuck ends under, securing with toothpicks if necessary.

Combine corn flake crumbs, Parmesan cheese, chili powder, salt, cumin and pepper in a medium-sized bowl. Dip each chicken piece in melted butter, then roll in crumbs. Place seam-side down in baking dish and drizzle with remaining melted butter.

Bake uncovered for approximately 30 minutes, or until done.

Serve on bed of shredded lettuce and top with salsa. Spanish rice as a side dish makes the meal truly Mexican.

—CAROL CRANE

Five Star
ENTRÉES
POULTRY

Chicken Kabobs

Yield: 4-6 servings

2 whole skinless, boneless
    chicken breasts, cut
    into 2-inch pieces
1 pint cherry tomatoes or
    2 to 3 tomatoes, cut
    into wedges
2 to 3 green peppers, cut
    into wedges
8 ounces fresh whole mushrooms
1 fresh pineapple, cut into
    2-inch chunks or 1 can
    (16 ounces) pineapple
    chunks, drained

MARINADE
1/2 cup soy sauce
2/3 cup vegetable oil
2 tablespoons sugar
2 tablespoons sherry
1 clove garlic, crushed

૎ Combine marinade ingredients and whisk well. Place chicken in marinade for 4 to 6 hours, being sure to use a non-aluminum pan.

Assemble kabobs on skewers, alternating chicken, tomatoes, peppers, mushrooms and pineapple. Baste with remaining marinade and grill over medium-high heat approximately 15 minutes per side.

— Lois Fishback

Grilled Chicken

with hot spices

Yield: 6 servings

1 roasting chicken (3 pounds)
2 teaspoons salt
1 tablespoon pepper
1 tablespoon sombal ulek* or
    ground chili spices or both
2 teaspoons grated onion
2 cloves garlic, minced
2 tablespoons dark soy sauce
2 teaspoons granulated brown
    sugar
2 tablespoons lemon juice
2 tablespoons peanut oil

Available in Indian/Indonesian markets.

૎ Cut chicken into pieces. Remove skin, if desired, and score to allow flavors to penetrate.

Combine all other ingredients in glass dish. Add chicken and refrigerate overnight.

Grill over medium-high heat until cooked through, approximately 30 minutes.

— Marilyn Althans

Low-Fat Chicken Enchiladas

Light, fresh and attractive.

YIELD: 2-3 SERVINGS

1-3/4 teaspoons olive oil
1/4 teaspoon sesame oil
1 onion, chopped
2 cloves garlic, chopped
1-1/2 pounds tomatillos,* peeled, washed and quartered
1 jalapeño pepper, chopped and seeded
1 cup water
1 large red onion, sliced
1 large red pepper, seeded and sliced
2 cups chicken stock or low-salt chicken broth
1 cup cooked and shredded chicken meat
1 teaspoon ground cumin
1 teaspoon chili powder
1/4 cup shredded cilantro
1/4 cup chopped Italian parsley
3 tablespoons cornstarch
1/2 cup water
4 to 6 flour tortillas

Available at specialty produce stores and in some supermarkets.

꿍 Heat 3/4 teaspoon olive oil and sesame oil in a heavy saucepan over medium-high heat. Add onion and garlic; sauté until brown. Add tomatillos, jalapeño and water. Cover, reduce heat and simmer for 15 minutes.

Heat 1 teaspoon olive oil in a medium frying pan over medium-high heat. Add onion and red pepper and brown until a caramel-like substance forms in the bottom of the pan.

Remove the tomatillo mixture from the saucepan to a blender or food processor. Blend, then strain to remove seeds and heavy skin. Return mixture to saucepan.

Divide chicken stock between the saucepan and the frying pan. Add chicken, cumin, chili powder, cilantro and parsley to the mixture in the frying pan and heat through over low heat.

Blend cornstarch with 1/2 cup water. Whisk two-thirds of it into the tomatillo mixture. Whisk remaining one-third into the chicken mixture.

Wrap tortillas in foil. Place in 350°F oven for approximately 10 minutes to heat through.

To serve, spoon some of chicken mixture in the center of each tortilla. Roll up, place on plate and top with tomatillo sauce.

— MARY WARD
COOKBOOK AUTHOR

Five Star
ENTRÉES
POULTRY

FRICASSÉE DE VOLAILLE AU VINAIGRE

*Sautéed chicken with
fresh vinegar sauce.*

YIELD: 8 SERVINGS

1/2 cup (1 stick) butter
2 frying chickens, cut into
    16 pieces
Salt and white pepper to taste
1/4 cup all-purpose flour
1/2 cup minced shallots
1/2 cup white wine vinegar
1 pound mushrooms, cleaned
    and sliced
1 pound tomatoes
1 cup heavy cream
Parsley for garnish

꙳ Preheat oven to 325°F. Melt butter in a large oven-proof skillet. Season chicken with salt and pepper and roll in flour. Shake off excess flour and brown in hot butter. Remove from pan.

Add shallots and sauté, but do not brown. Add vinegar and let sauce reduce.

Bring 2 cups of water to a boil in a medium saucepan and add mushroom slices. When water re-boils, remove mushrooms and place in skillet.

Drop tomatoes in boiling water to blanch, approximately 45 seconds. Remove skin and seeds. Chop and add to skillet. Add cream and bring to a boil.

Return chicken to pan. Cover and bake for approximately 15 minutes.

To serve, arrange chicken on platter and garnish with parsley.

Originally published in John Desmond's *Ma Cuisine.*

—JOHN DESMOND

ROAST CHICKEN
WITH ROSEMARY

Tender and moist.

YIELD: 4-6 SERVINGS

1 roasting hen (3 to 4 pounds),
    rinsed and patted dry
3 sprigs fresh rosemary or
    1 teaspoon dried
1/4 cup butter at room
    temperature
Salt and pepper to taste

꙳ Preheat oven to 450°F.

Place rosemary under breast skin and in cavity of chicken. Rub chicken with butter and then rub in salt and pepper.

Place chicken in roasting pan, breast-side up. Roast for 15 minutes. Reduce heat to 325°F and continue cooking for an additional 40 minutes. Remove from oven and allow to cool for 10 minutes before carving.

—MOLLY BARTLETT
SILVER CREEK FARM

Oven-Baked Free-Range Chicken with Maple Pecan Crust

Yield: 4 servings

2 free-range chickens
   (3 pounds each)
   or fryers
Salt and pepper to taste
2 tablespoons vegetable oil

MAPLE PECAN CRUST
1 cup finely ground pecans
1 tablespoon Dijon-style mustard
1 tablespoon maple syrup
1 tablespoon reserved chicken
   grease
1 lightly beaten egg white
2 tablespoons brandy
Salt to taste

PEPPER MIXTURE
1 cup ground black pepper
1/3 cup ground white pepper
1-1/2 tablespoons cayenne pepper

❧ Remove wings from chickens. Starting at the keel bone, run the tip of a knife between the breast meat and bone, back to the thigh, so that boneless breast and thigh meat separate in one piece. Leave on skin. Cutting from underside, remove thigh and leg bones. Repeat so that you have 4 boneless half-chickens.

To make pepper mixture, combine all ingredients. Cover tightly and store in a cool place.

Preheat oven to 400°F. Season chickens with salt and pepper mixture and sauté, skin-side down, in hot oil over medium heat. (Use a sauté pan large enough to hold chicken halves in single layer or transfer to roasting pan during baking time.)

Brown each bird to form a light crust, but do not burn. Turn halves, skin-side up, and place sauté pan in oven. Roast the birds for 8 minutes and remove from oven. Pour off all but 1 tablespoon grease; reserve for Maple Pecan Crust.

Combine all ingredients for Maple Pecan Crust and spoon onto each bird. Use the back of a spoon and cover the skin area with a thin coating.

Return pans to oven, about 8 minutes, until chicken is done. Keep warm.

Previously published in *The Mansion on Turtle Creek Cookbook*, Grove/Weidenfeld, copyright ©1987, by Dean Fearing, reprinted with permission.

— CHEF DEAN FEARING

Five Star
ENTRÉES
POULTRY

The Mansion on Turtle Creek
2821 Turtle Creek Boulevard
Dallas, TX 75219
214-559-2100

GRILLED DUCK BREASTS
WITH CRACKLINGS

Plan at least a day ahead.

YIELD: 6-8 SERVINGS

**4 whole boneless duck breasts,
   cut into 8 pieces**
1/2 cup Dijon-style mustard
1/2 cup balsamic vinegar
1-1/2 cups olive oil
1/2 teaspoon salt
1/4 teaspoon pepper
1-1/2 cups plum ketchup*

**Available at specialty food stores, or
substitute Oriental plum sauce.*

❂ At least 24 hours before serving, divide duck breasts; remove and save skin to make cracklings.

Mix mustard, vinegar, oil, salt and pepper and pour over duck breasts in non-metallic bowl or pan, making sure all meat is well coated. Cover and refrigerate 24 hours.

Remove duck breasts from marinade and grill over hot coals, approximately 10 minutes per side, basting liberally with plum ketchup.

To prepare cracklings, cut duck skin into thin strips and sauté in frying pan over medium heat until pieces are browned and crispy, approximately 30 minutes. Drain on paper towels and use as garnish. These can be prepared ahead and reheated at serving time.

—SALLY THOMSON

CRISP QUAIL
WITH PINEAPPLE AND GREEN ONION
YIELD: 4 SERVINGS

8 quail (4 ounces each),
    cut into quarters

MARINADE
2 tablespoons plum wine or
    sherry
2 tablespoons chopped fresh
    peeled ginger
1 tablespoon finely chopped
    garlic
1 tablespoon finely chopped
    green onion
1 teaspoon salt
1 teaspoon freshly ground
    white pepper

SAUCE
3/4 cup plum wine or port
1 tablespoon julienned fresh
    peeled ginger
1/2 cup brown stock (veal or
    brown chicken)
1/2 cinnamon stick
1 teaspoon chili oil
Salt
Freshly ground white pepper
2 tablespoons unsalted butter
Peanut oil for deep frying
1 cup rice flour

GARNISHES
6 green onions, trimmed and
    cut in half lengthwise
1/4 fresh pineapple, cut
    lengthwise, peeled, trimmed
    and cut into 10 thin slices

Place the quail quarters on a plate and toss with the marinade. Let marinate 1 to 6 hours, refrigerated.

To prepare the sauce, combine the wine and ginger in a medium skillet over high heat and reduce by half. Pour in the stock with the cinnamon stick and cook until the sauce thickens. Add the chili oil and season lightly with salt and pepper. Whisk in butter and correct seasoning to taste. Keep warm.

Heat about 3 inches of peanut oil to 350°F in a deep, heavy saucepan or deep-fat fryer.

Pour the rice flour into a small bowl and make a thick batter using 1/2 to 3/4 cup water. Transfer the quail from the marinade to a clean plate, reserving the marinade. Pour enough of the batter over the quail to coat well, reserving a little batter.

Deep-fry quail until golden, 2 to 3 minutes. **Do not overcook**. Drain on a clean towel and toss in the reserved sauce. Quail is best when still pink on the inside.

Coat the green onions with the remaining batter and fry until golden, 1 or 2 minutes. Drain on clean paper towels.

To serve, arrange the pineapple slices in a circle around the outer edges of a large oven-proof plate. Warm in the oven. Pile the quail in the center and poke the green onions into the quail at various intervals. Serve immediately.

Previously published in *A La Carte*, Random House, copyright ©1991, by Wolfgang Puck, reprinted with permission.

— CHEF WOLFGANG PUCK

Five Star
ENTRÉES
POULTRY

Chinois on Main
2709 Main Street
Santa Monica, CA 90405
213-392-9025

Eureka
1845 South Bundy
Los Angeles, CA 90025
213-447-8000

Granita
23725 West Malibu Road
Malibu, CA 90265
213-456-0488

Postrio
545 Post Street
San Francisco, CA 94102
415-776-7825

Spago
8795 Sunset Boulevard
Los Angeles, CA 90069
213-652-3706

Cornish Hens with Plum Sauce

Yield: 4 servings

4 Cornish hens
1/2 cup plum jam
1/3 cup soy sauce
1/4 cup orange juice
2 cloves garlic, minced
1/4 teaspoon crushed anise seed

🦢 Preheat oven to 375°F. Clean hens and discard the giblets. Rinse, drain and dry well. Place hens, breast-side down, on a rack in a foil-lined pan. Combine jam, soy sauce, orange juice, garlic and anise seed. Baste hens with sauce, inside and out.

Cover hens loosely with foil and bake for approximately 1 hour, basting occasionally. Remove foil and continue baking for an additional 30 minutes, basting often with the remaining sauce.

Serve with wild rice.

—Janet Mahon

Guinea Hen

Yield: 2 servings

1 guinea hen (2 to 2-1/2 pounds), quartered
3 tablespoons butter
4 to 5 shallots, chopped
Salt and pepper to taste

🦢 Preheat oven to 450°F.
Melt butter in heavy skillet and add shallots. Stir until brown and transfer to oven-proof dish.

Sauté quartered hen in skillet, over medium-high heat, approximately 5 minutes.

Place in oven-proof dish with shallots and bake, loosely covered, approximately 15 minutes.

—Molly Bartlett
Silver Creek Farm

Coq au Riesling

Yield: 4 servings

4 Cornish hens, about
    1-1/4 pounds each
Salt and pepper to taste
1/4 cup coarsely chopped shallots
4 sprigs fresh thyme
1 cup Riesling wine
2 tablespoons olive oil
16 white pearl onions,
    blanched for 10 minutes
1-1/4 cups fresh or canned
    chicken stock
10 large white mushrooms,
    cut into 1/2-inch cubes
4 carrots, cut into 1/2-inch cubes,
    and blanched for 10 minutes
1-1/2 tablespoons chopped fresh
    tarragon
6 thick slices of bacon, diced
3 turnips, cut into 1/2-inch cubes
    and boiled for 4-5 minutes

❧ To make spaetzle, place the eggs, yolks and water in a bowl and blend with a whisk. Using a rubber spatula, blend the flour and seasonings.

Bring 4 quarts of salted water to a boil. Pour the spaetzle mix into a colander over the boiling water. Press the mixture through the holes of the colander with a rubber spatula. Cook for 1 minute. Remove with a large slotted spoon into a bowl of ice water. When cooled, remove and drain. Toss lightly with olive oil.

Cut each Cornish hen into 6 serving pieces and season with salt and pepper. Place in a bowl, add shallots and thyme and mix well. Add the wine, cover and marinate for 12 hours.

SPAETZLE
3 whole eggs
3 egg yolks
1-1/2 cups of water
2-1/2 cups plus 1 tablespoon
    all-purpose flour
1/2 teaspoon salt
1/4 teaspoon white pepper
1/4 teaspoon nutmeg

Remove the pieces of Cornish hen, strain and reserve the marinade.

Heat the olive oil over medium heat in a skillet large enough to hold the pieces in one layer. Place the pieces skin-side down and brown on all sides for about 5 minutes.

Add the onions, carrots, turnips, mushrooms and bacon. Cook for about 8 to 10 minutes. Remove hens and keep warm.

Discard the fat, leaving the onions, mushrooms, carrots, turnips and bacon. Add the reserved marinade and chicken broth. Cook until reduced to about 1 cup.

Add the Cornish hens and the tarragon. Bring to a boil and serve immediately.

—CHEF DEBRA PONZEK

Five Star
ENTRÉES
POULTRY

Montrachet
239 West Broadway
New York, NY 10013
212-219-2777

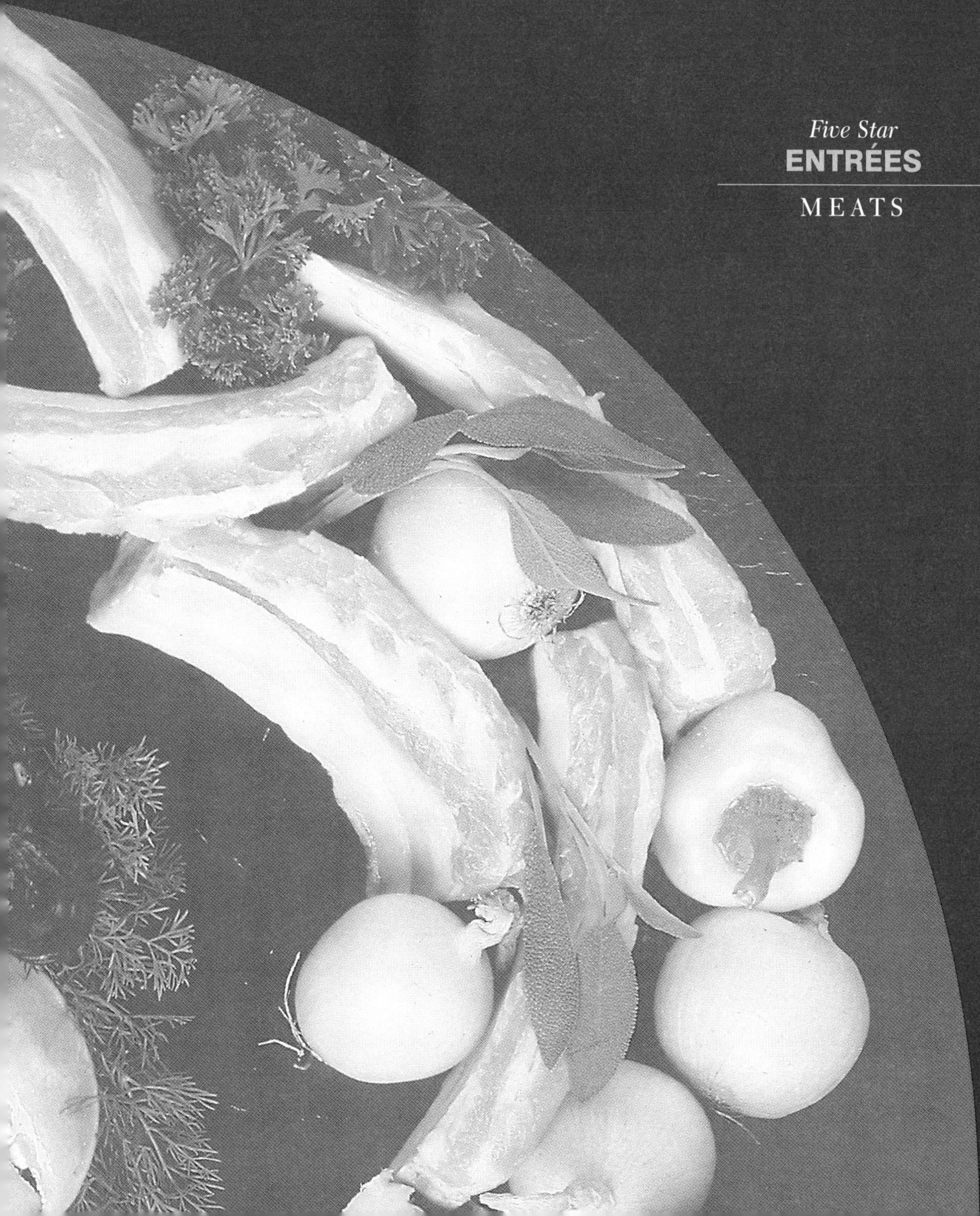

Five Star
ENTRÉES

MEATS

VEAL MARSALA
YIELD: 6-8 SERVINGS

1-1/2 pounds veal cutlet, thinly
    sliced and well pounded
1/2 teaspoon salt
1/4 teaspoon pepper
1 teaspoon garlic powder
1/4 cup all-purpose flour
1/4 cup vegetable oil for frying
1 cup sliced mushrooms
1 tablespoon olive oil
1/8 teaspoon tarragon
1/8 teaspoon oregano
1/4 cup chicken broth
1/2 cup Marsala

ॐ Sprinkle salt, pepper and garlic powder on both sides of veal. Dredge the veal in flour, being sure to coat both sides of the cutlet.

Add vegetable oil to a large skillet. Brown both sides of veal in skillet over medium-high heat. Remove veal and drain skillet of excess oil.

Meanwhile, sauté mushrooms over medium heat in a small saucepan; set aside.

Add one tablespoon of olive oil to the veal skillet, along with the tarragon and oregano. Cook over medium-high heat for 1 minute. Stir in chicken broth and Marsala.

Add veal slices and mushrooms, reduce heat and simmer about 4 to 5 minutes or until sauce is thickened and reduced.

Serve with wild rice.

— DR. SOSAMMA BERGER

VEAL SCALLOPS
WITH EGGPLANT AND TOMATO
YIELD: 2 SERVINGS

4 slices (1/4-inch thick) eggplant, skinned, salted and pressed 1 hour
6 tablespoons clarified margarine
3 ounces olive oil
6 veal scallops (2 ounces each), sliced 1/4-inch thick and pounded thin
1 tablespoon diced shallots
1/3 cup thinly sliced mushrooms
2 thin slices prosciutto, julienned
1 large tomato, peeled, seeded and julienned
1/8 teaspoon fine herbs
2 ounces Madeira
5 ounces Espagnole sauce,* glacé de viande or other thick, beef sauce
4 tablespoons unsalted butter
1 teaspoon chopped parsley
Salt and freshly ground pepper to taste
6 tablespoons all-purpose flour

*See page 201 for recipe.

ই Pat dry and lightly flour the pressed eggplant.

Heat 2 tablespoons each of the clarified margarine and olive oil in a medium-size skillet until a light haze forms over it. Add the dusted eggplant, salt and pepper to taste and brown on each side. Remove from skillet and keep warm.

Heat remaining margarine and olive oil in a large skillet until a light haze forms over it. Lightly flour veal scallops, place in skillet, season with salt and pepper and lightly brown on one side.

Turn and remove excess oil. Add shallots, mushrooms, prosciutto, tomatoes and herbs and sauté for 2 minutes. Add Madeira over high heat and deglaze pan. Add Espagnole sauce and fresh butter. Cook until butter is incorporated into the sauce. Adjust seasonings.

—CHEF CARL QUAGLIATA
GIOVANNI'S RESTAURANT
CLEVELAND, OHIO

Five Star
ENTRÉES
VEAL

SAUTÉED VEAL
WITH WILD MUSHROOMS, PORT WINE AND PROSCIUTTO
YIELD: 4 SERVINGS

1-1/2 pounds veal round or loin, thinly sliced
1 cup all-purpose flour
4 tablespoons vegetable oil
1 tablespoon chopped garlic
1 tablespoon chopped shallots
1 pound wild mushrooms (morels, shiitake, oyster, etc.), sliced
2 cups port wine
8 thin slices prosciutto
Salt and pepper
1 cup shredded Swiss or Gruyère cheese

&em; Place veal between pieces of waxed paper and pound lightly to a 1/4-inch thickness.

Heat oil in a skillet over medium-high heat. Dredge veal in flour and sauté in skillet until brown on both sides, about 2 minutes per side. Remove from skillet and drain.

Add garlic, shallots and mushrooms to skillet and cook for 2 to 3 minutes. Add port wine and simmer until liquid is reduced to a half cup. Season to taste.

Arrange veal on a large oven-proof platter. Place prosciutto slices on top of veal and cover with shredded cheese. Brown under broiler for 1 minute and serve with mushrooms.

— HERBERT KAISER

VEAL CHOPS
IN ZINFANDEL WITH GARLIC BUTTER
YIELD: 4 SERVINGS

4 veal chops, sliced 1-inch thick
1/4 cup all-purpose flour
Salt and pepper to taste
1/4 cup olive oil
2 tablespoons butter
1/2 cup Zinfandel
1 tablespoon fresh basil
1 tablespoon chopped fresh parsley
1 teaspoon dried thyme

GARLIC BUTTER
1 small head garlic, unpeeled and broken into cloves
2 tablespoons olive oil
1/4 pound butter
1 tablespoon chopped parsley

&em; Dust veal with flour, salt and pepper. Heat a large skillet over high heat and add oil and butter. Add veal and sauté on both sides. Add wine and sauté for 15 minutes.

To make garlic butter, place garlic in olive oil and sauté over medium-high heat for 15 minutes. Remove from pan and peel garlic. Blend garlic, butter and parsley in food processor. Roll in parchment or waxed paper and chill for 1 hour.

To serve, sprinkle chops with basil, parsley and thyme and top with a thin slice of garlic butter.

— LORETTA PAGANINI
LORETTA PAGANINI
SCHOOL OF COOKING

BREAST OF VEAL

A great picnic idea.

YIELD: 6 SERVINGS

1 whole breast of veal
3 tablespoons peanut oil
1 tablespoon chopped parsley
2 medium onions, sliced
1/2 teaspoon thyme
1 tablespoon tarragon
1/2 cup dry white wine
1 cup veal or chicken stock
2 bay leaves
Salt and freshly ground pepper
    to taste

⁅ Heat 2 tablespoons oil in a large skillet over high heat and braise veal until brown on all sides. Remove and place in roasting pan.

Add 1 tablespoon peanut oil to skillet along with parsley, onions, thyme and tarragon and sauté for about 3 minutes. Add wine and continue cooking an additional 2 minutes. Add stock, bay leaves, salt and pepper, stirring well. Simmer for 10 minutes.

Pour sauce over veal breast, cover tightly, and cook in 350°F oven for approximately 2 hours. Baste veal every 20 minutes, being careful not to overcook. (Veal is done when it can be pierced with a fork and feels tender.) Refrigerate. Serve cold.

—JANE WOOD

VEAL MEDALLIONS
STUFFED
WITH RED PESTO

A winner!

YIELD: 4 SERVINGS

4 boneless veal rib eye medallions
    (6 ounces each)
4 cloves garlic, minced
6 sun-dried tomatoes, minced
4 tablespoons minced fresh basil
2 tablespoons grated Asiago or
    Parmesan cheese
1 teaspoon black pepper
1/4 pound thinly sliced pancetta
    or prosciutto
1 tablespoon olive oil

⁅ Cut pocket in each medallion. Combine garlic, sun-dried tomatoes, basil, cheese and pepper. Stuff one-fourth of this mixture into the pocket of each veal medallion.

Wrap stuffed medallions with a slice of pancetta or prosciutto. Panfry in olive oil over medium heat 4 minutes per side or roast in 375°F oven for approximately 12 minutes.

Serve with angel hair pasta.

—RANDAL JOHNSON

Five Star
ENTRÉES

VEAL

VEAL DE BUCKEYE

For those cold Ohio nights.

YIELD: 6 SERVINGS

1-1/2 pounds veal, cut into
 1-1/2-inch cubes
4 tablespoons butter, divided
1 medium onion, minced
1 tablespoon chopped fresh
 parsley
1 tablespoon all-purpose flour
1 cup beef bouillon, warmed
1 cup dry white wine
 (Chardonnay or
 Sauvignon Blanc)
1/8 teaspoon dried parsley
1/8 teaspoon dried thyme
1/8 teaspoon dried sage
1/8 teaspoon dried rosemary
1/8 teaspoon dried savory
1 bay leaf
Salt and pepper to taste
1 cup tomato sauce
1 cup mushrooms, sliced
Fresh parsley for garnish

Brown veal cubes in 2 tablespoons butter in heavy skillet over medium-high heat. Add onion and parsley and cook until onion is translucent, about 3 minutes.

Add flour and cook for about 1 minute, stirring constantly.

Combine bouillon and wine and bring to a boil. Add to veal. Add seasonings, cover and simmer over low heat for approximately 1 hour.

Add tomato sauce and continue cooking until veal is tender and sauce is reduced, well blended and smooth, approximately 45 minutes.

Sauté mushrooms in remaining butter over medium-high heat and add to veal. Remove bay leaf. To serve, sprinkle with fresh parsley.

Serve with buttered noodles.
You may substitute 1 teaspoon fresh parsley, thyme, sage, rosemary and savory for dried herbs.

— DAN ELLIOTT

ROAST VEAL
WITH HERBS

YIELD: 6 SERVINGS

MARINADE
1 teaspoon parsley
1 teaspoon thyme
1 crushed bay leaf
3 tablespoons vegetable oil
1 teaspoon salt
1 tablespoon chopped green
 onion
1/4 teaspoon pepper
1/8 teaspoon nutmeg
1 tablespoon steak sauce

2-1/2-pound veal roast, boned
 and rolled
1 cup sliced mushrooms
1 tablespoon margarine
1 tablespoon all-purpose flour
1 tablespoon cider vinegar

Combine marinade ingredients in large bowl; add veal roast and mushrooms; refrigerate 24 hours, turning occasionally.

Wrap veal, mushrooms and herbs in heavy aluminum foil; place in roasting pan and roast at 350°F, approximately 2-1/4 hours or until tender.

Remove roast from oven, scrape off mushrooms and herbs and slice thin.

Melt margarine in saucepan over medium heat. Add flour, vinegar, mushrooms, herbs and meat juices. Bring to a boil, stirring constantly.

Pour over veal slices and serve extra gravy on the side.

— MRS. MARK UPSON, JR.

Veal Paprikás
Yield: 6 servings

1/2 cup butter or margarine
2 medium onions, diced
1 clove garlic, minced
2 pounds veal shoulder, cut
    into 1-inch cubes
1 cup whole tomatoes, drained
    and chopped
1/2 cup chicken broth
1 tablespoon sugar
1 teaspoon salt
1 teaspoon paprika
1/2 teaspoon ground black pepper
1/4 cup all-purpose flour
2 cups sour cream

❧ Melt butter or margarine in a large heavy soup pot or Dutch oven. Sauté onions and garlic over medium-high heat until tender, about 5 minutes.

Add veal; cover and cook over low heat for 20 minutes, stirring occasionally. Add tomatoes, chicken broth, sugar and seasonings. Cover and simmer over low heat until veal is tender, about 1-1/4 hours.

Combine flour and sour cream in a small bowl, blend until smooth and slowly add to the veal, stirring constantly. Simmer over low heat for 5 to 6 minutes or until thickened. Do not boil.

Serve hot over rice, noodles, dumplings or spaetzle.

—William E. Hartley

Five Star
ENTRÉES

VEAL

Medallions de Boeuf
au Poivre Vert

1-1/2 cups veal stock or unsalted chicken broth
8 beef medallions, 4 ounces each
2 tablespoons unsalted butter
2 tablespoons minced shallots
1/4 cup green peppercorns
1/4 cup plus 2 tablespoons (3 ounces) Madeira
1/2 cup heavy cream
Salt and white pepper to taste

❧ Bring veal stock to a boil in a heavy saucepan. Reduce heat and simmer until reduced by half. Remove from heat.

Season medallions with salt and white pepper. Melt butter in a heavy skillet and sauté medallions on both sides, for about 2 minutes per side for rare or 4 minutes per side for medium. Transfer meat to platter and keep warm.

Sauté shallots and green peppercorns in a saucepan for 1 minute. Add Madeira and cook another minute. Add reduced veal stock and cream. Simmer until sauce is reduced by half. Adjust seasonings and pour sauce over medallions. Serve immediately.

—JAMES L. MILLER, CEC, HGT
AMERICAN CULINARY FEDERATION
CLEVELAND CHAPTER, INC.

LARRY FORGIONE'S GRILLED FLANK STEAK MARINATED IN BEER

YIELD: 4 SERVINGS

1 flank steak (approximately
    2 pounds)
Vegetable oil
Salt
Freshly ground black pepper
8 tablespoons (1 stick) unsalted
    butter, at room temperature,
    cut into small pieces

MARINADE

12 ounces amber beer
1-1/2 cups chicken or veal stock
1/2 teaspoon fresh thyme
1 cup peeled, seeded and
    chopped tomatoes
1 teaspoon Worcestershire sauce
5 drops Tabasco
1 bay leaf
1/2 teaspoon freshly ground
    black pepper
1/2 teaspoon salt
1/4 cup chopped parsley

To make marinade, combine and thoroughly mix all the ingredients in a glass or porcelain dish large enough to hold the meat in a single layer.

Put the steak in the marinade, cover and refrigerate for 4 to 12 hours. Turn the meat from time to time.

Prepare a charcoal fire, or preheat the broiler. Remove the steak from the marinade and pat dry. Rub the meat with a little oil and season with salt and pepper.

Pour the marinade into a saucepan and bring to a boil, skimming off any foam that rises to the surface. Lower the heat and simmer for 15 to 20 minutes until the marinade is reduced by about half. Continue to skim off the fat as necessary.

Remove the bay leaf from the marinade and stir in the butter, one piece at a time, making sure each piece is completely incorporated before adding the next. Keep the sauce warm until ready to serve.

Grill the steak over the hot charcoal fire or under the broiler for 3 to 4 minutes on each side for medium-rare. Remove the steak from the grill, spoon the sauce over each steak and serve immediately.

Copyright ©1988 Larry Forgione.

— CHEF LARRY FORGIONE

Five Star
ENTRÉES

BEEF

An American Place
4 Mill Street, Rt. 9
Rhinebeck, NY 12572
914-871-1766

GERMAN BRISKET OF BEEF

Fine family fare.

YIELD: 4 SERVINGS

1-1/2 pounds beef brisket
Vegetable oil for frying
1/4 teaspoon pepper
Salt to taste
2 onions, sliced
4 celery stalks with leaves,
    chopped
1 can beer
1 jar (12 ounces) chili sauce

❧ Sear meat in a little oil in
a Dutch oven over high heat.

Turn meat, fat-side up, salt,
pepper and cover with onions,
celery, beer and chili sauce. Cover
and roast for 3-1/2 to 4 hours
in a 325°F oven. Serve with
remaining sauce.

— MARILYN ALTHANS

BEEF IN BEER

YIELD: 6-8 SERVINGS

1 tablespoon corn oil
2 pounds beef round
    or end of round rump,
    cut into 1/4-inch slices
2 large yellow onions, quartered
1 heaping tablespoon all-
    purpose flour
1 cup (1/2 pint) strong brown
    ale or beer
1/2 teaspoon dried thyme
1 bay leaf
1 large clove garlic, crushed
Salt and pepper to taste
1 cup grated Cheddar cheese
1/2 cup croutons

❧ Preheat oven to 300°F.
Heat oil in large oven-proof
dish over medium-high heat.
Brown meat on all sides and
remove to a plate. Add onions
and fry until brown.

Return meat and juices to
oven-proof dish. Lower heat and
sprinkle in the flour. Stir in beer
and add thyme, bay leaf, garlic
and seasonings.

Cover with a tight-fitting
lid and cook in the oven for
approximately 2 hours or until
the meat is very tender. When
cooked, remove lid, add croutons
and grated cheese, and broil for
1 minute or until cheese has
melted and browned slightly.

— DIANE WHITTINGHAM

MOM'S BEST MEATLOAF

Not just another meatloaf.

YIELD: 6-8 SERVINGS

2 pounds ground chuck
8 slices bacon, fried, drained
    and crumbled
1 large onion, minced
1-1/2 cups soft bread crumbs
1/4 cup evaporated milk or half
    and half
1/4 cup chili sauce or ketchup
1 tablespoon Worcestershire
    sauce
1 tablespoon steak sauce
1 teaspoon salt
1/8 teaspoon pepper
1/4 teaspoon thyme
1/8 teaspoon sage
1/8 teaspoon ginger
1 egg or 1/2 cup egg substitute

❧ Mix all ingredients in a
large bowl.

Pack into a 9 × 5 × 3-inch
loaf pan. Cover with foil and
bake in 350°F oven for approximately 1 hour.

Uncover and drain liquid.

Return meatloaf to oven and
bake, uncovered, for an additional
30 minutes. Remove from oven
and allow to stand 5 to 10 minutes
before turning out of pan.

Leftovers make great sandwiches.

— KATHLEEN HUGHES

Sauerbraten

Plan ahead.
Marinates three to four days.
Yield: 8 servings

4 pounds boneless chuck roast

MARINADE
3 cups white distilled vinegar
4 cups cold water
2 onions, sliced
3 small bay leaves
3 whole cloves
8 whole black peppercorns
Seasoned salt to taste

2 tablespoons butter
2 tablespoons vegetable oil

GRAVY
1/4 cup all-purpose flour
1/2 cup cold water
1/2 cup California Burgundy

~ Combine marinade ingredients in a saucepan and bring to a boil. Let cool to room temperature.

Place the meat in a crock or stainless steel pan and pour marinade over meat. Cover and refrigerate for 3 to 4 days, turning the meat at least once a day. Remove the meat from the marinade and drain thoroughly. Strain the marinade and save.

Melt butter and oil in a heavy saucepan over medium heat. Add meat and brown on all sides. Set aside.

Place marinade in saucepan and bring to a slow boil over medium-high heat.

Place meat in an oven-proof dish. Pour marinade over meat, cover and bake in a 300°F oven for 3 hours or until meat is tender. Remove to platter and keep warm.

To make gravy, pour cooking liquid into saucepan, skim off fat and bring to a boil. Make a smooth paste of flour and water and add slowly to boiling liquid until gravy thickens. Add wine and heat through, stirring constantly, about 2 minutes.

Serve with potato pancakes, spaetzle or buttered noodles.

—Mr. and Mrs.
Wilhelm Herzberger
Old Austria Restaurant

Five Star
ENTRÉES

BEEF

SZEGEDIN GOULASH

YIELD: 6 SERVINGS

2 medium onions, chopped
1/4 teaspoon minced garlic
2 teaspoons olive oil
2 pounds pork, cubed
2 tablespoons all-purpose flour
2 teaspoons paprika
1 teaspoon salt
1/2 teaspoon pepper
1 pound sauerkraut, drained
    and rinsed
1 cup boiling water

છે Heat a large skillet over medium-high heat and simmer onions and garlic in olive oil for 5 minutes or until onions are limp and brown. Add meat and brown. Cover and simmer for 30 minutes. Add flour, paprika, salt and pepper and continue cooking over low heat for 10 minutes. Add sauerkraut and boiling water and simmer for 20 minutes.

— BEA ZIMMERMAN

SWEET AND SOUR BEEF STEW

YIELD: 4-5 SERVINGS

1-1/2 pounds beef stew meat
2 tablespoons vegetable oil
1 cup sliced carrots
1 cup sliced onion
1 can (8 ounces) tomato sauce
1/4 cup brown sugar
1/4 cup cider vinegar
1 tablespoon Worcestershire
    sauce
3/4 cup water
1 teaspoon salt
1 tablespoon cornstarch

છે Brown meat in oil over medium-high heat. Add carrots, onion, tomato sauce, brown sugar, vinegar, Worcestershire sauce, 1/2 cup water and salt. Cover and cook over low heat approximately 2 hours or until tender.

Combine cornstarch and 1/4 cup cold water until smooth and add to beef. Cook and stir until thick and bubbly.

Serve over spinach noodles.

— LAUREEN NOWAKOWSKI

PORK AND SAUERKRAUT BUJDOSO

YIELD: 6 SERVINGS

5 pounds pork, cubed
1 jar (32 ounces) sauerkraut
1 can (29 ounces) tomato sauce
2 cups (16 ounces) sour cream
3 cloves garlic, crushed
8 tablespoons caraway seeds
Black pepper to taste
Parsley for garnish

છે Brown pork in oil over medium-high heat. Place in a 3-quart, oven-proof dish. Drain and rinse sauerkraut; add to pork. Stir in tomato sauce and sour cream. Add garlic and caraway seeds, stirring well. Bake for at least 3 hours at 325°F.

Serve with mashed potatoes.

— CANDY WEIL

Stuffed Cabbage

A Serbian Christmas tradition.

Yield: 10-12 servings

1 pound ground pork
1 pound ground chuck
5 medium onions, finely chopped
1/2 cup rice
2 eggs
1 teaspoon pepper
1 teaspoon salt
2 heads cabbage
1 can sauerkraut
1/4 pound bacon, cooked
    and crumbled
1/2 pound smoked ribs

TOMATO SAUCE*
3 tablespoons vegetable oil
3 tablespoons all-purpose flour
4 tablespoons milk
2 cans (8 ounces each)
    tomato sauce
1/4 teaspoon salt
1/4 teaspoon sugar
1/4 teaspoon paprika
2-1/2 cups water

In a hurry? Substitute 2 cans tomato soup and 2 cans water.

Brown ground meats. Remove meat with a slotted spoon and place in a large bowl.

Sauté onions in meat drippings over medium-high heat. Add onions, uncooked rice, eggs, salt and pepper to meat mixture, stirring well. Take cabbage and bore out the cores. Place them in boiling, salted water for 5 minutes or until water returns to a boil. Drain and detach cabbage leaves from the core.

To make tomato sauce, heat oil in a skillet over a moderate flame. Add flour and stir well. Cook approximately 3 minutes and add milk. The mixture should get very thick. Whisk in milk and tomato sauce. Add seasonings and thin further with 2 to 2-1/2 cups water.

Line a $13 \times 9 \times 2$-inch baking pan with cabbage leaves and a half can of sauerkraut. Take one cabbage leaf and place 1 teaspoon of the meat mixture in the middle. Fold in ends of cabbage leaf and roll leaf with meat into a neat, well-packed cylinder. Place in pan on top of cabbage leaves and sauerkraut and continue making cabbage rolls. Arrange cabbage rolls in layers with smoked ribs and bacon. Pour tomato sauce over the rolls; spread remaining sauerkraut on top. Bake in 325°F oven for 2 to 3 hours or until cabbage is cooked.

—Sonja T. Zivic

Five Star
ENTRÉES

PORK & BEEF

PORK LOIN
WITH ROSEMARY
YIELD: 6-8 SERVINGS

1 boneless pork loin roast,
    approximately 3 pounds
1 tablespoon fresh rosemary
2 cloves garlic, minced
1/4 cup extra virgin olive oil
Juice of 1 lemon

೪☙ Combine rosemary, garlic
and oil. Pour over pork roast,
refrigerate and marinate 4 to
6 hours or overnight.
    Grill over medium heat for
30 minutes or roast in 350°F oven
for 30 to 45 minutes. Squeeze
lemon juice over cooked meat
before serving.

— JOYCE NEIDITZ-SNOW

STUFFED
SPARERIBS
WITH APPLE DRESSING
YIELD: 4 SERVINGS

2 sides spareribs, equal in size
Salt and pepper to taste

APPLE DRESSING
6 apples, peeled and sliced
1 teaspoon cinnamon
1/4 teaspoon nutmeg
3/4 cup sugar
1 cup raisins
8 slices of bread, cubed and
    moistened with water

೪☙ Mix all of the ingredients
for apple dressing and stir gently.
    Arrange dressing between
the slabs of spareribs. Tie or
fasten the ribs together with
skewers. Salt and pepper ribs.
    Bake in 350°F oven for
about 45 minutes. Turn ribs to
brown on other side. Continue
cooking for a total of 2 hours,
or until pork is well browned
and cooked through.

— MRS. S. M. MADISON

MARINATED GRILLED
PORK TENDERLOIN
Fresh mint and
hoisin sauce marinade.
YIELD: 6 SERVINGS

2 pounds pork tenderloin

MARINADE
4 tablespoons hoisin sauce
4 tablespoons tamari or soy sauce
3 tablespoons water
1/3 cup molasses
3 cloves garlic, minced
1 tablespoon minced fresh ginger
1/4 cup minced fresh spearmint

೪☙ Mix marinade ingredients
thoroughly. Pour over pork
tenderloin to coat well. Cover
and marinate for 4 to 8 hours
in refrigerator.
    Remove tenderloin and cook
on the grill over medium-high
heat for 15 minutes on each
side. Baste occasionally. (This
may also be oven-roasted for
30 minutes at 400°F. Be sure
to sear meat in a sauté pan
before baking.)

— PATTY ARTINO

Pork Roast
Yield: 6-8 servings

Pork shoulder roast (about
   6 pounds), boned, rolled
   and tied; reserve bones
1-1/2 tablespoons vegetable oil,
   divided
1 teaspoon salt
1/2 teaspoon pepper
1/4 teaspoon thyme
1/4 teaspoon ground fennel
1/4 teaspoon oregano
All-purpose flour
3/4 cup chicken broth
1 cup apple cider
1/3 cup dry white wine
2 cloves garlic, minced
1/2 teaspoon nutmeg
1 cup sour cream

Rub pork shoulder with 1/2 tablespoon of oil. Mix salt, pepper, thyme, fennel and oregano. Roll meat in seasonings and then in enough flour to coat all sides. Heat remaining tablespoon of oil in a Dutch oven over medium-high heat and brown meat on all sides.

Add chicken broth, cider, wine, garlic and nutmeg to Dutch oven along with the reserved pork bones. Cover, reduce heat, and simmer for approximately 2-1/2 hours.

Remove roast from pan and let rest in a warm oven for 5 to 10 minutes before slicing. Discard pork bones. Thicken gravy with flour and boil for about 2 minutes. Remove from heat and whisk in sour cream. Warm sauce but do not boil.

Slice the meat and arrange on a serving platter. Serve gravy with meat.

— Kitty Unger

SAUTÉED PORK
WITH LEEK AND
ROQUEFORT SAUCE
YIELD: 4-6 SERVINGS

2-1/2 pounds pork tenderloin
3 teaspoons butter, divided
2 teaspoons olive oil, divided
2 medium leeks
1/2 cup chicken broth
1/2 cup dry white wine
1/2 cup crumbled Roquefort
    cheese
Salt and pepper

𑁋 Cut tenderloin on the
diagonal into 1/2-inch pieces.
Pound to 1/8-inch thickness
between sheets of waxed paper.
Heat 1 teaspoon butter and
1 teaspoon oil in a non-stick
skillet over medium-high heat.
Add pork, in two batches, and
cook 2 minutes on each side.
Remove from pan and keep warm.

Cut off and discard 4 inches
of green leek top. Split leeks
lengthwise and chop coarsely.
Cook leeks in 1 teaspoon oil
and 1 teaspoon butter until soft,
about 4 minutes. Add chicken
broth and wine and boil until
liquid has almost evaporated,
about 5 minutes. Remove from
heat and stir in 1 teaspoon butter
and Roquefort cheese. Season
to taste. Pour over pork slices
and serve.

—DIANE RITCHIE

INDONESIAN
MARINATED
PORK LOIN
Cool summer fare.
YIELD: 4 SERVINGS

1-1/2 pounds pork loin, cooked
    and trimmed of all visible fat
2 tablespoons diced onion
2 tablespoons chopped fresh
    cilantro
1 tablespoon light brown sugar
1/4 teaspoon black pepper
1/2 teaspoon minced garlic
1/8 teaspoon red pepper or
    hot pepper sauce
5 tablespoons lemon juice
1/4 cup lite soy sauce

𑁋 Slice cooked pork loin paper
thin and place in a glass dish.

Combine remaining ingre-
dients in a mixing bowl and mix
well. Pour over sliced pork loin.
Cover and refrigerate at least
5 hours or overnight. Serve cold.

—MARY ANN LANG

TWICE-COOKED PORK

YIELD: 4 SERVINGS

1/2 pound boneless pork butt
3 cups water
1 piece (1-1/2-inch) ginger root
3 scallions
2 cloves garlic
1/3 cup vegetable oil
1/2 red pepper, cut in 1-inch cubes
1/2 green pepper, cut in 1-inch
    cubes
1/3 head cabbage, cut in 1-inch
    cubes
8 button mushrooms, sliced
Salt to taste
1-1/2 teaspoons sugar
3 tablespoons hoisin sauce
1/2 teaspoon hot bean paste
    (optional)
Sesame oil

❧ Bring water to a boil in a saucepan large enough to hold pork butt. Add 2 quarter-size slices of ginger, 1 whole scallion and pork. Continue to boil gently 30 minutes, being careful not to overcook pork. Remove from liquid and cut pork across the grain into thin slices.

Dice remaining ginger root, scallions and garlic. Add to oil and set aside.

Heat wok, add 2 tablespoons of flavored oil and stir-fry peppers over high heat 1 to 2 minutes; remove from wok.

Add more oil as needed to wok and stir-fry cabbage, mushrooms, salt and 1 teaspoon sugar. Cook until cabbage softens; remove from wok.

Add remaining seasoned oil to wok. Add pork slices and stir-fry for 2 to 3 minutes. Add all vegetables and mix well. Add hoisin sauce and hot bean paste. Sprinkle with 1/2 teaspoon sugar and stir to coat all vegetables. Sprinkle with sesame oil and serve.

—ROSE WONG
PEARL OF THE ORIENT RESTAURANT
SHAKER HEIGHTS, OHIO

Five Star
ENTRÉES

PORK

SATAY GRILLED PORK
WITH PEANUT BUTTER SAUCE
A delightful hint of Indonesian flavors.
YIELD: 4 SERVINGS

2 pounds pork, cut into
    1-inch cubes

MARINADE
1/2 cup soy sauce
2 cloves garlic, crushed
1/4 teaspoon pepper
2 to 3 tablespoons sugar
2 tablespoons lemon juice

PEANUT BUTTER SAUCE
1 medium onion, finely chopped
2 cloves garlic, crushed
1/2 teaspoon crushed red pepper
3 tablespoons vegetable oil
1 cup peanut butter, smooth or
    crunchy
1 to 1-1/2 cups milk, divided
1 tablespoon lemon juice
1 medium piece dried galingale*
2 leaves daum jeruk purut*
    or 1/2 teaspoon grated
    lemon peel (optional)
Salt and sugar to taste

*Available in Oriental or Indian
specialty stores.*

❦ Combine marinade ingredients and place in a non-metallic bowl. Add pork cubes and refrigerate overnight.

To make Peanut Butter Sauce, fry onion, garlic and pepper in vegetable oil over medium-high heat until onion is limp. Add peanut butter, 1 cup milk, lemon juice, galingale and daum jeruk purut; mix well. Reduce heat and simmer until thickened, stirring constantly. Be careful warming this sauce. If the sauce becomes too thick, stir in the remaining milk. Add salt and sugar to taste. If the heat is too high a skin will form on top. Remove and discard galingale.

Skewer pork and grill over hot coals until golden brown, basting frequently with marinade. Serve with rice and Peanut Butter Sauce.

—MRS. JERRY LOTH

Spicy Honey-Glazed Baby Pork Ribs

Yield: 4-6 servings

2 sides (about 3 pounds) baby pork ribs

MARINADE
1 cup soy sauce
1 cup sake
1 teaspoon ground dried chili flakes
4 tablespoons honey
2 tablespoons minced fresh garlic
2 tablespoons minced fresh ginger
6 tablespoons sesame oil

Mix all the ingredients for the marinade in a bowl. Place the ribs in a container just large enough to hold them, one side on top of the other. Pour the marinade over the ribs, cover with plastic wrap or aluminum foil and let marinate in the refrigerator overnight.

Preheat the oven to 300°F. Place half the marinade in baking pan with ribs. Bake for 2 hours or until the meat is tender, turning ribs frequently. Glaze the ribs under a preheated broiler or on a wood-fired grill for 3 to 4 minutes. Remove the ribs and cut each side into individual pieces.

To serve, arrange the ribs in an overlapping fashion on each plate or on a large serving platter. Spoon the warm marinade over them.

Previously published in *The Wolfgang Puck Cookbook*, Random House, copyright ©1986, by Wolfgang Puck, reprinted with permission.

— CHEF WOLFGANG PUCK

Five Star
ENTRÉES
PORK

Chinois on Main
2709 Main Street
Santa Monica, CA 90405
213-392-9025

Eureka
1845 South Bundy
Los Angeles, CA 90025
213-447-8000

Granita
23725 West Malibu Road
Malibu, CA 90265
213-456-0488

Postrio
545 Post Street
San Francisco, CA 94102
415-776-7825

Spago
8795 Sunset Boulevard
Los Angeles, CA 90069
213-652-3706

Pecan-Crusted Pork Cutlet

Ginger mayonnaise is excellent!

YIELD: 6 SERVINGS

2 pounds boneless pork cutlets
   or sliced pork tenderloin,
   trimmed
All-purpose flour
2 cups bread crumbs
1 cup finely chopped pecans
2 eggs, beaten
Peanut oil for frying
Green onions for garnish

MARINADE
1/3 cup sherry
1/3 cup soy sauce
4 medium green onions, minced
3 tablespoons peeled and
   minced ginger

GINGER MAYONNAISE
Ginger (1-inch piece), peeled
1 large clove garlic
2 egg yolks at room temperature
4 teaspoons cider vinegar
1/4 teaspoon salt
3/4 cup plus 2-1/2 teaspoons
   peanut oil
1-1/2 teaspoons sesame oil
4 drops hot chili oil
1 Italian plum tomato, seeded
   and diced
1 small green onion minced

Pound pork between sheets of waxed paper to 1/4-inch thickness and pat dry.

Combine marinade ingredients and pour over pork. Place in a non-metallic dish and refrigerate at least 2 hours or overnight.

To make Ginger Mayonnaise, mince ginger and garlic in container of food processor. Add egg yolks, vinegar and salt; process until well blended.

Combine oils in a measuring cup. Turn on processor and add the oils through the feed tube in a slow, steady stream. Continue processing for about 1-1/2 minutes or until the sauce is thickened. Transfer to a bowl and add tomatoes and green onion. Cover and refrigerate at least 1 hour.

Drain pork and pat dry. Dredge in flour and shake off excess. Mix bread crumbs and pecans and place in a shallow dish. Dip flour-dredged pork in eggs and then in bread crumb mixture. Arrange cutlets on a platter and refrigerate for at least 30 minutes.

Heat 1 inch of peanut oil in a heavy skillet over medium-high heat. Cook pork in batches, being careful not to crowd, until crisp and brown, about 3 minutes per side. Arrange on a platter and serve with Ginger Mayonnaise and green onion fans for garnish.

To make green onion fans, slice 2 to 3 inches off the bottom of a green onion. Make vertical slits about 1/2 inch deep at both ends and place in cold water. The ends will curl and get crispy.

—LYNNE SMITH

GRILLED VENISON LOIN
MARINATED IN ROASTED GARLIC AND FRESH THYME, SERVED WITH A THAI BARBECUE SAUCE
YIELD: 4 SERVINGS

1 venison loin, approximately
    2 pounds

**ROASTED GARLIC
AND THYME OIL**
1 head of garlic, peeled
1-1/2 cups olive oil
1 bunch fresh thyme, chopped
    or 1 tablespoon dried

THAI BARBECUE SAUCE
1 orange, peeled and chopped
1/2 cup honey
3 tablespoons soy sauce
1 cup tomato paste
2 to 3 scallions, chopped
3 cloves garlic, minced
1 tablespoon chili paste*
3/4 cup hoisin sauce*
1 tablespoon rice wine vinegar*

Available in Oriental food stores.

⁍ Preheat oven to 400°F. Roast garlic in olive oil for about 20 minutes or until garlic is soft. Let cool and add thyme. Marinate venison loin in roasted garlic and thyme oil for at least 3 hours.

Combine all ingredients for Thai Barbecue Sauce and mix well. Set aside.

Grill venison loin over medium-high heat about 3 minutes per pound per side for medium-rare. Top with Thai Barbecue Sauce and place in preheated 400°F oven for 8 to 10 minutes. Let rest 10 minutes before slicing.

—CHEF RALPH DIORIO

Five Star
ENTRÉES

PORK & GAME

Sammy's
1400 West 10th Street
Cleveland, OH 44113
216-523-1177

LATIN AMERICAN CHILI STEW

Works for chicken, beef, pork, venison or rabbit.
The secret's in the sauce.

YIELD: 4-6 SERVINGS

1 roasting chicken, cut in
    serving pieces
    or 2-1/2 pounds meat, cubed
3 tablespoons vegetable oil
2 to 4 dried ancho chilies,
    stemmed and seeded*
4 to 6 cloves garlic
1 whole onion, quartered
1 cup water
1 pound chorizo (the type that
    crumbles)**
1 piece (2 inches) stick cinnamon
3 whole cloves
1 teaspoon dried oregano
2 bay leaves
Salt and pepper to taste
2 cups chicken broth
Fresh coriander for garnish

Ancho chilies are flat, round and dark red. They are spicy rather than hot.

**Available at Latin American markets.*

∾ Brown chicken or meat in oil over high heat and remove to heavy casserole or saucepan.

Place ancho chilies, garlic, onion and water in container of food processor and process until the mixture reaches the consistency of a paste. Add this mixture to the meat.

Remove chorizo from casing (it dissolves as it cooks). Add chorizo, remaining seasonings, chicken broth and enough water to leave 1 inch of meat above surface. Bring to a boil. Reduce heat, cover and simmer until tender, about 45 to 60 minutes for chicken or 2 hours for meat.

Uncover the last 15 to 20 minutes to reduce sauce. Sprinkle with coriander.

Serve with brown rice, flour tortillas and salad.

— MAYNARD THOMSON

MARTHA RAYMOND'S MULLIGATAWNY

Company dinner. Can be made with leftover meats.

YIELD: 6 SERVINGS

2 onions, chopped
1 cup chopped celery
1/4 cup chopped carrots
1 apple, chopped
1 green pepper, chopped
1-1/2 cups (12 ounces) sliced
    mushrooms (optional)
4 tablespoons butter
1/2 cup all-purpose flour
4 cups beef or chicken broth
1/8 teaspoon ground cloves
1/4 teaspoon ground mace
    or nutmeg
1 tablespoon curry powder
1 tablespoon parsley flakes
Salt and freshly ground pepper
    to taste
1 cup canned tomatoes, drained
2-1/2 cups cooked chicken,
    turkey, lamb or beef

∾ Sauté onions, celery, carrots, apple, green pepper and mushrooms in butter until the onion is golden.

Mix in flour, using enough to give the consistency of gravy when the liquid is added. Add broth or stock, seasonings and tomatoes. Simmer 1 hour and add cooked meat.

Serve over cooked rice with chutney on the side.

— ANNE MCERLEAN

GRILLED LAMB CHOPS WITH CHILE CASCABEL

YIELD: 4 SERVINGS

1-1/2 ounces (about 12 medium) dried chiles cascabel, stemmed and seeded or substitute an equal weight of dried chile quajillo, or 1 ounce dried chile chipotle, chile mora or chile morita, stemmed and seeded

1 pound (10 to 12 medium) fresh tomatillos, husked and washed

3 large cloves garlic, unpeeled

2 tablespoons rich-tasting lard, bacon drippings or olive oil

2 cups meat broth, plus a little more if necessary

Salt to taste

12 lamb rib chops
Fresh coriander for garnish

੭☙ Toast the chiles, a few at a time, on a griddle or heavy skillet over medium heat, pressing them flat for a few seconds with a metal spatula, then flipping them over and pressing again. When they send up their aroma and change color, they're ready. Cover with boiling water, weight with a plate to keep them submerged, and soak for 30 minutes. Set aside.

Lay the tomatillos on a baking sheet and roast 6 inches below a preheated broiler, until soft and blackened in spots, 4 to 5 minutes on each side.

Roast the garlic on a griddle or heavy skillet over medium heat, turning occasionally until it is soft and blackened in spots, about 15 minutes. Cool, then slip off the skin.

To make sauce, drain the chiles and place them in a blender jar with the roasted tomatillos and garlic. Blend to a smooth purée, then pass through a medium-mesh strainer. Heat the lard, bacon drippings or oil in a medium-size saucepan over medium-high heat. When hot enough to make a drop of the purée sizzle, add it all at once. Stir constantly until the purée thickens and darkens, about 4 minutes. Add the broth, partially cover and simmer over medium-low heat for about 45 minutes. Season with salt. If the sauce has thickened beyond a light consistency, thin with a little broth.

One-half hour before serving, light a charcoal fire and let burn until the flames die down and the coals are still quite hot. Reheat the sauce in a covered saucepan. Grill the lamb chops for 2 to 4 minutes per side, to desired degree of doneness. Spoon a portion of the sauce onto each of four warm dinner plates. Arrange the grilled chops over the sauce and garnish with sprigs of fresh coriander.

Copyright ©1991, Rick Bayless

— CHEF RICK BAYLESS

Five Star
ENTRÉES
LAMB

Frontera Grill/Topolobampo
445 North Clark Street
Chicago, IL 60610
312-661-1434

RACK OF LAMB PERSILLÉ

YIELD: 4 SERVINGS

2 lamb racks (1-3/4 pounds each),
    trimmed of all but a thin
    layer of fat
Salt and pepper to taste
2 tablespoons chopped shallots
4 cloves garlic, chopped
6 tablespoons butter, softened
1 cup bread crumbs
1/2 teaspoon ground thyme
2 teaspoons chopped parsley
Salt and pepper to taste
2 bunches watercress for garnish

&~ Slice the thin layer of fat
over each rack of lamb so that
it can be lifted. Lift layer and
salt and pepper the lamb.

Combine shallots, garlic,
butter, bread crumbs, thyme,
parsley, salt and pepper and
mix well. Tuck the mixture
under the fat, next to the lamb.
Secure the fat at both ends and
in the middle with skewers.

Bake in 450°F oven for 30
minutes for medium-rare lamb.
Cook longer for well done. To
serve, arrange on a platter and
garnish with watercress.

*Serve with green beans and
broiled tomatoes.*

—CHEF MARTIAL VALENTIN
THE PEPPER PIKE CLUB

LAMB CHOPS À LA MAISON

YIELD: 4 SERVINGS

1/2 ounce (1 tablespoon) butter
12 single lamb chops
2 ounces mushrooms, sliced
1 ounce prosciutto, julienned
1 clove garlic, chopped
4 artichoke hearts, quartered
3 ounces (1/4 cup plus 2 table-
    spoons) white wine
6 ounces (3/4 cup) demi-glace
    or reduced beef stock
1/8 teaspoon oregano
2 teaspoons Dijon-style mustard

&~ Heat butter in a skillet over
medium-high heat. Add lamb
chops and cook both sides to
desired doneness. Remove from
pan.

Add mushrooms, prosciutto,
garlic and artichoke hearts and
cook for 30 seconds; add white
wine and allow it to reduce
by half.

Add demi-glace, oregano and
mustard and simmer for 1 minute.
Return lamb chops to skillet
and coat them with sauce; heat
through. Remove chops to serving
platter and top with remaining
sauce.

*Serve with brown rice and
a green salad.*

—DAVID HAUBERT, SOUS CHEF
KIRTLAND COUNTRY CLUB

*When similar recipes were submitted,
acknowledgement was given to each contributor.*

Lemon Mint Lamb Chops

Yield: 4 servings

8 loin lamb chops
3 tablespoons lemon juice
1/2 teaspoon salt
3 tablespoons olive oil
Handful of fresh mint, chopped
Freshly ground black pepper
    to taste

MINT BUTTER
1/2 cup unsalted butter
2 tablespoons lemon juice
Handful of fresh mint, chopped
Freshly ground black pepper,
    to taste

❧ Marinate lamb chops in lemon juice, salt, olive oil, mint and pepper.

While lamb marinates, prepare mint butter. Combine all ingredients in container of food processor and process until creamed and blended. Remove from processor and form into a cylinder. Wrap in waxed paper and chill until firm.

Broil or pan fry lamb chops 3 to 5 minutes on each side. Remove from heat and top each chop with a slice of mint butter. Serve on individual plates and garnish with fresh mint and lemon slices.

Variation on above—add 5 cloves of garlic, crushed, and 1/2 teaspoon dried or 1 tablespoon fresh rosemary to marinade.

— Molly Bartlett
SILVER CREEK FARM

— Laura Thomson

Five Star
ENTRÉES

LAMB

Butterflied Leg of Lamb Shashlik

Yield: 8 servings

1 leg of lamb (approximately 5 pounds), butterflied

1/2 teaspoon salt
1/2 teaspoon freshly ground black pepper
1 tablespoon minced fresh basil
1 tablespoon minced fresh oregano
1 tablespoon minced fresh parsley
2 cloves garlic, minced
1/4 cup soy sauce
1/2 cup dry red wine
1/4 cup red wine vinegar
1/2 cup extra virgin olive oil

❧ Place lamb in a large shallow pan. Mix ingredients and pour over meat. Marinate meat in refrigerator for 24 hours, turning every 6 hours and basting occasionally. Remove from refrigerator and bring to room temperature before grilling.

Grill over hot coals for approximately 25 minutes, turning once at 12 minutes. Remove from grill and let stand for 10 minutes before carving.

This cooking time is for rare lamb. If you prefer your meat well done, cook longer. Internal temperature for rare lamb is 130°F; for medium lamb 140°F.

—Joyce Neiditz-Snow

Marches Style Lamb

A delicious blend of flavors.

Yield: 6 servings

3 pounds lamb stew meat or ground lamb
1 tablespoon extra virgin olive oil
1 teaspoon chopped garlic
2 teaspoons finely chopped rosemary leaves
1 cup undrained canned tomatoes
1 cup dry white wine
Salt and pepper

❧ Heat a large skillet over medium heat. Sauté the lamb in olive oil. Remove from pan and set aside.

Add garlic to skillet and sauté until softened, about 1 minute. Add rosemary.

Return lamb to skillet; add tomatoes and wine. If using lamb stew meat, cover and simmer for 1 hour; if using ground lamb, simmer uncovered for 20 minutes. Season to taste.

—John Horn

LAMB CURRY

Authentic Indian curry.

YIELD: 4-6 SERVINGS

4 tablespoons vegetable oil
1/2 teaspoon mustard seed
1 large onion, diced
3 teaspoons crushed garlic
1-1/2 tablespoons grated ginger
2 to 3 tablespoons coriander
  powder
1 tablespoon crushed poppy seed
1/4 teaspoon crushed or ground
  cardamom
1-1/2 tablespoons paprika
1/4 teaspoon cumin powder
1/2 teaspoon turmeric
1/2 to 3/4 teaspoon cayenne
  pepper
1/4 teaspoon ground cloves
1 tablespoon curry leaves
  (optional)
1 large bay leaf, cut into
  small pieces
2 to 3 pounds lamb cubes
1/4 to 1/2 cup yogurt
2 to 3 medium-size ripe
  tomatoes, diced
1/2 to 1 cup water
Salt to taste

❧ Heat oil over medium heat. Add mustard seed and heat until cracked. Add onion and cook until browned.

Lower heat, add garlic and ginger and sauté. Add coriander powder, poppy seed, cardamom, paprika, cumin, turmeric, cayenne, ground cloves, curry leaves and bay leaf and stir for 30 seconds to 1 minute.

Add lamb cubes, increase heat and stir meat, mixing well with the seasonings. Stir in yogurt, tomatoes, water and salt, mixing well.

Cover and cook, stirring occasionally, until the meat is tender and gravy is somewhat thick. Remove from heat.

Serve with rice and garnish with chopped coriander leaves or parsley.

— DR. SOSAMMA BERGER

Five Star
ENTRÉES

LAMB

ESTELLE'S TOURTIÈRE

Attractive, aromatic meat pie.

YIELD: 8 SERVINGS

EGGLESS PÂTE BRISÉE
2 cups of flour (combine
  2/3 high protein flour and
  1/3 cake flour)
1-1/2 sticks unsalted butter,
  chilled and cut into
  1/4-inch pieces
1/3 cup ice water

FILLING
1 tablespoon unsalted butter
1 tablespoon vegetable oil
1 medium onion, chopped
1 large clove garlic, minced
1 pound ground meat (veal, pork,
  beef, sausage or mixture)
3 medium potatoes, peeled, diced
  and cooked in boiling water
  until very tender. Drain,
  reserving cooking liquid.
1 teaspoon dried thyme leaves
  or 1 tablespoon fresh thyme
1 teaspoon cinnamon
1 teaspoon ground cloves
Salt and freshly ground pepper
  to taste
Freshly ground nutmeg to taste

EGG WASH
1 whole egg beaten
Salt to taste

To make eggless pâte brisée, place the flour on a work surface and toss with the butter cubes and salt. Quickly work the flour and butter into crumbs with your fingertips. Draw a line down the center of the flour-butter mixture and add water. Toss and work lightly with your fingers again.

Gather the dough into a rough ball. Using the heel of your hand, push down and away from the outer edge of the dough ball, thereby smearing small sections of flour and butter together. Gather together and repeat. Form the dough into a flattened disk and chill for 1 hour before rolling.

To make filling, heat the butter and oil in a heavy sauté pan until they foam. Sauté the onion and garlic over gentle heat until soft and translucent.

Add the ground meat, breaking it into small pieces with a fork as it cooks. Add cooked potatoes, seasonings and enough potato liquid to make a soupy mixture. Cook slowly for a few minutes to develop flavors, adding more potato liquid as it evaporates. Correct seasoning and cool before filling pie crust. Filling should be quite spicy.

Preheat oven to 375°F. To assemble Tourtière, divide the dough in half and roll into two circles, 1/8-inch thick. Fit one pastry round into a deep, 9-inch pie plate. Add the cooled meat filling and top with the second pastry circle. Trim excess pastry, seal the edges and flute. Brush the top with egg wash. Trim pastry scraps to decorate the top as desired and brush decorations with egg wash. Bake on the bottom oven rack for 40 minutes or until golden. Cool and serve slightly warm or at room temperature.

Both pastry and meat filling may be prepared 2 to 3 days in advance; wrap and refrigerate. Both may be frozen with good results for one month. Tourtière is best assembled just prior to baking. Prepare as "pub pies" using large muffin tins, or as hors d'oeuvres using tiny muffin tins.

—HOLLY COLLINS

AMISH POT PIE

Fun to make, fun to eat.

YIELD: 4-6 SERVINGS

1 chicken, cut in pieces
6 to 8 cups water
2 ribs celery
3 parsley sprigs
1 teaspoon salt
1/2 teaspoon pepper
3 carrots, sliced 1/4-inch thick
2 large potatoes, cut in 1-inch
    dice
2 tablespoons snipped
    fresh parsley

DOUGH
1 egg
3 tablespoons heavy cream
1 tablespoon butter, melted
1 teaspoon salt
1-1/2 cups all-purpose flour

❧ Place chicken, water, celery and parsley sprigs in Dutch oven. Add salt and pepper, cover and bring to a boil. Skim off foam, reduce heat and simmer until chicken is tender.

Remove chicken from oven, cool and bone. Strain broth, discarding celery and parsley.

Return chicken and broth to Dutch oven, add carrots and potatoes and simmer gently, 10 to 15 minutes, while preparing dough.

Whisk egg, cream, butter and salt; combine with flour to form a dough.

Knead briefly and roll out so it is very thin; cut into 1-3/4-inch squares. Use a cookie cutter to make different shapes, if you wish. Drop squares into boiling broth, adding slowly to keep at a constant boil. Add snipped parsley, stir, cover and boil approximately 15 minutes. Adjust the seasonings.

Try it with the Lettuce Salad with Roquefort and Beets or Hren Horseradish and Beet Relish (see recipes on pages 89, 126) for color and variety.

—FANNIE KLINE

Five Star
ENTRÉES

MIXED MEATS

TERIYAKI MARINADE
YIELD: 1-1/2 CUPS

1/4 cup soy sauce
1/2 cup red wine
1/2 cup corn oil or combination
     of corn oil and olive oil
2 tablespoons minced candied
     ginger
1 tablespoon curry powder
2 tablespoons ketchup
1/2 teaspoon pepper
2 large cloves garlic, minced

• Add all ingredients to a jar
and shake well.

*Excellent for grilled tenderloin,
chicken or vegetables.*

—DR. JERRY M. SHUCK

STEAK MARINADE
A good all-around marinade.
YIELD: 1 CUP

1/3 cup balsamic vinegar
1/3 cup dark soy sauce or light
     soy sauce plus 1-1/2 table-
     spoons molasses
3 tablespoons sesame oil
1 tablespoon garlic powder or
     2 to 3 cloves garlic, minced
1-1/2 tablespoons five-spice
     powder*
1 teaspoon crushed red pepper
     or more to taste
1 teaspoon coarsely ground
     black pepper

*Available at Asian groceries and
Chinese markets.*

• Mix all marinade ingredients.
Pour over meat and marinate
several hours, turning occasionally. Grill meat, basting with
additional marinade, if desired.

—DR. MICHAEL MAGUIRE

Sauce Espagnole

Rich, brown sauce.

YIELD: 8 CUPS

2 tablespoons butter
1/4 cup all-purpose flour
5 pints (10 cups) beef stock
1/2 cup chopped mushrooms
1 cup diced celery
1 cup diced onion
1 cup diced carrots
2-1/2 pounds crushed tomatoes

෨ Combine butter and flour in a saucepan and cook over medium-high heat to make a brown roux, about 5 minutes. Add beef stock and bring to a boil. Add remaining ingredients, reduce heat and simmer for 4 hours or until sauce is reduced to approximately 8 cups.

Cool. Pass mixture through a sieve or cheesecloth. Store in jars and refrigerate.

This recipe can be used with Veal Scallops with Eggplant and Tomato, see page 173.

—THE COOKBOOK COMMITTEE

RON'S BAR-BEE-QUE SAUCE

Improves with age!

YIELD: 1-1/2 — 2 QUARTS

1/4 cup pickling spices
1 large onion or 1 bunch
    scallions, sliced
1 tablespoon chopped garlic
1/2 cup (1 stick) butter
1/2 cup (1 stick) margarine
1 cup lemonade (4 tablespoons
    of frozen concentrated
    lemonade to 1 cup of water)
1 cup beer
1 cup sugar
1 cup brown sugar
1 cup honey
1 quart apple cider vinegar
1 bottle (14 ounces) ketchup
1 can (12 ounces) tomato paste
1 can (15 ounces) tomato sauce
1 teaspoon salt
1 tablespoon chili powder
1 tablespoon Worcestershire
    sauce
1 tablespoon Italian seasoning
1 teaspoon black pepper
1 teaspoon hot sauce or
    1/2 teaspoon for a
    milder sauce
1 tablespoon red pepper

➥ Place pickling spices in cheesecloth and bind tightly with string. Set aside.

Sauté onions, garlic, butter and margarine in a large, heavy pot. Add remaining ingredients and mix well. Add pickling spices in cheesecloth and simmer for about 2 hours or until the sauce is reduced by one-fourth.

Remove pickling spices. Add additional hot sauce, lemonade and salt to taste. Refrigerate.

— RON JAMES

Black Russian Barbecue Sauce

Cocoa makes the difference.

YIELD: 3 CUPS

4 tablespoons butter
1 medium onion, chopped
2 cloves garlic, minced
2 tablespoons white vinegar
1 cup strong black coffee into
 which 1 teaspoon cocoa
 has been dissolved
1/2 cup beer
1 cup chili sauce
1/4 cup soy sauce
Juice of 1/2 lemon
Grated peel of 1/2 lemon
2 tablespoons Worcestershire
 sauce
2 tablespoons steak sauce
Hot pepper sauce to taste
1 tablespoon dry mustard
1/2 teaspoon celery seed
1/2 teaspoon thyme
1/4 teaspoon turmeric
1/4 teaspoon marjoram
1/4 teaspoon paprika
1/4 teaspoon red pepper
1/4 teaspoon powdered ginger
2 tablespoons horseradish
2 bay leaves
2 teaspoons cornstarch

Melt butter in a saucepan and sauté onion over medium-high heat until tender. Add garlic and sauté for an additional 2 minutes. Add vinegar. Reduce heat and add remaining ingredients. Simmer for at least 1 hour, stirring occasionally. Remove bay leaf and serve or store in refrigerator.

—ANDY KROTINGER

Five Star
ENTRÉES

SAUCES

ROASTED SWEET RED PEPPER SAUCE

*Great pizza topping.
A change from the
usual tomato sauces.*

YIELD: 1-1/2 QUARTS

5 to 6 large red peppers, roasted
1 large red onion, sliced
3 cloves garlic
1-1/4 cups olive oil
1 tablespoon salt
1 teaspoon freshly ground
    black pepper

∾ Roast the red peppers by
cooking them in a hot oven until
browned. Remove from oven
and place in a brown paper
bag; seal to allow peppers to
steam for 20 minutes. Peel and
seed the cooled peppers.

Sauté onions and garlic in
olive oil until the onions are
soft. Remove from pan and cool.

Place peppers, onion, salt
and pepper in container of food
processor and purée. Do **not** add
hot onions into cold peppers.
Be sure all ingredients are at
the same temperature.

— JULIE SHARY
PLAYERS PIZZA
LAKEWOOD, OHIO

CORIANDER CHUTNEY

YIELD: 8 SERVINGS

1 large bunch fresh coriander
Juice of 1 lime
1/4 cup raisins or currants
3 tablespoons chopped green
    onions
2 inches fresh ginger root, peeled
3 garlic cloves, peeled
1 teaspoon salt
1 fresh red or green chili,
    seeds removed
1/4 cup water or more to
    bind mixture

∾ Combine all ingredients
in container of food processor
and blend until almost a purée.
Cover and refrigerate until
ready to serve.

*Excellent with curries and
cold meats.*

— LAURA THOMSON

Salsa Verde Cruda

Fresh green tomatillo sauce.

YIELD: ABOUT 1-1/2 CUPS

8 ounces (5 or 6 medium) fresh
   tomatillos, husked and
   washed or 1 can (13-ounces)
   tomatillos, drained
Fresh hot green chiles to taste
   (roughly 2 chiles serranos or
   1 chile jalapeño), stemmed
5 or 6 sprigs fresh coriander
   (cilantro), roughly chopped
1/2 small onion, chopped
Salt, about 1/2 teaspoon

To prepare, boil fresh tomatillos in salted water to cover until barely tender, 8 to 10 minutes; drain. Canned tomatillos only need to be drained.

To make purée, place the tomatillos in container of blender or food processor. If you want a milder sauce, seed the chile(s), then chop into small bits and add to the tomatillos along with the coriander and chopped onion; if using a blender, stir well. Blend or process to a coarse purée.

To finish the sauce, scrape into a sauce dish, thin to a medium-thick consistency with about 1/4 cup water, then season with salt. Let stand for about 1/2 hour before serving for the flavors to blend.

This sauce is best eaten within 2 hours after preparation because the onion can get strong.

Previously published in *Authentic Mexican*, William Morrow and Co., Inc., copyright ©1987, by Rick Bayless and Deann Groen Bayless, reprinted with permission.

—CHEF RICK BAYLESS

Five Star
ENTRÉES

SAUCES

Frontera Grill/Topolobampo
445 North Clark Street
Chicago, IL 60610
312-661-1434

Five Star
DESSERTS

Marbleized Chocolate Squares

Yield: 16 squares

2 squares (2 ounces) unsweetened
  chocolate
1 square (1 ounce) semisweet
  chocolate
1/3 cup plus 1 tablespoon
  unsalted butter
1/4 teaspoon instant coffee
2 eggs
1 cup sugar
1/2 cup all-purpose flour
2 teaspoons vanilla
1/8 teaspoon salt
1/3 cup chopped walnuts or
  pecans (optional)

&> Preheat oven to 350°F.
Lightly grease a 9 × 9-inch
square pan.

Melt chocolate, butter and
coffee in the top of a double
boiler or in microwave until
smooth. Cool.

Beat eggs with a wire
whisk and add sugar. Add flour,
1 teaspoon vanilla, salt and
nuts to egg mixture. Divide
batter in half. Add melted
chocolate mixture to one half,
and 1 teaspoon vanilla to the
other half.

Pour vanilla batter into
prepared pan. Spoon chocolate
batter over vanilla batter. Swirl
a knife through the batter until
a marbleized pattern emerges.
Do not over-swirl. Bake for
approximately 25 minutes or
until a toothpick inserted in
center comes out clean.

— Hannah Thomson

White Chocolate Brownies

Yield: 25-30 squares

1 cup (2 sticks) unsalted butter
10 ounces white chocolate
  morsels or chunks, broken
  in pieces
1 cup sugar
4 teaspoons vanilla
4 large eggs
2 cups all-purpose flour
1 cup coarsely chopped
  macadamia nuts

&> Preheat oven to 325°F.
Line a 13 × 9 × 2-inch pan with
foil, including sides, and lightly
grease.

Melt butter and chocolate
in microwave or over low heat
until mixture is smooth, stirring
several times. Remove from
heat. Stir in sugar and vanilla.

Beat eggs lightly, add to
chocolate mixture and stir well.
Do not be concerned if mixture
appears curdled. Add flour and
nuts, stirring just to combine.
Pour batter into prepared pan
and bake 30 to 35 minutes or
until pale golden.

Cool completely and lift
out of pan with foil; peel away
foil and cut into squares.

— Helen B. Greenleaf

BOURBON CHOCOLATE PECAN CAKE
YIELD: 10 SERVINGS

1 cup (2 sticks) unsalted butter
8 ounces bittersweet or
    semisweet chocolate
1-1/2 cups sugar
1 cup unsweetened cocoa
6 large eggs
1-1/2 cups coarsely chopped
    toasted pecans
1/3 cup good bourbon

GLAZE
4 ounces bittersweet or
    semisweet chocolate
1/2 cup (1 stick) unsalted butter
1/2 cup coarsely chopped
    toasted pecans

Five Star
DESSERTS
CHOCOLATE

੨᠊ Preheat oven to 350°F. Butter sides and bottom of a 9-inch, round cake pan. Line bottom with a circle of parchment, making sure it lies flat.

To make batter, melt butter and chocolate over simmering water. Stir until very smooth. Set aside to cool.

Mix the sugar, cocoa and eggs just until the egg whites are broken up and ingredients are well combined. (A mixer with paddle attachment is best for the job because it doesn't incorporate air. You may also use a hand whisk or very low speed on a beater-type electric mixer.)

Add the chocolate-butter mixture and mix only until combined. Stir in pecans and bourbon.

Pour batter into prepared cake pan. Place pan inside a larger pan and pour about an inch of hot water into outer pan. Bake until cake is firm to the touch, about 45 minutes. (The surface may crack a little.) Remove from oven and cool on a rack to room temperature. Wrap in plastic wrap and refrigerate overnight.

The following day, place the cake upside down on a wire rack with a sheet of parchment or waxed paper underneath to catch the drips. Remove the parchment circle.

To make glaze, melt chocolate and butter over simmering water. Stir until completely smooth. Cool about 5 minutes.

Drizzle spoonfuls of glaze along edges of cake so that it drips down and coats the sides. When sides are covered, spoon the rest of glaze on top of cake and smooth it with a spatula.

Cover sides of the cake with pecans, pressing them gently against the glaze with your open palm. Refrigerate until 30 minutes before serving.

Also published in *Baking with Jim Dodge*, published by Simon and Schuster, © 1991.

—CHEF JIM DODGE
SAN FRANCISCO, CALIFORNIA

GERMAN CHOCOLATE PIE

YIELD: 8 SERVINGS

1 package (4 ounces) German
  chocolate
1/4 cup margarine
1-2/3 cups evaporated milk
1-1/2 cups sugar
3 tablespoons cornstarch
1/8 teaspoon salt
2 eggs
1 teaspoon vanilla
1 unbaked 9-inch pie shell
1-1/3 cups flaked coconut
1/2 cup chopped pecans

☙ Preheat oven to 350°F.
  Melt chocolate and margarine over low heat. Remove from heat and gradually blend in milk.
  Mix sugar, cornstarch and salt in medium bowl. Beat in eggs and vanilla. Gradually blend in chocolate mixture.
  Pour into pie shell. Combine coconut and nuts and sprinkle over chocolate filling. Bake 40 minutes. Cover with foil and bake an additional 15 to 20 minutes. Serve warm.

— LINDA MILLER

ANITA'S SURPRISE CHOCOLATE CAKE

Dense, dark and delicious.

YIELD: 16 SERVINGS

FILLING
1/4 cup sugar
1 teaspoon vanilla
8 ounces cream cheese, softened
1 egg
1/2 cup shredded coconut
6 ounces chocolate morsels

CAKE
2 cups sugar
1 cup corn oil
2 eggs
2 teaspoons baking powder
2 teaspoons baking soda
2 cups all-purpose flour
3/4 cup unsweetened cocoa
2 teaspoons salt
1 teaspoon vanilla
1 cup buttermilk
1 cup strong coffee
1/2 cup chopped walnuts

GLAZE
1 cup confectioners sugar
3 tablespoons unsweetened
  cocoa
2 tablespoons butter, softened
2 teaspoons vanilla
1 to 3 tablespoons hot water

☙ Preheat oven to 350°F. Grease and lightly flour a bundt or tube pan.
  To prepare filling, beat sugar, vanilla, cream cheese and egg until smooth. Stir in coconut and chocolate morsels. Set aside.
  To prepare cake, beat sugar, oil and eggs at high speed for 1 minute. Add remaining cake ingredients, except nuts, and continue beating at medium speed for 3 minutes. Stir in nuts. Batter will be thin.
  Pour two-thirds of the batter into prepared pan. Spoon the filling mixture over the batter, being careful to keep it away from the walls of the pan.
  Pour remaining batter over filling and bake for 55 minutes. Turn oven temperature down to 325°F and continue baking an additional 15 minutes.
  Cool in pan, upright, for approximately 30 to 45 minutes. Remove from pan and cool on a wire rack.
  To prepare glaze, stir all ingredients to blend and beat at high speed for 1 minute. Drizzle over cake and serve.
  Cake can also be frosted. Prepare frosting by doubling the glaze ingredients and using 2 to 3 tablespoons hot water.

— DR. LINDA W. SHUCK

TRUFFLES
YIELD: 208 TRUFFLES

GANACHE CREAM
4 pounds, 4 ounces dark
chocolate
4 cups (1 quart) heavy cream
1/2 cup sugar
1/2 cup (1 stick) butter

TEMPERED CHOCOLATE
12 ounces dark chocolate

&✒ Option: To make a variety of flavored truffles, add 1 to 1-1/2 ounces of liqueur and an additional 2 ounces of melted chocolate to every 1 pound of Ganache Cream. Please note that this recipe makes approximately 7 pounds Ganache Cream.

Chop chocolate, place in a large bowl and set aside. Rinse a large copper or stainless steel pot with cold water and drain. (This forms a water seal which prevents the cream from burning.) Combine cream, sugar and butter in pot and bring to a good rolling boil. Continue boiling for 1 to 2 minutes.

Remove from heat and add chopped chocolate. Stir with a spoon or wooden paddle. Do **not** whisk, as you will incorporate air which can reduce the shelf life of the truffle. Stir until smooth and strain if necessary. Liqueur and additional chocolate may be added at this time.

Place saran wrap directly on top of the Ganache Cream so that no crust forms and refrigerate, preferably overnight.

When ready to make truffles, place Ganache Cream in a pastry bag and pipe approximately 1/2 ounce for each truffle onto parchment or waxed paper. Let set up.

To temper chocolate, heat 8 ounces of chocolate to 120°F over a steaming water bath. Add finely shaved or chopped chocolate until mixture is reduced to a temperature of 90°F.

Roll each piped truffle into a ball, then hand roll each truffle with tempered chocolate to apply a thin coating. Let set up. (The coating may crack since you are combining hot and cold ingredients.) Repeat the process, adding a final coating to the truffle.

TIPS FOR WORKING WITH CHOCOLATE

All manufacturers' brands have different formulations, depending upon the quality and blend of cocoa beans used, the amount of cocoa, butter, sugar, etc.

MELTING CHOCOLATE

Moisture and direct and excessive heat can affect chocolate and cause denaturing, which is a seizing or thickening.

Chocolate has to reach 115°F so that all crystals melt and compounds of cocoa butter equalize. Chocolate should never be heated above 120°F because when too warm, it becomes grainy.

- Never melt chocolate over direct heat.
- Chocolate may be melted over a water bath that is 120°F.
- To speed up the melting process, chop the chocolate into small pieces to allow more surface area.
- Stir frequently, bringing back to 90°F.

—CHEF ALBERT KUMIN

Vie de France Bakery Yamazaki, Inc.
International Pastry Arts Center
525 Executive Boulevard
Elmsford, NY 10523
914-347-3737

This recipe is featured on the color cover of the Desserts section tab.

ÉCLAIRS

YIELD: 12 SERVINGS

CREAM PUFFS
1 cup water
1/2 cup (1 stick) sweet butter
1/8 teaspoon salt
1 cup all-purpose flour
4 large eggs

CUSTARD FILLING
1/2 cup sugar
2 tablespoons cornstarch
1 tablespoon all-purpose flour
1/8 teaspoon salt
3 large egg yolks
1 cup heavy cream
1 cup milk
1 teaspoon vanilla

MOCHA FROSTING
4 tablespoons butter
2 teaspoons instant espresso
  coffee powder
1 cup confectioners sugar
2 tablespoons heavy cream

CHOCOLATE FROSTING
1 cup confectioners sugar
1/3 cup Dutch cocoa
1 tablespoon butter, melted
1 teaspoon vanilla
3 to 4 tablespoons boiling water

Preheat oven to 400°F.

To make cream puffs, place water, butter and salt in a 1-quart saucepan and bring to a boil. Remove from heat and stir in flour. Beat with a wooden spoon. Return to stove and continue cooking over moderate heat until dough forms a stiff ball and leaves the sides of the pan. Remove from heat and beat in eggs, one at a time, until shiny. Do not overbeat.

Squeeze dough from pastry bag into 4-inch lengths spaced 2 inches apart on ungreased baking sheet and bake 30 minutes or until golden. Prick the puffs with a knife to allow steam to escape. Turn off heat and leave in oven 10 to 15 minutes to dry out centers.

To make custard filling, combine sugar, cornstarch, flour and salt in top of double boiler. Beat in egg yolks and 1/4 cup cream. Cook over moderate heat. Heat remaining cream and milk in a small saucepan, being careful not to boil; add to cream-sugar-egg mixture and stir over hot (not boiling) water until custard is very thick. Remove from heat and add vanilla. Cool and cover top of custard with plastic wrap to prevent skin from forming. Refrigerate.

To make mocha frosting, melt butter in small saucepan. Add espresso and sugar, stirring with a wire whisk. Add cream and continue to whisk.

To make chocolate frosting, combine sugar, cocoa, butter and vanilla. Stir in boiling water. Cool until thickened.

To serve, split cream puffs, fill with custard and spoon desired frosting over them.

—JOAN FOUNTAIN

Chocolate Crème Brûlée

Yield: 8 servings

CRÈME BRÛLÉE
1/2 cup milk
2 cups heavy cream
1/2 cup sugar
2 vanilla beans, cut in half
    lengthwise
8 egg yolks

CHOCOLATE MOUSSE
5 ounces semisweet chocolate,
    coarsely chopped
1/2 cup (1 stick) cold unsalted
    butter, cut in pieces
5 eggs, separated
Pinch of salt
1/4 cup sugar
1/2 cup granulated brown
    sugar, sifted

❧ Preheat oven to 300°F.

To prepare the Crème Brûlée, place the milk, cream, sugar and vanilla beans in a saucepan. Heat until the mixture comes to a boil. Remove from heat and set aside to infuse for 30 minutes.

Remove the vanilla beans and scrape out the soft interior into the cream mixture. Add the egg yolks and whisk until well combined. Strain and divide equally among eight (8 ounces each) quiche dishes.

Place dishes in a water bath and bake until an inserted knife comes out clean, about 1 to 1-1/2 hours. Remove from water bath and cool.

To prepare the Chocolate Mousse, place chocolate in a heavy-bottomed saucepan over low heat. When chocolate is just melted, add butter and stir with a wooden spoon until butter is melted. Remove from the heat and stir in the egg yolks, one at a time.

Beat the egg whites with the salt until soft peaks start to form. Sprinkle in the sugar and continue beating until stiff but not dry. Carefully fold in the chocolate. Divide the mousse equally among the quiche dishes, smoothing it evenly over the Crème Brûlée with a spatula. Cover dishes with plastic wrap and chill until set.

To serve, preheat the broiler. Sprinkle the brown sugar evenly over the chocolate mousse. Caramelize the sugar by melting with a propane torch or in a salamander until golden-brown. Watch carefully as it burns easily.

Unfortunately, home broilers are generally not hot enough to have good results. It takes longer to caramelize the sugar, which melts the chocolate mousse.

Copyright ©1991, Michel Richard.

— Chef Michel Richard

Citrus
6703 Melrose Avenue
Los Angeles, CA 90038
213-857-0034

MOCHA RUM MOUSSE
YIELD: 6-12 SERVINGS

1 package (6 ounces)
    semisweet chocolate morsels
5 tablespoons hot coffee
4 eggs, separated
1/4 cup rum
1/8 teaspoon cinnamon

☞ Place chocolate morsels, hot coffee, egg yolks, rum and cinnamon in blender or container of food processor and process on high for 1 minute. Refrigerate 1 hour.

Beat egg whites until stiff; carefully fold into chocolate mixture. Refrigerate until firm (at least 1 hour).

Transfer to 6 serving dishes or 12 demitasse cups.

—SHIRLEY SHAPERO

HELGA STANG'S DAISY COOKIES
OR CHOCOLATE SPRITZ
YIELD: 36-50 COOKIES

DOUGH
2 cups all-purpose flour
2/3 cup sugar
1 or 2 packages (9 grams each)
    vanilla sugar or 2 to
    4 teaspoons homemade
    vanilla sugar*
1/8 teaspoon salt
1 egg yolk
1 cup cold unsalted butter, cut
    into 1/8-inch bits
Place cracked vanilla bean in sugar in closed container for several days.

☞ Preheat oven to 325°F. Generously grease baking sheets. Sift flour into large bowl. Add sugar, vanilla sugar and salt.

Make a well in center of ingredients and drop in the egg yolk. Add butter bits and quickly knead all ingredients into a smooth dough.

To make Daisy Cookies, turn dough out on lightly floured surface. Divide dough into thirds and roll each into a sheet approximately 1/8-inch thick. Using a 2- or 3-inch daisy-shaped cutter, cut sheet into daisies. Transfer to prepared cookie sheets, leaving a 1-inch space between cookies.

Bake 15 to 20 minutes or until light golden brown. Place one chocolate disc in the center of each daisy. Transfer to cake rack to cool.

Squeeze dots of melted white chocolate through pastry tube on each dark chocolate disc.

**DECORATION FOR
DAISY COOKIES**
(Decorates 1 recipe of dough)
8 ounces semisweet or milk
    chocolate discs or chocolate
    nonpareils
10 white chocolate discs,
    melted (available in candy
    supply stores)

**DECORATION FOR
CHOCOLATE SPRITZ**
(Decorates 1 recipe of dough)
4 ounces semisweet chocolate,
    melted with 4 ounces milk
    chocolate
1/2 cup blanched almonds,
    toasted at 300°F for 15 to
    20 minutes and finely grated
    (may use food processor)

To make Chocolate Spritz, roll the dough into 3-inch long ropes about 1/4–1/2-inch thick. Transfer to prepared cookie sheets and shape each rope into an "S." Using the tines of a fork, ridge and flatten the "S" into 1/8–1/4-inch thickness. Bake 15 to 20 minutes or until light golden brown. Cool on cake rack. Coat both ends of the "S" with melted chocolate. Sprinkle finely grated almonds over soft chocolate and allow to harden.

These can be stored in airtight containers between layers of waxed paper at a cool room temperature for several weeks.

—HELGA STANG
COOKBOOK AUTHOR AND
PASTRY CHEF

SACHERTORTE

A Viennese classic for chocolate lovers.

YIELD: 10 SERVINGS

8 ounces semisweet chocolate
1 cup (2 sticks) unsalted butter, softened
3/4 teaspoon salt
2 teaspoons vanilla
1 cup sugar
2 cups very finely ground walnuts
1/3 cup all-purpose flour
8 eggs, separated
2/3 cup strained apricot jam

ICING
1/2 cup heavy cream
2 teaspoons instant coffee
6 ounces semisweet chocolate
Whipped cream for garnish

🐦 Preheat oven to 350°F. Butter and flour a 9-inch spring-form pan and line the bottom with parchment paper.

Melt chocolate and let cool. Cream butter with the salt, vanilla and sugar. Toss together the walnuts and flour. Add egg yolks, one by one, to the butter-sugar mixture. Stir in the chocolate and flour-nut mixture.

Beat the egg whites to soft peaks and stir one-third of the whites into the chocolate-flour-nut mixture to lighten the batter. Fold in the remaining whites.

Pour the batter into the prepared pan and bake 1 hour. Let cool in the pan for 20 minutes and then push down the puffed-up sides so that they are flush with the middle. Remove sides of the pan and invert the cake on a rack set over waxed paper. Cool completely.

Heat the apricot jam and brush over the top and sides of the cooled cake. Let glaze set at least 1/2 hour before icing the cake.

To ice the cake, scald the cream in a small saucepan. Whisk in the coffee and add the chocolate. Stir 1 minute over the heat, then remove and continue to stir until the chocolate has completely melted. Pour over cake and spread evenly with a spatula. Chill the cake on its rack until the icing is completely set. Bring to room temperature before serving.

A pretty garnish would be candied violets around the perimeter or sprigs of fresh holly. Don't forget to serve a bowl of whipped cream to pass with Sachertorte.

— KATHY FLEEGLER

CHOCOLATE TOWER

YIELD: 8 SERVINGS

CHOCOLATE MOUSSE
5-1/2 ounces dark chocolate
3 tablespoons unsalted butter
1/4 cup heavy cream
10 egg whites, at room
    temperature
4 tablespoons superfine sugar
Parchment paper
2 ounces dark chocolate, melted
5 ounces white chocolate, melted

ESPRESSO SAUCE
1 cup half and half
1/2 vanilla bean
12 espresso beans
4 egg yolks
3-1/2 tablespoons sugar

GARNISH
3 tablespoons vanilla sauce
16 slices fresh figs
8 strawberry fans
12 blackberries, halved
2 cups raspberries
8 mint sprigs

❧ For the mousse, slowly melt the dark chocolate and the butter in a double boiler, stirring occasionally to blend. Whip the cream until stiff and set it aside. In a stainless steel mixing bowl whip the egg whites with the sugar until stiff peaks form. In a steady stream, fold the melted chocolate and butter mixture into the stiff egg whites, scraping the bottom of the bowl until the chocolate is fully incorporated into the whites. Fold the whipped cream into the chocolate-egg mixture and keep the mousse well chilled.

Cut 8 parchment paper strips, 3-1/2 inches high and 5 inches wide. Roll the strips into tubes fastened with tape, stand them up and fill them, using a pastry bag, with the chocolate mousse. Place them in the freezer, for 3 to 4 hours, until frozen, and carefully unwrap each one. Cut 8 parchment paper strips, 5 inches high and 5 inches wide. With the melted dark chocolate, drizzle a crisscrossed pattern on these paper strips, allowing the chocolate to set up slightly. Carefully pour the melted white chocolate over the crisscrossed pattern of the dark, but only over a 3-1/2-inch by 5-inch area, which will allow for the basket effect on the top of the chocolate tower. Lay each frozen mousse onto a chocolate-coated strip, and wrap it around the chocolate mousse cylinder while it is still pliable. Refrigerate and remove the paper after 5 minutes. Keep in refrigerator for a minimum of 6 hours to soften the frozen

mousse before serving.

For the sauce, bring the half and half, with the vanilla and the espresso beans, to a simmer. In a stainless steel bowl, mix the egg yolks and the sugar. Temper the egg yolk and sugar mixture by adding 1/4 of the scalded half and half; stir well, pour in the remaining half and half, and cook gently over a double boiler, stirring constantly. When the sauce is thick enough to coat the back of a spoon, strain out the beans and let cool.

To serve, rim the inside edge of each plate with a line of vanilla sauce covered with drops of the espresso sauce, bringing the tip of a small knife through each drop to create the heart-shaped pattern. Stand each of the chocolate towers up in the center of a plate; garnish the plates with the fresh figs and berries. Fill the basket top of the towers with raspberries and finish them with a sprig of mint.

Previously published in *Art Culinaire*, Culinaire, Inc., copyright ©1991, by Franz Mitterer, reprinted with permission.

— CHEF CHRISTOPHER GROSS

Christopher's and Christopher's Bistro
2398 East Camelback Road #220
Phoenix, AZ 85016
602-957-3214

RASPBERRY AND PISTACHIO PHYLLO BON BONS

YIELD: 4 SERVINGS

2 cups milk
1/2 cup sugar
3 tablespoons cornstarch
4 egg yolks
1/4 cup pistachio paste
8 sheets phyllo dough
1/2 cup (1 stick) sweet butter,
    melted and cooled
1 cup fresh raspberries

Five Star
DESSERTS
CHOCOLATE & FRUIT

❧ To make pastry cream, heat the milk to a simmer. Mix the sugar and cornstarch, add the yolks and mix until smooth. Slowly add 1/2 cup hot milk to the sugar-yolk mixture. Whisk until smooth; pour the yolk mixture into the milk and bring to a boil, whisking constantly. Cool and add the pistachio paste.

To assemble, lay a sheet of phyllo on a dry surface and **lightly** brush with the melted butter. Repeat with 3 more sheets. Repeat entire process with remaining 4 sheets of phyllo dough. Cut the sheets in quarters and place 1-1/2 tablespoons of the pastry cream in the center. Top with a few berries. Crimp like a bon bon. Make all 8 pieces. Brush with butter and bake at 375°F for 8 to 10 minutes.

Serve immediately with choice of ice cream.

— CHEF GARY COYLE

The Rittenhouse Hotel
210 West Rittenhouse Square
Philadelphia, PA 19103
215-546-9000

PINEAPPLE ZIP

Light and refreshing.

YIELD: 4 SERVINGS

2 cups diced fresh pineapple
1/2 cup orange juice
2 tablespoons maraschino
     cherry syrup
1/4 cup confectioners sugar
1/8 teaspoon cinnamon

🦢 Combine all ingredients.
Cover and chill thoroughly.

— NEL BUCKLEY

FRESH FRUIT TORTE

An easy summer dessert.

YIELD: 8 SERVINGS

1/2 cup (1 stick) butter, softened
1 cup sugar
2 eggs
1 cup all-purpose flour
1 teaspoon baking powder
1 teaspoon vanilla
1-1/2 cups blueberries, sliced
     peaches, strawberries or
     any summer fruit
3 tablespoons sugar
1 tablespoon cinnamon
1/2 tablespoon grated lemon rind

🦢 Preheat oven to 350°F.
Cream butter and sugar and
beat in eggs. Add flour and
baking powder and beat
quickly. Add vanilla and mix
well. Pour into a 9-inch round
cake or springform pan. Cover
the top with fruit.

Mix sugar, cinnamon and
lemon peel and sprinkle over
torte. Bake for approximately
30 minutes or until crust is
lightly browned.

*Serve with French vanilla ice
cream or crème fraîche.*

— CAMILLE LaBARRE

ORANGE TARTS

YIELD: 10 SERVINGS

PASTRY
1 cup all-purpose flour
1/8 teaspoon salt
4 tablespoons unsalted butter
1-1/2 tablespoons solid
     vegetable shortening
3 tablespoons iced water

ORANGE FILLING
2 oranges
1 lemon
3/4 cup sugar
1/3 cup butter, melted
1 heaping teaspoon cornstarch
1/2 cup water

🦢 Preheat oven to 375°F.
Butter one muffin tin.

Sift flour and salt into a
bowl. Cut in butter and shortening until mixture is texture
of coarse crumbs.

Add only enough water to
make a soft dough. Form into
ball, wrap in waxed paper and
chill 1 hour.

Divide dough into 10 por-
tions, roll into squares and place
gently in prepared muffin tin.

To make filling, squeeze
oranges and lemon. Grate rind
of oranges and combine with
juices, sugar, butter and cornstarch dissolved in water.

Fill tarts half full and bake
about 40 minutes, until filling
is delicately congealed but not
stiff. Crust should be pale and
puffy. Watch carefully and
reduce heat if cooking too fast.
Cool before serving.

— MRS. CHILTON THOMSON
  ORANGE FILLING
— ROMA POLLOCK TURNBOW
  PASTRY

*When similar recipes were submitted,
acknowledgement was given to each contributor.*

Pear Tart

Yield: 8-10 servings

2 sheets frozen puff pastry,
    thawed
1 egg white, lightly beaten
1-1/2 cups raspberry jam
3 tablespoons butter or
    margarine
2 tablespoons Chambord or
    raspberry liqueur
3 firm Bosc pears
1/4 cup sugar
1/2 pint fresh raspberries
Fresh mint leaves for garnish

➣ Preheat oven to 425°F.

Roll pastry into two 11-inch rounds on a chilled, floured surface. Lift one round onto a flat baking sheet. From the second round, cut a 1-inch wide ring to form a rim for the tart. Brush part of the egg white on a 1-inch band of the outer edge of the pastry round on the baking sheet, being careful not to drip over the edges. Place pastry ring on top and put in freezer 15 minutes.

Melt jam and butter over medium heat. Add the Chambord and cook until the liqueur boils off.

Peel, core and brush pears with lemon juice. Slice pears lengthwise from top to bottom to keep pear shape. Arrange in a spiral on tart shell, coating each layer with jam mixture and sprinkling with sugar. Leave 1/4-inch between fruit and shell. Brush exposed pastry with egg white.

Bake 10 minutes. Reduce heat to 375°F and bake for 20 more minutes.

Cool on a rack and remove tart to serving dish. Garnish with fresh raspberries and mint leaves.

This dessert may be prepared several hours ahead and kept at room temperature.

—Joan Kekst

Five Star
DESERTS

FRUIT

LEMON ANGEL PIE

YIELD: 10-12 SERVINGS

CRUST
1 cup sugar
1/4 teaspoon cream of tartar
4 egg whites

FILLING
8 egg yolks
1 cup sugar
2 tablespoons (about 4 lemons)
   grated lemon peel
6 tablespoons fresh lemon juice
1/4 teaspoon salt
4 cups heavy cream
Confectioners sugar

๛ Preheat oven to 275°F. Generously grease a 9-inch pie plate. Sift sugar with cream of tartar.

Beat egg whites at medium speed until stiff, but not dry. Slowly add sugar mixture and beat until smooth and glossy. Spread meringue over bottom and up sides of prepared pie plate, about 1/4-inch thick on bottom and 1-inch thick on sides. Bake for 1 hour or until light brown and crisp. Cool.

Heat egg yolks in top of double boiler. Stir in sugar, lemon peel, lemon juice and salt. Cook over boiling water, stirring until thickened, about 8 to 10 minutes. Cool.

Whip 2 cups of cream and fold into cooled lemon mixture. Pour into center of meringue shell, making sure all pockets are filled and smooth on top. Refrigerate 12 hours or overnight.

Beat remaining 2 cups cream with confectioners sugar to taste. To serve, top with sweetened whipped cream and garnish with fresh strawberries.

—DOLORES SINGER

Lemon Meringue Tarts

Yield: 8 servings

**SUGAR DOUGH TARTS
WITH GROUND ALMONDS**
1/2 cup (1 stick) butter
1/3 cup sugar
1 egg
1 egg yolk
2-1/2 cups flour
1/4 cup almond meal, sifted
1/8 teaspoon salt

LEMON MERINGUE
2/3 cup strained lemon juice
8 eggs, separated, whites at
    room temperature
1-3/4 cups sugar
5 tablespoons butter

૎ To make tarts, beat the butter and sugar until it lightens in color and becomes creamy. Add egg and egg yolk to the butter-sugar mixture, beating well.

Combine flour, almond meal and salt. Add one-quarter of this into the butter mixture, stirring well. Add the remaining flour mixture and stir just until blended. Refrigerate overnight before use.

To prepare lemon meringue, whisk the lemon juice, egg yolks and 3/4 cup of the sugar in the top of a double boiler. Cook until the mixture is warm.

Add the butter and continue whisking until the mixture thickens and resembles a thick hollandaise sauce, about 4 to 5 minutes. Refrigerate until cooled.

Preheat oven to 350°F. Divide tart dough into 8 portions and roll into circles. Place into 4 × 3/4-inch pastry rings or tart pans, gently pressing down. Bake for approximately 10 minutes until golden brown. Cool completely.

Fill each baked tart with 1/4 cup of the cooled lemon mixture; smooth with a spatula.

Place egg whites in bowl of electric mixer; beat until soft peaks form. With the mixer running, slowly add the remaining 1 cup sugar. Continue beating until stiff peaks form.

Spread the meringue over the lemon-filled tarts with a spatula, mounding in the center. Touch the meringue quickly and lightly several times to form peaks.

Place tarts under preheated broiler and broil until browned.

Copyright ©1991, Michel Richard.

— Chef Michel Richard

Five Star
DESERTS
FRUIT

Citrus
6703 Melrose Avenue
Los Angeles, CA 90038
213-857-0034

HALLE BROS. CO. TEAROOM FRUIT DRESSING

A Cleveland favorite.

YIELD: 2-1/2 CUPS

1 cup pineapple juice
1/4 cup lemon juice
3 eggs, beaten
1-1/2 cups sugar
1 cup heavy cream

❧ Mix fruit juices, eggs and sugar and place in the top of a double boiler. Cook until thickened. Strain through a sieve and cool in refrigerator.

Whip cream and fold into cooled mixture.

Light, flavorful complement for fresh fruit.

— PAT DeFABIO-SHIMRAK

STRAWBERRIES CARDINAL

YIELD: 4-6 SERVINGS

2 pints fresh strawberries
1 pint fresh red raspberries
1/4 cup sugar
1/2 cup water
Toasted almonds
Fresh mint

❧ Wash, hull and slice strawberries and place in champagne glasses.

Combine red raspberries, sugar and water in a small, heavy saucepan. Bring to a boil and simmer for 15 minutes.

Strain raspberry mixture through fine sieve. Return to heat and let raspberry mixture reduce and thicken until it coats the back of a spoon. Cool.

Pour raspberry mixture over strawberries and garnish with toasted almonds and mint sprigs.

—TOM PEPKA

LINDA AND FRED GRIFFITH'S SUMMER CHERRY FOOL

YIELD: 6 SERVINGS

3 cups puréed pitted cherries
  (about 6 cups before pitting)
1 cup heavy cream
2/3 cup sour cream
1/4 cup firmly packed light
  brown sugar
Zest of 1 lemon, finely minced
1/4 teaspoon freshly grated
  nutmeg
1/3 cup sweetened whipped
  cream
Whole cherries with stems
Mint leaves
1/2 cup toasted and chopped
  pecans

❧ Blend the fruit, creams, sugar, lemon zest and nutmeg thoroughly. Spoon mixture into serving bowls or parfait glasses. Chill for several hours.

To serve, put a dollop of whipped cream on top of each serving. Place a cherry and mint leaf on the cream. Sprinkle with nuts.

This can be made in the morning, but don't let it sit more than the day and don't freeze it.

—LINDA AND FRED GRIFFITH
COOKBOOK AUTHORS

MOTHER'S BIRTHDAY TORTE
A real beauty!
YIELD: 8-10 SERVINGS

9 egg whites
3/4 teaspoon cream of tartar
1/8 teaspoon salt
3 cups sugar
2-1/2 teaspoons vanilla
1-1/2 teaspoons white vinegar
4 cups (2 pints) heavy cream
1 pint strawberries

❧ Preheat oven to 325°F. Lightly grease two 9-inch cake pans with cutters or line pan with parchment paper.

Beat egg whites, cream of tartar and salt until very stiff. Slowly add sugar, 1-1/2 teaspoons vanilla and vinegar and continue beating. Divide batter into cake pans. Bake for 60 minutes. Let cool in pans for 5 minutes; remove and cool completely.

(To avoid crystallizing, leave meringue in cool oven for 2 to 3 hours after baking.)

To assemble torte, whip cream and 1 teaspoon vanilla. Slice one-third of the strawberries. Place one cooled meringue on a serving plate, trimming, if necessary, to fit. Cover with about 1-1/2 cups whipped cream and sliced strawberries. Invert second meringue, place on top of first and trim. Ice the top and sides with the remaining whipped cream, arrange whole strawberries on top and refrigerate.

This torte can be made with any seasonal fruit.

—MRS. HOWARD P. STEVENS

Five Star
DESKERTS
DESSERTS
FRUIT

223

APPLE CREAM PIE
YIELD: 6-8 SERVINGS

1 unbaked 9-inch pie shell
4 large, firm, red cooking apples
2 tablespoons lemon juice
1 cup brown sugar
3 tablespoons all-purpose flour
1/2 teaspoon cinnamon
1 cup heavy cream

❧ Preheat oven to 350°F. Fit one 9-inch, unbaked pie shell into a quiche pan. Set aside.

Peel and slice apples. Place in a bowl and coat with lemon juice. Mix brown sugar, flour and cinnamon in a small bowl. Drain lemon juice from apples and place them, rounded side up, in the pie shell. Sprinkle the apples with 3/4 cup of brown-sugar mixture.

Pour cream over pie and sprinkle with the remaining sugar mixture. Bake for 60 to 75 minutes or until crust is nicely browned. Remove from oven and allow to stand for at least 30 minutes. Serve warm.

—GAIL RESCH

FRESH PEACH SOUR CREAM PIE
YIELD: 6-8 SERVINGS

1 unbaked 9-inch pie shell
1/2 cup sugar
1/2 cup brown sugar
1/4 cup all-purpose flour
1 cup sour cream
5 to 6 fresh medium peaches, peeled and halved

❧ Preheat oven to 350°F.

Combine sugars, flour and sour cream. Mix until smooth and well blended.

Place peaches, cut-side down, in unbaked pie shell. Pour sugar mixture over fruit, lifting peaches if necessary to allow sugar mixture to spread everywhere. Bake for approximately 30 to 40 minutes until peaches are tender.

Cool before serving; refrigerate leftovers.

—PAMELA LaMANTIA

SUMMER FRUIT PLATTER PIE
Beautiful presentation.
YIELD: 8-10 SERVINGS

Pastry for double-crust
    9-inch pie
2/3 cup shredded Cheddar
    cheese
1 cup sugar
1/4 teaspoon salt
2 tablespoons cornstarch
1 cup orange juice
1/4 cup lemon juice
2/3 cup water
1/2 teaspoon grated orange peel
1/2 teaspoon grated lemon peel
1 pint fresh strawberries, halved,
    reserving 7 whole berries
3 fresh peaches, peeled
    and sliced
1-1/2 cups seedless green grapes
1 medium banana, cut into
    1/8-inch slices
Whipped cream for garnish

Preheat oven to 475°F. Prepare your favorite pastry recipe as directed, except before adding water, stir the shredded cheese into the flour mixture. Roll dough 1-inch larger than a 14-inch pizza pan (or pastry can be baked on a baking sheet). Ease the dough into the pan; flute edges. Prick bottom and sides. Bake approximately 8 minutes. Cool.

Stir sugar, salt and cornstarch in a small pan. Gradually add orange and lemon juices and water. Cook over medium heat, stirring constantly until mixture thickens and boils for 1 minute. Remove from heat and stir in orange and lemon peels. Cool.

Arrange strawberry halves around edge of pastry shell. Place peaches in a circle next to strawberries. Mound grapes in a circle next to the peaches, then arrange a circle of overlapping banana slices. Place whole berries in the center. Spoon sauce over the fruit and cut the pie into wedges.

Garnish with whipped cream and remaining sauce.

— KITTY GILLUND

Five Star
DESKTOP
DESSERTS

FRUIT

APPLES AU VIN

YIELD: 6-9 SERVINGS

6 large Granny Smith or other
  tart apples
1 cup plus 2 tablespoons light
  brown sugar
2 tablespoons fresh lemon juice
1 tablespoon lemon rind
1 cup dry red wine
1 stick cinnamon or 3/4 teaspoon
  cinnamon
1/8 teaspoon ground nutmeg

ह≥ Preheat oven to 350°F.
Butter 9 × 9 × 2-inch dish.
  Peel, core and slice apples
1/4-inch thick. Arrange in prepared pan.
  Mix sugar, lemon juice and
rind and set aside.
  Heat wine with cinnamon
stick, being careful not to boil.
When heated through, remove
cinnamon stick and stir into
sugar mixture. Pour over apples
and bake 20 to 30 minutes or
until tender.

*Serve hot as a side dish or with
vanilla ice cream.*

—MRS. PATRICIA ROSE

APPLE-NUT CAKE

Moist and full of flavor.

YIELD: 10-12 SERVINGS

2 cups all-purpose flour
2 teaspoons baking soda
2 teaspoons cinnamon
3/4 teaspoon salt
2 eggs
2 cups sugar
1 teaspoon vanilla
1/2 cup vegetable oil
1 cup chopped walnuts
4 cups peeled and finely
  chopped apples

ह≥ Preheat oven to 325°F.
Sift flour, baking soda, cinnamon
and salt into a large bowl.
  Beat eggs, sugar, vanilla
and oil in a small bowl until
thick and creamy. Stir into
flour mixture. Add nuts and
apples and mix well. Pour into
an ungreased 9 × 9-inch pan.
Bake for approximately 1 hour,
or until a toothpick inserted in
center comes out clean. Cool
on wire rack for 15 minutes
before slicing.

*Serve with ice cream or
whipped cream.*

—PEGGY RATCHESON

APPLE CRANBERRY PIE

Colorful combination.

YIELD: 6-8 SERVINGS

1 cup halved fresh cranberries
4 cups apples, washed, pared,
  cored and thinly sliced
  before measuring
1-1/4 cups sugar
3 tablespoons all-purpose flour
Pastry for one 9-inch pie and
  lattice strips
1/4 cup mincemeat
2 tablespoons orange juice
1/2 teaspoon salt

ह≥ Preheat oven to 400°F.
Mix apples and cranberries in
large bowl.
  Mix sugar and flour. Pour
1/4 cup of sugar and flour mixture in unbaked pie shell.
  Mix remaining sugar and
flour with apples and cranberries.
Add mincemeat, orange juice
and salt to fruit mixture and
place in pie crust.
  Cover top with pastry strips,
lattice style.
  Bake in preheated oven for
10 minutes. Lower heat to 350°F
and bake 30 to 40 minutes.

—JENNIFER LANGSTON

*When similar recipes were submitted,
acknowledgement was given to each contributor.*

Swedish Apple Dumplings

A yummy treat served with or without vanilla ice cream.

YIELD: 6 SERVINGS

6 baking apples, peeled
   and cored
6 tablespoons sugar

DUMPLING DOUGH
2 cups all-purpose flour
4 teaspoons baking powder
1/2 teaspoon salt
1/2 cup solid vegetable shortening
2/3 cup milk

SYRUP
1-1/2 cups brown sugar
1 cup water
4 tablespoons margarine
1/2 teaspoon cinnamon

❧ Preheat oven to 400°F. Butter a 13 × 9 × 2-inch pan. Peel and core apples, leaving them whole; set aside.

Mix flour, baking powder and salt in a medium bowl. Cut in shortening until mixture resembles coarse crumbs. Pour in milk and stir with a fork until the dough holds together. Turn onto a lightly-floured surface and roll into a 12 × 8-inch rectangle. Cut in half lengthwise, then in thirds crosswise, making six 4-inch squares.

Place an apple in the center of each dough square and sprinkle with sugar. Fold the four corners of dough together at the top to enclose the apple.

To make syrup, combine sugar, water, margarine and cinnamon in a medium saucepan and bring to a boil. Continue cooking on low heat for 5 minutes.

Place dumplings in prepared baking pan, approximately 1 inch apart. Pour syrup over dumplings and bake for 15 minutes. Reduce heat to 300°F and continue baking for an additional 45 minutes.

Remove from pan and serve warm.

—BETTY JACKSON
—ELSIE KAINRAD

Five Star
DESSERTS
FRUIT

COLD LIME SOUFFLÉ

Light and delicious.

YIELD: 8 SERVINGS

1 envelope unflavored gelatin
1/4 cup cold water
4 egg yolks, lightly beaten
1 cup sugar, divided
1/2 cup fresh lime juice
1 cup heavy cream
6 egg whites
1/8 teaspoon salt
Lime slices for garnish

ᔡ Sprinkle gelatin over water.
Put egg yolks in top of
double boiler. Add 1/2 cup
sugar and lime juice and mix.
Cook over simmering water
until hot and thick enough to
coat spoon. Add gelatin. Strain
into bowl and cool. Whip
cream to soft peaks.

Beat egg whites with
pinch of salt until foamy. Add
remaining 1/2 cup sugar and
beat until stiff peaks form. Fold
whipped cream into lime base.
Carefully fold into egg whites.

Pour into a prepared 1-quart
soufflé dish with greased collar.
(To make soufflé collar, use
greased waxed paper. The collar
should come 2 to 3 inches above
the rim of the dish. Secure
with paper clips.) Refrigerate
4 to 6 hours.

To serve, garnish with
swirls of whipped cream and
top with a slice of lime.

—KATIE LORETTA

SANTA FE SUNSETS

Elegant served in crystal goblets.

YIELD: 10 SERVINGS

10 oranges
1/2 cup Tequila
1/4 cup Cointreau
1/4 cup orange juice
    concentrate
1/2 cup heavy cream
1/2 cup sugar
1 tablespoon lemon juice
Pomegranate seeds, and mint
    for garnish

ᔡ Cut off top third of the
oranges and scrape out the
pulp. Place pulp in blender
container and process until
smooth. Freeze in a shallow
pan until solid.

Break up the frozen orange
pulp and place in blender container with the remaining ingredients. Process until puréed.
Pour into oranges and freeze
until solid. Garnish with mint
and pomegranate seeds.

—DIANA ARMSTRONG

CRÈME BRÛLÉE
YIELD: 8 SERVINGS

2 cups heavy cream
1 cup half and half
1/2 cup superfine sugar
5 egg yolks
2 teaspoons vanilla extract
Granulated sugar for topping

ⅎ Preheat oven to 300°F. Combine heavy cream and half and half in a saucepan, bring to boil and remove from heat.

Combine the superfine sugar and egg yolks in a large mixing bowl and beat with a wire whisk until foamy. Add the vanilla and blend.

Whisk the egg mixture rapidly (never stopping for a second) and pour into the hot cream mixture; continue mixing briskly until mixture is well blended and smooth.

Strain the mixture through a fine sieve into shallow gratin dishes to within 1/8-inch from top. Place the dishes in a baking pan and pour hot water into pan until it is halfway up the sides of the dishes. Bake 35 to 40 minutes or until a small knife inserted in the middle comes out just barely sticky. Check often so water does not boil over into custard or top does not burn.

Remove dishes from water and cool. Cover with plastic wrap and refrigerate at least 3 hours or until custard is well chilled. Sprinkle tops of custard with granulated sugar, then caramelize sugar with a torch.

—CHEF LUCIEN VENDÔME

Five Star
DESSERTS
FRUIT

Stouffer Hotels and Resorts
Corporate Office
29800 Bainbridge Road
Solon, OH 44139
216-248-3600

APRICOT BREAD PUDDING
WITH APRICOT SAUCE
YIELD: 12 SERVINGS

1 cup candied apricots
1/2 cup kirsch, Framboise or
    other fruit liqueur
1/2 cup currants
1/2 pound French bread
6 tablespoons butter
5 large eggs
4 large egg yolks
1 cup sugar
1 teaspoon vanilla
1 quart milk
1 cup heavy cream
2 tablespoons confectioners sugar
2 tablespoons strained apricot
    jam (optional)

APRICOT SAUCE
2 cans apricot halves
Apricot brandy or other fruit
    liqueur to taste

Butter a 3-quart soufflé dish or other oven-proof baking dish.

Chop the candied apricots and soak in the liqueur for at least 30 minutes.

Soak the currants in boiling water to cover for 5 minutes. Drain.

Cut the bread into 1/4-inch slices and butter one side of each piece.

Whisk the eggs, yolks, sugar and vanilla.

Heat milk until just about to boil and add the heavy cream. Remove from heat and whisk into the egg mixture.

Spread the apricots, liqueur and drained currants on the bottom of the soufflé dish. Place the bread, buttered-side up, over the fruit. You will need to overlap the slices to make them fit.

Strain the egg-milk mixture through a very fine sieve over the bread. Let sit for about 30 minutes for the bread to absorb some of the liquid. The bread will float, so press it down a few times.

Place the dish into a larger baking dish and pour a few inches of boiling water into the larger dish. You have now made a bain-marie. Place into a preheated 375°F oven for about 1 hour or until custard is set. You can test by inserting a skewer in the center. Bits of custard may cling to the skewer, but it should not be liquid.

Sprinkle confectioners sugar on top and glaze the top under the broiler. For variety, brush some apricot jam over the top.

To make Apricot Sauce, drain the apricot halves, reserving some of the syrup. Place the apricots in container of a food processor and purée. Add a little syrup if it seems too thick and flavor to taste with the brandy or liqueur. Warm and serve with the warm Apricot Bread Pudding.

—SUSIE HELLER

APRICOT BARS
YIELD: 16 BARS

2/3 cup dried apricots
1/2 cup (1 stick) butter or
    margarine, softened
1/4 cup sugar
1-1/3 cups sifted all-purpose flour
1/2 teaspoon baking powder
1/4 teaspoon salt
1 cup packed brown sugar
2 eggs, well beaten
1/2 teaspoon vanilla
1/2 cup chopped nuts
Confectioners sugar (optional)

➳ Preheat oven to 350°F. Lightly grease an 8 × 8 × 2-inch pan.

Rinse apricots, place in saucepan, cover with water and boil 10 minutes; drain, cool and chop.

Mix butter, sugar and 1 cup flour until crumbly. Pack into pan. Bake approximately 25 minutes until lightly brown.

Sift remaining 1/3 cup flour, baking powder and salt.

Gradually beat brown sugar into eggs, add sifted flour mixture and blend well. Add vanilla, nuts and apricots. Spread over baked layer.

Bake approximately 30 minutes or until done. Cool in pan, cut into bars and roll in confectioners sugar.

—ANAH PYTTE

Five Star
DESSERTS
FRUIT

BISQUE TORTONI
Fancy frozen delight.
YIELD: 8-10 SERVINGS

1/3 cup sifted confectioners
    sugar
1 teaspoon vanilla
3 tablespoons sherry
1/4 teaspoon salt
2 cups (1 pint) heavy cream,
    whipped
2 egg whites
2 tablespoons sugar
1 cup macaroon crumbs
1/4 cup slivered and toasted
    almonds
4 candied cherry halves

❧ Fold confectioners sugar,
vanilla, sherry and salt into
whipped cream.

Beat egg whites until foamy.
Add sugar, one tablespoon at a
time, beating after each addition,
until whites are stiff but not dry.
Fold egg whites and macaroon
crumbs into cream mixture.
Spoon mixture into 1/2-cup size
paper soufflés or paper cups.
Sprinkle tops with almonds
and garnish with half a cherry.
Freeze until firm.

—ANAH PYTTE

CZECHOSLOVAKIAN COOKIES
YIELD: 16 SQUARES

1 cup (2 sticks) butter, softened
1 cup sugar
2 egg yolks
2 cups all-purpose flour
1 cup finely chopped nuts
1/2 cup blackberry jelly*

*Any kind of jam, preserves or jelly
can be used in this recipe.*

❧ Preheat oven to 325°F.
Lightly grease an 8-inch
square pan.

Cream butter and sugar.
Add egg yolks, blending well
after each addition. Gradually
add flour. Fold chopped nuts
into dough.

Press half the dough into
the prepared pan. Spread with
jelly, sprinkle with remaining
dough, pressing down dough to
cover jelly layer. Bake for 45 to
50 minutes. Cool and cut into
squares.

—MARY RYDZEL

SCHOCOLATEN BROT

Chocolate Hazelnut Cookies.

YIELD: 3 DOZEN

CHOCOLATE DOUGH

1 cup all-purpose flour
1/8 teaspoon baking powder
1/8 teaspoon salt
4 ounces finely grated dark
    chocolate bar
1/3 cup sugar
2 packages (9 grams each)
    vanilla sugar
1 egg yolk, reserve white
1/2 cup (1 stick) cold unsalted
    butter, cut into 1/8-inch bits
1 cup blanched hazelnuts

BUTTER DOUGH

1 cup all-purpose flour
1/8 teaspoon baking powder
1/8 teaspoon salt
1/4 cup granulated sugar
1 package (9 grams each)
    vanilla sugar
1 egg yolk, reserve white
1/2 cup (1 stick) cold unsalted
    butter, cut into 1/8-inch bits

❧ To make chocolate dough, sift flour and baking powder on a flat surface. Add salt, grated chocolate, sugar and vanilla sugar. Make a well in the center and drop the egg yolk into the well. Add butter bits and knead all ingredients into a smooth dough. Knead in the hazelnuts. Shape dough into a 9 × 3 × 1-inch-thick rectangle. Moisten with beaten egg white.

Prepare butter dough in the same fashion and roll into a 9-inch square. Wrap around moist chocolate dough. Wrap in waxed paper and chill over-night in refrigerator.

Preheat oven to 325°F. Coat baking sheets with short-ening. Slice dough into 1/8- or 1/4-inch thick slices with a sharp knife. Transfer to prepared baking sheets, leaving a 1-inch space between each slice. Bake in the middle of oven for 14 to 18 minutes or until golden. Transfer to cake rack to cool.

These can be stored in an airtight container at a cool room temperature for several weeks.

—HELGA STANG
COOKBOOK AUTHOR
AND PASTRY CHEF

SWISS RASPBERRY PASTRY
YIELD: 20-25 SERVINGS

4 cups sifted all-purpose flour
2 cups (4 sticks) butter or
   margarine
1 cup sugar
3 egg yolks and 1 egg white
1 egg
Rind and juice of 1 lemon
1 cup (8 ounces) raspberry jam
1/2 cup (4 ounces) currant jam
Confectioners sugar

⬥ Preheat oven to 350°F. Lightly grease a 13 × 9-inch pan.

Mix flour, butter or margarine, sugar, egg yolks, whole egg, lemon rind and juice in a large bowl. Reserve one-fourth of the dough for the top of pastry. Roll out remaining dough on a lightly-floured surface. Line the bottom and sides of prepared pan with dough. Mix raspberry and currant jams and spread over the top of the pastry dough.

Form the remaining pastry dough into long ropes about 1/4-inch in diameter. Roll each out on a lightly-floured surface. Place the strips of dough on top of the pastry in a crisscross fashion.

Brush with egg white and bake for approximately 40 minutes. Cool and sprinkle with confectioners sugar. Cut into diamond shapes and serve.

— MRS. ANNETTE GROSS

BLUEBERRY PIEROGI
YIELD: 8-10 SERVINGS

2 medium potatoes, cooked,
   mashed and cooled
3 eggs
1/2 cup water
3 cups all-purpose flour
1 pint fresh blueberries
1/2 cup sugar
1/2 cup (1 stick) butter
1/4 cup fine dry bread crumbs
Sour cream, thinned with
   milk for topping

⬥ Combine potatoes, eggs, water and flour and knead until dough is light and smooth. Roll out on a thickly-floured board and cut into 3-inch squares.

Mix berries and sugar; spoon 1 teaspoon onto each square. Fold into triangles and press edges together well to seal. Cook in boiling, salted water until pierogi rise to surface, then cook 2 minutes more.

Remove from water with a slotted spoon and place on a serving platter.

Melt butter, add bread crumbs and brown slightly. Spoon over pierogi and serve with sour cream.

— BETTY PROCOP

When similar recipes were submitted, acknowledgement was given to each contributor.

RUSSIAN TEA BISCUITS

YIELD: 80 BISCUITS

DOUGH
4 cups all-purpose flour
3/4 cup sugar
3 teaspoons baking powder
1/2 cup (1 stick) margarine, melted
1/4 cup vegetable oil
3 eggs plus 1 yolk, reserving white
1/4 cup orange juice
2 teaspoons vanilla

FILLING
3/4 cup sugar
1 teaspoon cinnamon
1/2 cup ground walnuts
Golden raisins
Raspberry jelly

❧ Combine all dough ingredients, except the reserved egg white, and mix well. Divide dough into six balls and refrigerate overnight.

Preheat oven to 325°F. Grease cookie sheets.

Combine ingredients for filling and mix well.

Working with one dough ball at a time, roll out on a heavily-floured board into a 6- to 7-inch square. Spread with raisins and jelly, sprinkle with filling and roll up jelly-roll fashion.

Slice into 1/2-inch pieces and brush with beaten egg white. Bake on prepared sheets 30 to 35 minutes or until light brown.

Remove from cookie sheets immediately and cool.

—EUDICE BROWN
—DORIS KAPLAN

Five Star
DESSERTS

BEE STING CAKE

YIELD: 10 SERVINGS

BATTER
2 eggs
1 cup sugar
1 teaspoon vanilla
1 cup all-purpose flour
1 teaspoon baking powder
1/2 cup milk
1 heaping tablespoon butter

TOPPING
10 tablespoons brown sugar
4 tablespoons melted butter
4 tablespoons heavy cream
1 cup shredded coconut
1 teaspoon vanilla

ভ্ Preheat oven to 350°F. Grease an 8 × 8-inch pan.

Mix eggs, sugar, vanilla, flour and baking powder.

Bring milk and butter to a boil and mix with batter mixture. Pour into prepared pan and bake about 30 minutes.

Mix topping ingredients and spread on cake while cake is still warm. Broil until topping is bubbly and brown.

—SHIRLEY SHAPERO

STANCHFIELD COFFEE CAKE

A breakfast or tea-time treat.

YIELD: 6-8 SERVINGS

1-1/2 cups sugar
2 eggs
1 cup flour
1 teaspoon baking powder
1/2 teaspoon salt
1/2 cup hot milk
1 tablespoon cinnamon
1/2 cup chopped pecans
1/2 cup butter, melted

ভ্ Preheat oven to 350°F. Grease and lightly flour an 8 × 8-inch pan.

Beat 1 cup of sugar and eggs until creamy and thick, at least 3 minutes.

Sift flour, baking powder and salt in a large bowl. Add to sugar and egg mixture. Add hot milk and mix well. Pour into prepared pan.

Mix remaining 1/2 cup of sugar with cinnamon and sprinkle over batter. Top with pecans. Bake for approximately 25 minutes or until a toothpick inserted in the center comes out clean.

Remove from oven and immediately drizzle with 1/2 cup melted butter. Cool on wire rack for 15 minutes before serving.

—GAIL RESCH

GRAMMA B's CLOVE CAKE

YIELD: 12 SERVINGS

1 cup (2 sticks) butter
2-1/2 cups sugar
5 medium eggs, beaten
3 cups all-purpose flour
1 tablespoon ground cloves
1 tablespoon cinnamon
1/2 teaspoon salt
1 teaspoon baking soda
1 cup sour milk*

To sour milk, add 1 tablespoon of vinegar to 1 cup of milk.

🐦 Preheat oven to 350°F. Butter and flour a 10-inch tube pan.

Cream butter and sugar and add eggs.

Combine dry ingredients and alternate adding dry ingredients and milk to creamed mixture. Pour into prepared pan and bake about 50 to 60 minutes.

Cool in pan.

—MRS. WILLIAM BINGHAM

AUNT JANE's SHAKER POUND CAKE

YIELD: 15 SERVINGS

1/2 cup plus one teaspoon unsweetened cocoa
1/2 teaspoon baking powder
1/4 teaspoon salt
3 cups all-purpose flour
1 cup (2 sticks) butter
1/2 cup solid vegetable shortening
3 cups sugar
5 eggs
1-1/4 cups milk
1-1/2 ounces unsweetened chocolate squares
1 teaspoon vanilla

🐦 Preheat oven to 350°F. Grease a 10-inch tube pan and dust with 1 teaspoon cocoa.

Mix cocoa, baking powder, salt and flour and set aside.

Beat butter, shortening and sugar at medium speed for 5 minutes. Add eggs, one at a time, beating after each addition.

Mix at low speed, adding flour mixture in 4 additions, alternating with milk in 3 additions.

Shave chocolate squares into batter, add vanilla and mix until blended. Turn into prepared pan and bake for 1 hour and 15 to 20 minutes.

Cool 20 minutes before removing from pan.

—BETH MIRMELSTEIN

Five Star
DESERTS

CAKE

237

PUMPKIN ROLL
Something different for Thanksgiving dinner.
YIELD: 10-12 SERVINGS

3 eggs
1 cup sugar
1 teaspoon lemon juice
2/3 cup solid pack pumpkin
1 teaspoon baking powder
2 teaspoons cinnamon
1 teaspoon ginger
1/2 teaspoon nutmeg
1/2 teaspoon salt
3/4 cup all-purpose flour
1 cup chopped nuts
1 cup heavy cream, whipped

FILLING
1 cup confectioners sugar
1 package (8 ounces) cream
   cheese
4 tablespoons margarine
1 teaspoon vanilla

Preheat oven to 350°F. Line a 15 × 10-inch jelly-roll pan with waxed paper and lightly grease.

Beat eggs at high speed. Gradually add sugar. Stir in lemon juice and pumpkin. Set aside.

Sift baking powder, cinnamon, ginger, nutmeg, salt and flour in a large bowl.

Mix pumpkin mixture with dry ingredients. Pour mixture into prepared pan. Sprinkle with nuts and bake for 15 minutes.

Turn cake out onto tea towel dusted with confectioners sugar. Remove waxed paper. Beginning at long end, roll up, jelly-roll fashion, and cool for 30 minutes.

Combine filling ingredients and beat well. Unroll cake and spread with filling; roll again. Serve with whipped cream.

—DEANNA BOGACKI
—KATHRYN HILLARD

When similar recipes were submitted, acknowledgement was given to each contributor.

238

BANANA CAKE SQUARES

YIELD: 16 SQUARES

5 tablespoons sour cream
1 teaspoon baking soda
1/2 cup (1 stick) unsalted butter
    or margarine
1-1/4 cups sugar
2 eggs
1-1/2 cups cake flour
1/4 teaspoon salt
1-1/2 cups (about 3 large)
    mashed, over-ripe bananas
1 teaspoon vanilla
Confectioners sugar for garnish

❧ Preheat oven to 350°F. Lightly grease an 8 × 8-inch baking pan.

Mix sour cream and baking soda in small bowl; set aside.

Cream butter and sugar in large bowl. Add eggs and beat with mixer until light.

Sift flour and salt onto waxed paper; set aside.

Add sour cream mixture to butter and egg mixture and beat with mixer. Add mashed bananas, flour mixture and vanilla. Continue beating for approximately 3 minutes.

Pour into pan and bake approximately 40 minutes; cool. Cut into 16 squares. If desired, sprinkle top with confectioners sugar.

—SHARON EPSTEIN

DATE PUDDING

YIELD: 6-8 SERVINGS

1 cup chopped dates
1 tablespoon butter
1 teaspoon baking soda
1 cup boiling water
1 egg, lightly beaten
1/8 teaspoon salt
1 cup sugar
1 cup all-purpose flour
1/2 cup chopped nuts
1 teaspoon vanilla
2 bananas, sliced
1 cup heavy cream, whipped with
    sugar and vanilla to taste

❧ Preheat oven to 350°F. Lightly grease a 9-inch square pan.

Pour boiling water over dates, butter and baking soda. Set aside to cool.

Stir in egg, salt, sugar, flour, chopped nuts and vanilla and beat until smooth. Pour into prepared pan and bake for about 30 minutes. Cool.

To serve, remove cake from pan, cut into 1-inch squares and layer with sliced bananas and sweetened whipped cream.

This looks lovely in a glass bowl. Leftover cake squares can be frozen.

—ALMA KAUFMAN

Five Star
DESSERTS

CAKE

POTICA I
TRANSLATED IT MEANS
"SOMETHING ROLLED IN."

A rich nut bread made to celebrate Slovenian holidays.
We offer two versions: this first version makes a larger quantity in one stage.

YIELD: 3-4 LOAVES

DOUGH
1-1/4 cups milk
3/4 cup (1-1/2 sticks) unsalted
　　butter
2 packages active dry yeast
　　or 1 cake (1-1/4 ounce) yeast
1 tablespoon sugar
1/4 cup warm water
4 egg yolks, reserve whites for
　　nut filling
3/4 cup sour cream
7 to 8 cups unbleached white
　　flour
3/4 cup sugar
1 tablespoon salt
1 tablespoon grated lemon rind

WALNUT FILLING
2-1/2 pounds walnuts, finely
　　ground
2-1/2 cups sugar
3/4 cup (1-1/2 sticks) unsalted
　　butter
1-1/2 cups half and half
3/4 cup honey
1 tablespoon rum or vanilla
　　flavoring
1 tablespoon grated lemon rind
4 egg whites
1-1/2 cups golden raisins,
　　plumped (optional)
1/4 cup dark rum (optional)

EGG WASH
1 egg
1 tablespoon milk

&❧ Heat milk and butter in saucepan until butter melts. Cool to lukewarm.

Sprinkle yeast and sugar over lukewarm water in a small bowl. Stir to mix; let stand until foamy.

Beat egg yolks slightly in another bowl and mix with sour cream.

Place 7 cups flour, sugar, salt and lemon rind in a large bowl. Make a well in center. Add egg yolk-sour cream mixture, lukewarm milk-butter mixture and foamy yeast. Mix with wooden spoon until all liquid is absorbed and well blended. Add just enough reserved flour to form a soft dough.

Turn dough onto floured board and knead until smooth and elastic, approximately 10 minutes, working in more of the reserved flour as needed. Dough should be soft. (An electric mixer with a dough hook may be used.)

Shape dough into a ball and place in large, well-greased bowl, turning to coat. Cover, let stand in a warm, draft-free place until doubled in bulk, approximately 1 hour.

While dough is rising, prepare nut filling and grease three 12 × 4 × 4-inch loaf pans.

To make Walnut Filling, place ground walnuts in a large bowl. Sprinkle sugar over them.

Melt butter in half and half. Heat to just below boiling. Pour hot half and half and butter mixture over nuts and sugar. Add honey, flavoring and lemon rind. Mix until well blended.

Beat egg whites until glossy and peaks are formed. Fold into nut mixture.

Raisins can be plumped by soaking in hot water and draining or soaking in rum overnight.

When dough has doubled, turn onto center of large floured cloth. (A clean white sheet folded in half works well.) With rolling pin, roll until dough is a 36 × 26-inch rectangle. It will be about 1/8-inch thick.

Spread walnut filling evenly over dough, leaving about 1 inch free of filling at furthest long end. If using plumped raisins, drain and sprinkle them evenly over walnut mixture.

Starting from longer end, roll up, jelly-roll style, stretching the dough as you roll. When rolled about halfway, pierce the roll at the top with a paring knife about every 3 inches across the roll. The length of the roll should be about 36 inches to fit into 3 well-greased 12 × 4 × 4-inch loaf pans.

Cut roll with a knife to fit into each pan. You may use round pans or any size pan you wish, but pan should be at least 4 inches high and 3 inches wide to allow for expansion.

Beat egg with milk and brush the egg wash over the top of the rolls. Pierce again at 3-inch intervals, but not quite through. Cover and let rise in a warm, draft-free place until doubled, approximately 1 hour.

Bake in preheated 325°F oven for approximately 1 hour, until medium brown or until a toothpick inserted in center comes out clean.

Remove from oven. Let stand 15 minutes, remove from pans and cool completely on wire racks. Each loaf should yield about 20 slices.

— JEAN KRIZMAN

POTICA II

A simpler version made in two stages, using a refrigerated dough method.

YIELD: 2 LOAVES

YEAST MIXTURE
2 packages (1/4 ounce each)
    dry yeast
1/2 cup water
1 tablespoon sugar

EGG MIXTURE
2 egg yolks
1 cup half and half

DOUGH MIXTURE
4 cups unbleached white flour
3 tablespoons sugar
1 tablespoon salt
1/2 cup (1 stick) unsalted butter

FILLING
1-1/2 pounds walnuts, finely
    ground
1 cup half and half
1/2 cup (1 stick) unsalted butter
1 cup sugar
1/2 cup honey
1 teaspoon vanilla
2 egg whites
1 cup raisins, plumped
3 tablespoons rum (optional)

❧ Crumble yeast into water, add sugar and mix; let stand until foamy.

To make egg mixture, beat egg yolks slightly, adding half and half; set aside.

To make dough, combine flour, sugar and salt. Cut butter into flour and mix with a fork until mealy. Add egg mixture and yeast mixture with wooden spoon and stir until well mixed and dough forms. Transfer to floured board and knead until dough is smooth.

Place in well-greased bowl and cover or place in plastic bag with closure. Refrigerate for at least 6 hours or overnight.

When ready to use, remove from refrigerator and let stand at room temperature until dough is pliable, approximately 1 hour.

Meanwhile, combine all ingredients for walnut filling, following the same procedure as in Potica I.

Roll out dough on floured cloth into a 26-inch square. Spread nut mixture over entire dough, leaving 1 inch of edge free of nut mixture. Sprinkle with an additional 1 cup sugar and 1 cup plumped raisins.

Roll by hand, jelly-roll style, stretching dough as you roll. Pierce dough with knife when rolling. Place in two greased 12 × 4 × 4-inch pans. Let rise.

Bake at 350°F for 1 hour. Let stand 15 minutes, remove from pans and cool completely on wire racks.

—JEAN KRIZMAN

GRANDMA ESTHER'S STRUDEL
YIELD: 20 SERVINGS

1 cup solid vegetable
    shortening
1/2 cup sugar
1/2 teaspoon salt
5 eggs
3-1/2 to 4 cups all-purpose flour
3 teaspoons baking powder
1/3 cup orange juice
1 cup sugar
2 teaspoons cinnamon
1 cup (8 ounces) cherry
    preserves
1 cup (8 ounces) orange
    marmalade
1 cup (8 ounces) strawberry
    preserves
1-1/2 cups yellow raisins
1 cup shredded coconut
1 cup chopped nuts
2 tablespoons grated lemon
    rind
2 tablespoons lemon juice

Preheat oven to 325°F. Lightly grease a 14 × 10-inch pan.

Cream shortening, sugar and salt. Add eggs, one at a time, beating after each addition. Add 1 cup flour, baking powder and orange juice, mixing well. Gradually add the remaining flour and mix well.

Meanwhile, mix sugar and cinnamon in a small bowl and set aside.

Place dough on lightly-floured surface and divide into 3 equal portions. Roll out one portion and fit into the bottom and sides of prepared pan.

Spread dough with cherry preserves, one-half of the orange marmalade, 3/4 cup raisins, 1/2 cup coconut and 1/3 cup nuts. Sprinkle with 1/3 cup cinnamon-sugar mixture, 1 tablespoon grated lemon rind and 1 tablespoon lemon juice.

Roll out second portion of dough and place over fillings. Repeat the process for filling, except substitute strawberry for cherry preserves.

Roll out last portion of dough and place over fillings. Sprinkle with the remaining chopped nuts and cinnamon-sugar. Carefully cut the **top layer only** into diagonals.

Bake for 50 to 60 minutes.

—BETH SIMON

Five Star
DESSERTS

Torta od Lešnika

Hazelnut Torte.

YIELD: 6-8 SERVINGS

HAZELNUT TORTE
8 eggs, separated
1/2 cup sugar
1/2 cup ground hazelnuts
1/2 cup all-purpose flour
1 teaspoon baking powder

YELLOW TORTE
4 eggs, separated
4 tablespoons sugar
4 tablespoons all-purpose flour
1 teaspoon baking powder

FILLING
1 cup milk
3 tablespoons flour
1 cup (2 sticks) unsalted butter
1 cup confectioners sugar
1 teaspoon vanilla

GARNISH
1 cup ground walnuts
Red and green candied
cherries

❧ Preheat oven to 350°F. Lightly grease and flour three 9-inch cake or torte pans.

To make hazelnut torte, beat egg yolks and sugar in a large bowl until thick and lemon-colored. Add hazelnuts, flour and baking powder, mixing well.

Fold in stiffly beaten egg whites and pour into two prepared pans. Bake for 30 minutes or until a toothpick inserted in center comes out clean. Cool.

To make yellow torte, beat egg whites until stiff; set aside. Beat egg yolks and sugar until thick and lemon-colored. Add flour and baking powder. Fold in egg whites, pour into prepared pan and bake for 30 minutes or until toothpick inserted in center comes out clean.

To make filling, cook milk and flour in a saucepan over low heat until thick. Cool. Beat butter, sugar and vanilla in a small bowl. Add milk mixture, blending well.

To assemble torte, place one hazelnut torte on a serving platter and frost with some of the filling. Add the yellow torte layer, frost, and top with the remaining hazelnut layer. Frost the top and sides of the assembled torte. Garnish with ground walnuts and red and green candied cherries.

For a more dramatic looking torte, split all torte layers in half and double the filling recipe. This will give you a six-layer torte.

—SONJA T. ZIVIC

Baklava

Yield: 36 servings

1 pound finely chopped
   walnuts
1 cup sugar
1 tablespoon cinnamon
1 package (1 pound) phyllo
   dough, thawed
2 cups (4 sticks) sweet butter,
   melted or 1 cup (2 sticks)
   sweet butter, and 1 cup
   (2 sticks) margarine, melted
Plain bread crumbs to taste

SYRUP
3/4 cup sugar
3/4 cup honey
1-1/2 cups water
Rind and juice of 1/2 lemon

Preheat oven to 350°F.

Combine walnuts, sugar and cinnamon.

Take eight sheets of thawed phyllo dough from package. Place one sheet on an ungreased cookie sheet. Brush with melted butter and lightly sprinkle with bread crumbs. Cover with another layer of phyllo dough and repeat this process until you have eight layers of prepared phyllo dough.

Spread walnut mixture over the top of the entire sheet and drizzle with melted butter.

Continue adding eight more sheets of dough, brushing each layer with butter and bread crumbs. Brush top sheet generously with butter.

Cut into diamond-shaped pieces or squares and bake for 40 to 45 minutes or until golden brown.

To make syrup, combine sugar, honey, water, lemon juice and lemon rind. Bring to a slow boil and cook for 20 minutes. Remove rind and chill syrup.

To serve, spoon cold syrup over top of baklava.

—Mary Jo Zingale

Five Star
DESSERTS

NUT ROLLS

Easy and great tasting.

YIELD: 4 ROLLS

2 packages active dry yeast
1 cup lukewarm water
4 tablespoons sugar
1 cup (2 sticks) margarine
4 cups all-purpose flour
3 eggs, separated
1 teaspoon salt
Confectioners sugar

FILLING
1/2 cup milk
1 pound ground walnuts
3/4 cup sugar
1 tablespoon margarine
1 teaspoon lemon juice

🐦 Sprinkle yeast over water; add sugar and set aside.

Cut margarine into flour until crumbly. Make a well in the flour; add egg yolks, salt and yeast mixture. Mix until it forms a ball of dough; divide into quarters.

To make filling, heat milk until warm. Stir in nuts; add sugar, margarine and lemon juice. Cool slightly.

Roll dough into rectangle on floured board, using standard cookie sheet as a guide.

Spread one-fourth of the filling on dough and roll up. Repeat with other three pieces of dough. Place all four rolls seam-side down on one cookie sheet.

Beat egg whites until frothy. Brush tops of rolls with beaten egg whites. Let stand 1 hour in a warm place.

Bake in a 350°F oven for approximately 30 minutes or until tops are brown.

To serve, slice and sprinkle each piece with confectioners sugar.

—MARY ANN MAJORAS

FROSTED PECANS
YIELD: 4 CUPS

4 cups (1-1/4 pounds) pecan halves
2 egg whites
1 cup sugar
1/8 teaspoon salt
1/2 cup margarine

ᓭ Heat pecans in 325°F oven for 5 minutes.

Beat egg whites with sugar and salt until stiff peaks form. Fold in heated pecans.

Melt margarine in 15 x 10 x 1-inch pan. Spread with nut mixture and bake in 350°F oven for 30 minutes, stirring every 10 minutes.

Cool and store in airtight container.

— ELIZABETH MARTIN

HERMIT PRALINE ICE CREAM SAUCE
Reminiscent of New Orleans.
YIELD: 6-8 SERVINGS

1/2 cup (1 stick) butter
1/8 cup chopped pecans
1/8 cup chopped walnuts
1/8 cup chopped peanuts
1/2 cup firmly packed brown
  sugar
1/4 cup corn syrup
1/2 cup sour cream

ᓭ Melt butter over low heat. Add chopped nuts, sugar and corn syrup and cook for 10 minutes over low heat. Remove from heat, let cool slightly and add sour cream slowly. Serve over ice cream.

Can be made ahead of time and warmed in the microwave.

—TOM PEPKA

Five Star
DESSERTS

INDEX OF RECIPES

ACKNOWLEDGEMENTS

It takes a lot of talented and generous people to put together a collection such as this.
We would like to offer special thanks and appreciation to the following:

Anne Abbott
Kay Abegglen
Melania Adamcio
Cheryl Adams
Ruth Adams
Heather Agle
Alice Alexander
Mrs. Emmett Allen
Marilyn Althans
Madeline Alunni
Madelyn Alvarez
Marcella Anderson
Betty Andre
Gayla Andreale
Diana Armstrong
Debra Arthur
Phyllis Arthur
Patty Artino
Sue Austin
Marilyn Bachman
Cydney Weingart Baddeley
Cynthia Bailey
Cindi Baker
Kathy Baker
Vern Barbour
Bonnie Barenholtz
Mary Barkey
Clair Barkley
Hanna Bartlett
James T. Bartlett
Molly Bartlett
Chef Rick Bayless
Helen Behrend
Mack Bell
Zakiyyah Bergen
Dr. Irving Berger
Merianne Berger
Ruthanne Berger
Dr. Sosamma Berger
Mary Berndt
Beatrix Berne
Chef Renato Bertolo
Donna Biacsi
Melinda Bickers
Margie Biggar
Jonas Bilunas
Jean Bingay
Mrs. William Bingham
Nancy S. Black
Becky Blair
Suzanne Blaser
Mollye Block
Rena Blumberg
Nancy Blumenthaler
Frances Bode
Deanna Bogacki
Mrs. Donald Boggs
Barbara Bohlman
Bo Loong Restaurant
Bonnie Davis Catering
Maria Bowerfind
Laurel Shie Bowles

Dorothy Bowman
Evelyn Boyd
RoseMarie Brigneli
Linda Broda
Phyllis Cohen Brody
George Brookes
Bonnie Broseman
Eudice Brown
Karran Brown
Chef Zachary Bruell
Grace Brumfield
Helen Brzoska
Rose Mary Buchman
Carol Buck
Nel Buckley
Sue Bumgardner
Margaret Burand
Mary F. Burgess
Joella Decell Burgoon
Judy Post Burke
Jodi Burkhart
Edna Burkle
Mary Beth Byrne
Cafe Sausalito
Peggy Caldwell
Gail Calfee
Ann Calkins
Rosy Cancela
Carolyn Caplan
Susan Cargile
Mrs. Roland D. Carlson
Cindy Carr
Ellen Carr
Russell F. Catanese
Mildred K. Cesan
Stanley L. Cesan
Jan Chapman
Chrisian Chavanne
Cheese Cellar
Sandra Cherniack
Ann L. Chernosky
Shirley Chessin
Jenny Chin
Jean Chockley
Carolyn E. Christopher
Mary Ellen Christiansen
Ann Cicarella
Barbara Clark
Ryn Clarke
Sally Cockayne
Faye Cohen
Lottie Cohn
Carol Colbert
Rosemary Coleman
Barbara Bratel Collier
Claire Collier
Holly Collins
Mrs. David F. Conley
Joan A. Conrad
Judith Copeland
Carol Crane
Gina Crimi

Sue Cristal
Alice Cronquist
Mrs. Charles Crouse
Barbara Custar
Czech Catholic Union
Debbie Daberko
Jane Daroff
Dr. Paul Dauchot
Ellen Daus
Chris Davis
Mrs. David E. Davis
Leola DeBarr
Sarah DeFino
Chef Robert Del Grande
Dan Denihan
Maria DeRoia
John Desmond
Florence DiGeronimo
Chef Ralph DiOrio
Tonda DiPlacido
Mari DiVincenzo
Sherry Docs
Chef Jim Dodge
Frances Domino
M. Louise Donato
Patty Doyle
Melissa Drane
Sherry Dres
Arleen Drier
Megan Driver
Ann Dunn
Becky Dunn
Carol Dunn
George J. Dunn
Ruth Dunn
Ann Marie Dvorak
Ann Earley
Barbara Eaton
Florence Ede
Patricia Edmonds
John Edwards
Katie Edwards
Lee Edwards
Ms. Eicher
Dan Elliott
Laurie Elmets
Brenda Embrescia
Sharon Epstein
Barb Erdelack
Leigh Fabens
Patricia Fagan
Kaylie Donahue-Fanfare
Marie Fasig
Robert Fatica
Chef Dean Fearing
Mary Fedak
Chef Susan Feniger
Donna Ferrante
Larry Ferrone
Phyllis Fersky
Bess J. Ficken
Ruth Finkelstein

Lea Fischbach
Lois Fishback
Judy Fishman
Helen Fitzgerald
Mary K. Flaherty
Kathy Fleegler
Marcia Floyd
Mrs. James Flynn
Mrs. James Forbes
Aileen Ford
Margaret Ford
Chef Larry Forgione
Joan Fountain
Dr. Evangeline Franklin-Nash
Betty Freed
Janet French
Marguerite Frieson
Jeanne Lange Fuller
Margaret A. Fuller
Carol Spark Fulop
Barbara Fulton
Florence Funta
Lydia Furman
Rebecca Gabriel
Mary Lou Gaffney
Edith Gagliardo
Susan Gall
Clarence Gallmann
Henry Geer
Diane Geha
Ann Gelehrter
Leonore Geller
Fran Gellin
Judy Genco
Pat George
Ida Geraci
Elaine German
Chef Emilio Manuel Gervilla
Nina Freedlander Gibans
Barbara Gibbs
Marie E. Gilchrist
May Gilchrist
Ann Gillespie
Kitty Gillund
Helen Gladwin
Sharon Glaser
Connie Kmieck-Gleason
Margaret T. Gobeille
Margie Goldberg
Joe Gombarcik
Colleen Woods Gotherman
Sr. Jane Grady
Gillian Graham
Lily Graham
Normajean Granito
Laura Sterkel Grant
Marty Grasberger
Mrs. Marc E. Graves
D. Allan Gray
Denise Grcevich
Helen B. Greenleaf
Greenwood Caterers

John Greenwood
Claudia Gregorek
Fred Griffith
Linda Griffith
Nancy Griffith
Randy Grodin
Chef Christopher Gross
Elaine Gross
Mrs. Annette Gross
Pamela Grosscup
Alyson Grossman
Marie C. Grossman
Kathy Groves
Claudia Gruen
Kathy Gwinn
Alex Gyekenyesi
Katherine Haffke
Holly Hallman
Nancy Halpin
Marj Halter
Bonnie Hami
Colleen Hanna
Susan Hannah
Lou Harding
Judy Hardy
Wafa Harik
Mary Harrell
William E. Hartley
Jean Hartson
Iris Harvie
David Haubert
Jan Hauenstein
Stephanie Hawliezek
Dee Dee Hayes
Marjorie A. Heller
Susie Heller
John Hellman
Emily Henninger
Ginna Hermann
Rice Hershey
Mr. and Mrs. Wilhelm Herzberger
Bernice Hess
Betty Hess
Ms. P. Hester
James Hewlett
Diane Gasior Hienton
Kathryn Hillard
Mrs. Dale Hilton
Helen Z. Ho
Bernice Hoffman
Gloria Hoffman
Robert Holloway
Pam Holmes
Pat Holmes
Ann Holtzman
Sibley Hoobler
John Horn
Patricia Hosang
Hough Bakeries, Inc.
Lil Howard
Terry Howard
Carey Flinn Howells
Mrs. Elton Hoyt
Alex Hudson
Julie Hudson
Kathleen Hughes
Vince Hulsman
Betty Hume

Carla Iudica
Betty Jackson
Ruth Jacobowitz
Sheila Jacobs
Gail Jacobsohn
Gertrude Jaffee
Pat James
Ron James
Judy Jenkins
Hazel Jennings
Helen Jensen
Pat Johnson
Randal Johnson
M. Johnstone
Dottie Jones
Ethel Jones
Kim Jones
Bill Joseph
Helen L. Judge
Nancy Marie Judge
Jonathan S. Juhasz
Jolan Kadar
Mrs. William Kail
Muffy Kain
Elsie Kainrad
Herbert Kaiser
Dick Kaplan
Doris Kaplan
Nonie Kaplan
Chef Seth Kaspy
Douglas Katz
Linda Katz
Alma Kaufman
Carol Kealy
Joyce M. Kearns
Nancy Keithley
Joan Kekst
Chef Thomas Keller
Peggy Kennerly
Ellie Kerester
Jane Kern
Sharon Keys
Debby Kimmey
Mary Jane King
Irene Kita
April Kleme
Gloria Klein
Mary Klein
Stephen Klein
Agnes B. Kleinhenz
Esther Kline
Fannie Kline
Terri Kline
Tobie Kogan
Janet Kohn
Ruth Koller
Bambi Kramer
Jean Krizman
Anita Krotine
Andrew Krotinger
Margaret Krudy
Chef Albert Kumin
Karen Kurak
Camille LaBarre
Toni Lagnese
James J. LaMantia
Nancy LaMantia
Pamela LaMantia

Maureen Ann Lamb
Jennifer Lang
Carolyn Lang
Mary Ann Lang
Thea Lange Spiegel
B. J. Langer
Mary Langer
Jennifer Langston
Pamela Lapish
Gail Larson
Cathy Laswell
Patsy Lease
Mrs. Leonard B. Lebby
Nan Leibold
Daina Lesheim
Stephen Leskovec
Rett Lewandowski
Althea Hughes-Lewis
Robert Lin
Dr. Agnes Lina
Shirley Linkow
Arretta Loas
Loretta Lobaza
Hope Lomas
Katie Loretta
Mrs. Jerry Loth
Pearlene Lovelady
Kay Lowe
Sandy Luby
Clara Ludesher
William Lux
Mary Susan Lyon
Rosemary Macedonio
Dan MacLachlan
Mrs. S. M. Madison
Michele Maggio Schroeder
Dr. Michael Maguire
Loraine Mahnic
Janet Mahon
John Majoras
Mary Ann Majoras
Victoria Majoras
Kathy Malone
Phyllis Mancino
Anne Manning
Barbara Mapstone
Carole Marciano
Anne Marcus
Joseph E. Martanovic
Elizabeth Martin
Hazel Martin
Jeffrey C. Marvin
Mrs. William D. Masters
Lynne Mathias
Chef Kazuto Matsusaka
Dr. Jim Mayes
Mrs. Janet Mayes
Mike McAllen
Lois McCartan
Ellen McChesney
Chris McCullough
Nina McDaniel
Angela McDougal
Anne McErlean
Pat McManamon
Mrs. Gordon Meacham
Louise Mediati
Elizabeth Meehan

Skippy Mehlman
Barbara Meisel
Rosemary Merchant
Carol J. Michel
Sharon Mick
Andrew Mikuszewski
Elizabeth Miller
James L. Miller
Linda Miller
Marjorie Miller
Robert and Pam Miller
Chef Mary Sue Milliken
Sandra Jean Mills
June Mincek
Marie Mingo
Chef Paul Minnillo
Beth Mirmelstein
Josephine Misic
Eugene Mitchell, Sr.
Barbara Mitroff
Kay Mlakar
Carol Moore
Paula Moore
Claire Morgan
Phil Morgan
Larry Morrow
Michelle Morse
Julie Moss
Paul Mraz
Joyce Munro
Candy Murdock
Donna S. Murray
Carol Neff
Gretchen Neff
Nina Neudorfer
Charles Neumann
Adell Newby
Mrs. Michael Nichols
Tina Nichols
Sally Nicklas
Shirley Nook
Ursula Norton
Laureen Nowakowski
Minnie Olgin
Sue Omori
Lydia B. Oppmann
Robin Oppmann
Nick Orlando, Jr.
Anna P. Osborne
Lois Osborne
Mrs. E. Osborne
Mrs. Lester Ovendorf
Mr. W. Glen Owens
Debra Ozan
Mary O'Loughlin
Anne O'Neil
Dee Dee O'Neil
Katherine Templeton O'Neill
Judy Pace
Loretta Paganini
Sherrie Pallotta
Anne Paquet
Madeleine Parker
Mrs. Theo. Parreco
Heidi Passow
Virginia Paterson
Nancy Patterson
Kathy Pavlish

Karen Payne
Pearl of the Orient
Mary Ann Pedone
Kathleen Pellegrin
Tom Pepka
Gertrude Pepper
Judith A. Percio
Ellen Petler
Grace J. Petot
Charlene Phelps
Geneva Phillips
Jane Pinkas
John L. Pistone II
Loretta Pitts
Pat Pogue
Chef William Poirier
Laura F. Pollock
Chef Debra Ponzek
Chef Alfred Portale
Helena Powell
Mrs. Evelyn Powers
Terri Powers
DeAnn Price
Betty Procop
Chef Wolfgang Puck
Anah Pytte
Carl Quagliata
Mrs. Mark A. Randol
Viki Rankin
Peggy Ratcheson
Marie Rauh
Sakinah Abdur Razzaque
Carolyn Reali
Toni Akers-Reaman
Mrs. K. J. Redig
Cynthia Reece
Ronald Reminick
Gail Resch
Jo Reynolds
Paula Rhodes
Chef Michel Richard
Charlotte Riley
Gerry Rini
Diane Ritchie
Marsha Ritley
Mrs. Donald Ritter
Riverside Cooking School
Howard Robbins
Mrs. Barbara C. Roe
Sheila Rombach
Marybeth Rooney
Sister Rosarie
Celeste Rose
Mrs. Patricia Rose
Mrs. Robert S. Rosenthal
Dr. Tena Tarler Rosner
Polly Rossborough
Hilary Rossen
Anna Rostafinski
Viola Roth
Dianne Rozak
Dr. R. L. Ruggles
Elizabeth A. Russell
James Russo
Flo Ryan
Mary Rydzel
Gary Sabath
Nancy Sabath

Susan Sack
Sue Sackman
Judith Salomon
Michelle L. Sanson
Vivian Sanson
Claudia Sansone
Jean Sarlson
Jon Marc Satterliee
Wendy Albin Sattin
Kit Sawyer
Patricia Scalzi
Diann G. Scaravilli
Susan Schenkelberg
Ellen Schermer
Chef Jimmy Schmidt
Maxine L. Schnabel
Marcia Schneider
Mary Beth Schneider
Marcy Schreibman
Michele Maggio Schroeder
John Schultze
Francesco Scortegagna
Sheryl Scortegagna
Roberta Sears
Mr. and Mrs. Dennis Seeds
Nancy Seidman
Patty Seink
Al Senger
Marilyn Serino
Sari Ben-Shachar
Maude Shafron
Shirley Shapero
Dr. William Shapero
Sue Shapiro
Julie Shary
Sandra Shedroff
Martin J. Shemensky
Nancy Shenker
Carol Sherwin
Sue Sherwin
Laura Shields
Pat DeFabio-Shimrak
Mrs. Asa Shiverick, Jr.
Carol Shkerich
Trisha Shonk
Dr. Jerry M. Shuck
Dr. Linda W. Shuck
Shujiro
Dr. Francis Silver
Silver Creek Farm
Beth Simon
Lynn Simon
Margaret Simon
Nancy Simpson
Dolores Singer
JoAnn Singer
Fred Sizer
Vivian Sizer
Emy Skufca
Vivian S. Slosberg
Barbara E. Smith
Chef Cleaven Smith, Jr.
Doug Smith
Gretchen Smith
Helen Smith
Dr. Howard A. Smith
June Smith
Lynne Smith

Mary Smith
Joyce Neiditz-Snow
Jane Sobonya
Laurie Soja
Judith Solomon
Chef Gabino Sotelino
Andrea Soto
Margie Sparks
Zona Spray
Arlene Spector
Bea Stadtler
Mrs. Myron Stanford
Helga Stang
Wendy Staniforth
Patricia Starrett
Nancy Stein
Kathy Stellato
Agnes Stern
Janet Sterrett
Mrs. Howard P. Stevens
Katherine S. Stevens
Lucretia Stoica
Mrs. Albert D. Sudetic
K. K. Sullivan
Nancy Sulzer
Pat Suster
Evelyn P. Swan
Clara Swiger
Mike Symon
Dr. Karen Szauter
Szechwan House
Shari J. Talisman
Lloyd Taplin
Charles Taylor
Colleen Lally-Taylor
Chef Richard Taylor
Jane Temple
Gene Tener
Isabel Tener
Sherry Tenno
Mrs. John Terrell
Karen Thompson
Alec Thomson
Mrs. Chilton Thomson
Hannah Thomson
Laura Thomson
Maynard Thomson
Sally Thomson
Berge Tookman
Jerry Toth
Mary B. Tracy
Di Treco
Merlene Treuhaft
Patricia Hagler-Tucker
Flora Tuisku
Roma Pollock Turnbow
Linda Y. Turner
Rosalie Tyner
Carole Ubinger
Kitty Unger
Mrs. David Upson
Mrs. Mark Upson, Jr.
Carrie Urbach
Chef Martial Valentin
Kim Valore
Peggy J. Van Buskirk
Diane Vanek
Chef Lucien Vendôme

Russell Vernon
Dinah Vince
Paul J. Vincent
Dianne Vogt
Charlotte Wagner
Jack Waldhelm
Dr. Albert Waldo
Anne C. Walters
James Waltrip
Chris Wamsley
Mary Ward
Donna Warner
Virginia Warnke
Anne Watson
Chef Jonathan Waxman
Marion Weaver
Susie Webb
Candy Weil
Debby Weiss
Florence Weiss
Jane Weiss
Jerome F. Weiss
Lois G. Wellman
Diane Welsh
Ann White
Sandy White
Sherry Whiting
Diane Whittingham
Karin Whyde
Jean Wiant
Trudy Wiesenberger
Caroline Wilford
Dr. Edward Wilkerson
Marg Williams
Sue Williams
Wanda Williams
Samuel Willman
Kathleen Winterich
Brian Wise
Tracy Woll
Rose Wong
Jane Wood
Barb Woodburn
Susan Wyler
Rosalie Engel Yarus
Kathie Young
Rebecca Reynolds-Young
Marilyn Youngner
Peter W. Zacher
Mrs. Jean Zarth
Alice Zimmerman
Bea Zimmerman
Mary Jo Zingale
Sonja T. Zivic
Barb Zola